S0-AFB-818

# TEST YOUR '80s CULTURAL LITERACY

*Carol Orsag Madigan*
*Ann Elwood*

**ARCO** • New York

## Photo Credits

## Front Cover

*All five photos:* AP/Wide World

## Back Cover

*Top left:* Amla Sanhgvi

*Top center:* AP/Wide World

*Top right:* NASA

*Bottom right:* © Stella Snead

First Edition

Copyright © 1990 by Carol Orsag Madigan and Ann Elwood

All rights reserved
including the right of reproduction
in whole or in part in any form

 **ARCO**

Simon & Schuster, Inc.
15 Columbus Circle
New York, NY 10023

DISTRIBUTED BY PRENTICE HALL TRADE SALES

Manufactured in the United States of America

1  2  3  4  5  6  7  8  9  10

**Library of Congress Cataloging-in-Publication Data**

Madigan, Carol Orsag.
Test your '80s cultural literacy / Carol Orsag Madigan, Ann Elwood.
    p.        cm.
   Includes bibliographical references.
   ISBN 0-13-911827-6
   1. History, Modern—1945–  —Examinations, questions, etc.
I. Elwood, Ann.  II. Title.  III. Title: Test your eighties cultural
literacy.
D848.M33  1990
909.82'2'076—dc20

89-17965
CIP

# CONTENTS

To Betty, John, Brook, Johnny, Linda, and Peg, with love

C.O.M.

To my friends and family, with thanks

A.E.

# *Acknowledgments*

We wish to express our gratitude to the following friends and colleagues who generously contributed their time and their talents to this book:

| | | |
|---|---|---|
| Lee Clayton | Peter Lichtgarn | Torene Svitil |
| Carol Dunlap | Jim Natal | Micheline Karas |
| Karen Pedersen | Diane Shepard | Lori Leyden |

In addition, we want to acknowledge and thank a very professional publishing team—Charles A. Wall, Pamela Byers, and Charles Levine.

# Introduction

This book, meant to encapsulate the decade just ended, tests your knowledge of trends and events almost too recent to be subjected to objective hindsight. It may seem fitting to take the tests as you put away the artifacts of the decade—a Cabbage Patch doll, a no-longer-state-of-the-art electronic gadget, a junk bond, or a Beijing protest T-shirt. If you are in the mood for reminiscing, this book will bring back memories. Whom did *you* play Trivial Pursuit with? How did you react to the hostage crisis? What was your first impression of Gorbachev—or Dr. Ruth? As you reminisce, you probably will realize that we can learn something from contemplating the 1980s.

It is a truism that we cannot without peril forget our past, even the most recent. And what better way to end a decade than with a judicious review? We have written this book aware that in doing such a review we risked choosing the trivial and ignoring the significant. Yet in an era in which time seems to have accelerated, it seems fitting to be boldly wrapping up the decade when it is hardly behind us.

We did not choose subjects for questions quixotically. The book is based on a search of print media for the past ten years, including year-end wrap-ups of the most important news stories by national news magazines. We have looked not just for the big, obvious changes but for the little ones that, through accretion, also led to change. And we have tried to present both sides of the picture—in a decade dominated by greed there was also Live Aid.

If you think you are somewhat culturally illiterate about the 1980s, it may not be entirely your fault. We *do* live in a world of information overload. Donald B. Rice, president and chief executive officer of the Rand Corporation, says that the volume of information is so staggering that "I often feel as if I'm drinking from a fire hose." Peter Large, author of *The Micro Revolution Revisited*, claims that "the total of all printed knowledge doubles every eight years."

It seems, too, that we have less time to pay attention to events outside our professional fields. If you doubt that, measure the height of the stack of magazines and books you don't have time to read. (Or have you assuaged your guilt by canceling your subscriptions?)

Also, in an age of information overload, where to get information looms as a vital decision. Studies show that Americans tend to get their news from television, not from a newspaper or news magazine. News comes in small bits— in sound bites and eye bites. Images constantly flash into our stream of consciousness and seem to push out the ones that just as rapidly preceded them. The information explosion has fragmented knowledge into shrapnel-like, disconnected bits. Some communications experts claim that fast-moving, graphic news does not compare well to print media, which does more to encourage interpretation and thought. Michael Schudsen, sociologist and chairman of communications at the University of California, San Diego, says, "The Evening News washes over you. With a newspaper, you're a little more . . . skeptical . . . in a way that encourages you to engage in debate or discussion." Todd Gitlin, professor of sociology at the University of California at Berkeley, who has spotted a "strategic ignorance initiative," says, "Not reading newspapers is part of a larger cultural flabbiness, a slickness . . . among the young that, yes, we have to worry about."

Perhaps the slickness is just another manifestation of information anxiety. Information anxiety, as defined by Richard Saul Wurman, author of the book of the same name, arises as the gap widens between what we understand and what we think we should understand, between available data and acquired knowledge. We worry about what others expect us to know, and we worry about how to discriminate between knowledge of permanent value and that which is merely of fleeting significance. The 1980s have put an ironic twist on George Orwell's *1984*, published forty years ago—

we have too much information, not too little. The fear is not that we do not have access to information but that we will be overcome by it.

We hope that this book will help you to sort through the data of the 1980s, to make some sense of the decade, and perhaps to alleviate some information anxiety. After all, if you did not pay much attention to the news of the 1980s, you *did* miss a great deal. Viewed in the light of predictions of the late 1970s, the decade brought about some major changes and surprises.

A 1975 book by Jerome Tuccille, *Who's Afraid of 1984? The Case for Optimism in Looking Ahead to the 1980s*, predicted a significant growth of leisure-class society in the United States. True? Maybe not, when you consider that the 1980s reinstated the forty-hour work week and deified the yuppie workaholic. In *The 80s: A Look Back at the Tumultuous Decade 1980–1989*, a parody written in 1979, the authors predicted that the world would grow to hate America, the Israelis would "take up" with the Arabs, pictures would replace print, and China would experience a Woodstock. Some hits, some misses.

In 1979 *Newsweek* asked a number of prominent people what trends they saw and what they predicted for the '80s. Historian Arthur M. Schlesinger, Jr., foresaw a zero-sum game of the economy, "where one person's gain is another person's loss," resulting in an alarming tension between the classes. Writer Octavio Paz thought that "love is becoming an abstraction." Betty Friedan feared that women would lose their gains in employment, and Vernon E. Jordan, Jr., president of the National Urban League, questioned whether this country was "really serious about equal opportunity for blacks." Kenneth Boulding was afraid that Americans were becoming mean-spirited. Senator Daniel Moynihan's question was "Will Russia Blow Up?" And John Hackett, author of *The Third World War*, wondered if peace with the Soviet Union was possible. Were they on the mark or not?

The same issue of *Newsweek* looked ahead to the "Wonders of '89"—technological advances made possible by research and development of the 1960s and 1970s. The big five were space technology, superconductivity, fiber optics, microprocessors, and recombinant DNA. Given the passage of time, we now know that space technology was hindered by the *Challenger* disaster. However, the 1987 Nobel Prize in physics went to two IBM scientists, Alex Müller and Georg Bednorz, for their breakthrough research in superconductivity. By the end of the 1980s phone companies were touting fiber-optic communication, the microchip had made possible great advances in home computing, and genetic engineers had inserted a foreign gene into corn in order to produce crops resistant to chemical pesticides. Some themes of the 1980s clearly stand out. Small was no longer considered beautiful. The notion of David Riesman (*The Lonely Crowd*) of "the more, the more" as a rule for human behavior seemed truer than ever. The decade saw the eclipse of traditional American liberalism. The United States was dominated by Ronald Reagan, Rambo, electronic religion, and an obsession with money. In the rest of the world several new democracies were born, and—not necessarily related—many countries experienced increasing terrorism. The two Olympic Games were shadowed by politics. Hirohito, Indira Gandhi, and Tito died; two more British princes were born. The decade saw the abrupt end of the sexual revolution and the advent of that dire threat, AIDS—again, not necessarily related.

Tom Shales, in the March 1986 issue of *Esquire*, was already calling the 1980s the "redecade"—a decade of "repeating, replaying, rerunning, retrieving, recycling, remaking of American culture." It was true that in these years in which we seemed to have so little time our ability to manipulate time increased enormously. Shales also claimed that the period of the 1980s, the sequel to the "Me Decade," had no style of its own because it was the decade of "one big electronic revue" of all of the other decades. And when he wrote the article, the "fax fanatic" had not yet been invented!

Greed reigned, and success meant making money. The 1980s witnessed the rise of paper-chasing deals and corporate raiders. Fascinated by wealth, we Americans were glued to our television sets to watch "Dallas," "Dynasty," and "Lifestyles of the Rich and Famous." Yuppies exaggerated the notion that one must know what's in and then go out and get it. Everyone wanted an MBA degree. Joseph Nocera called the 1980s, at least until the stock market crash, the Ga-Ga years, when the market "looked as if it would never stop rising." Was "Adam Smith" (a.k.a. business journalist George J. W. Goodman) right in calling the 1980s the "Roaring 80s" because they were reminiscent of the 1920s?

Like most other decades the 1980s did not have the chronological coherence we assign to them—things began to change before they ended. In 1988 *Newsweek* claimed the 1980s began with Election Day, November 4, 1980, when Carter lost, and ended on October 19, 1987, when the stock market collapsed. It was significant that in 1986–1987 "Dallas" dropped to number 11 and "The Cosby Show" became number 1. At the end of the decade stockbrokers and Yuppies, though not gone, were falling out of favor. Reagan stopped talking about "the evil empire" and began talking about friendship with Gorbachev. In the fall of 1986, Republicans lost the senate, and the Iran-*contra* scandal began coming out into the open. Cocaine, the achievers' drug, lost popularity to "ecstasy" and "grass," both hallucinogenics. The divorce rate leveled off, and some of us spotted a trend toward idealism and social responsibility.

## The Tests

We present twelve tests of forty questions each. The first test covers people in the news. The next two deal with big, mostly political events in the United States and the world. With the knowledge that these events are propped up and changed by the nonpolitical and seemingly small, we have included chapters such as Words and Language, Arts and Entertainment, Business and Economics, Science and Technology, Popular Culture, Sports, Celebrations and Milestones, Scandals, and Endings. Each question has four possible answers.

Here is an example:

**19.** In 1982 the ERA amendment to the U.S. Constitution failed ratification. The legislation concerned the rights of

    **a.** illegal aliens

    **b.** homosexuals

    **c.** women

    **d.** the poor

You may immediately recognize the right answer, or you may arrive at the right answer through the process of elimination.

Explanatory answers at the end of each test tell why the answer is correct and provide a capsule look at the issue covered in the question. In many cases, where appropriate, we have tried to entertain you, too. Here is an example of an explanatory answer:

**19. (c)** On June 30, 1982, the ERA (Equal Rights Amendment), which was intended to guarantee women's rights, failed to become part of the Constitution. The amendment read, "Equality of rights under the law shall not be denied or abridged by the United States or by any State on account of sex." Though approved ten years earlier by Congress, the amendment also needed ratification by thirty-eight states to become law. When the 1982 deadline came, however, only thirty-five states had approved the measure. The fight for ratification was led by the National Organization for Women (NOW).

Your scores will tell you, perhaps, where your heart and mind were in the 1980s and where the gaps in your knowledge are.

## Scoring Key

Each correct answer counts one point.

35–40:                    Excellent. You should write a book on how to assimilate information.

30–34:    Good. Though you are generally well informed, you might want to fill in the holes in your knowledge.

25–29:    Fair. Perhaps you were too busy to do much more than scan the headlines.

Below 25:    Poor. You were a 1980s Rip Van Winkle. Time for a cultural literacy tune-up.

## TEST 1

# *People in the News*

*I wish I had been Bob Geldof.*

—*PRINCE CHARLES*

1. During the 1980s, who became the first woman to manage a major presidential campaign?
   a. Elizabeth Dole
   b. Susan Estrich
   c. Jeane Kirkpatrick
   d. Kitty Dukakis

2. Who is "the Dapper Don," reputed mob boss and the head of New York City's Gambino crime family?
   a. John Gotti
   b. Paul Castellano
   c. Carlo Cambino
   d. Albert Anastasia

3. Why did Mary Cunningham leave the Bendix Corporation in October 1980?
   a. She was fired for insider trading.
   b. She resigned under pressure for having a friendship with the chairman.
   c. She was fired for industrial espionage.
   d. She left for a job at *Ms.* magazine.

4. Dr. C. Everett Koop took controversial stands on AIDS, smoking, and other health issues in the 1980s. What was his job title?
   a. director of the National Institutes of Health
   b. Surgeon General
   c. president of the American Medical Association
   d. director of Bethesda Naval Hospital

5. Why did the child in a nationally publicized dispute have three names—Sara, Melissa, and Baby M?
   a. She had a multiple personality disorder.
   b. She was the recipient of two heart transplants.
   c. She was the center of a lawsuit on surrogate motherhood.
   d. none of the above

**6.** Why did the practice of palimony lawyer Marvin Mitchelson suffer in the 1980s?

    **a.** Two former clients accused him of rape.

    **b.** The state bar accused him of professional offenses.

    **c.** California courts fined him $40,000 for filing unnecessary appeals.

    **d.** all of the above

**7.** In 1985 twenty-two-year-old Gary Kasparov became the youngest man to win

    **a.** a Pulitzer Prize in literature

    **b.** a position in the Soviet Politburo

    **c.** the world chess championship

    **d.** a Nobel Prize in science

**8.** After Dan Quayle was nominated as the 1988 Republican candidate for vice president, which of the following charges was (were) leveled at him by the press?

    **a.** He avoided the draft during the Vietnam War.

    **b.** He was a mediocre student.

    **c.** He was chosen because he resembled the film star Robert Redford.

    **d.** all of the above

**9.** Which of the eight Democratic candidates in the 1988 presidential race had never held an elected office?

    **a.** Richard Gephardt

    **b.** Bruce Babbitt

    **c.** Jesse Jackson

    **d.** Michael Dukakis

**10.** In 1986 the Kerr-McGee corporation reached an out-of-court settlement with the heirs of the woman who had been the subject of the 1983 movie titled

    **a.** *Missing*

    **b.** *The China Syndrome*

    c. *Silkwood*

    d. *State of Siege*

**11.** Which of these statements pertain(s) to Sally K. Ride?

    a. She was America's first woman in space.

    b. She is no longer with NASA.

    c. She was the only astronaut on the presidential commission that investigated the *Challenger* disaster.

    d. all of the above

**12.** What are the names of Chicago's first black mayor and the man elected after his death to complete his term?

    a. Harold Washington and Timothy C. Evans

    b. Eugene Sawyer and Richard M. Daley

    c. Harold Washington and Richard M. Daley

    d. Eugene Sawyer and Timothy C. Evans

**13.** Christine Craft spent much of the 1980s in a legal battle involving

    a. abortion

    b. sex discrimination

    c. surrogate motherhood

    d. an automobile accident

**14.** What is the name of the Associated Press correspondent who in March 1989 began his fifth year as a hostage in Lebanon?

    a. Terry Anderson

    b. Terry Waite

    c. Lawrence Martin Jenco

    d. David Jacobsen

**15.** Which of the following inanimate objects was *not* the nickname of a professional athlete in the 1980s?

    a. refrigerator

    b. microwave

    c. oil can

    d. carburetor

**16.** Samantha Smith became famous for

    a. becoming the recipient of a baboon heart

    b. being the youngest person admitted to Harvard

    c. writing a letter to Yuri Andropov and touring the Soviet Union at his invitation

    d. beating Chris Evert at Wimbeldon

**17.** Who was the unexpected winner of the 1987 Nobel Peace Prize?

    a. President Corazon Aquino of the Philippines

    b. President Raul Alfonsín of Argentina

    c. President Oscar Arias Sanchez of Costa Rica

    d. the World Health Organization

**18.** What nickname did the press give to Bernhard Goetz, who shot four black youths in New York City in December 1984?

    a. the "Urban Cowboy"

    b. the "Angel of Death"

    c. the "Subway Vigilante"

    d. the "Nightstalker"

**19.** Which country voted into power the political party of Benazir Bhutto, making her prime minister and the first woman to govern a Muslim country?

    a. India

    b. Pakistan

    c. Jordan

    d. Kuwait

**20.** In 1980, Synanon leader Charles Dederich and two other men pleaded no contest to charges of attempted murder with a deadly weapon. What weapon did they use?

    a. a handgun

    b. a rattlesnake

    c. rat poison

    d. a hypodermic needle

**21.** What common health problem did Kitty Dukakis bring to the nation's attention?

    a. breast cancer

    b. chronic fatigue syndrome

    c. cross-addiction

    d. anorexia

**22.** In November 1985 authorities jailed the religious leader Bhagwan Shree Rajneesh on what charges?

    a. extortion

    b. tax evasion

    c. violation of immigration laws

    d. possession of drugs

**23.** Who became the first black chairman of either of the major political parties?

    a. Lee Atwater

    b. Jesse Jackson

    c. Andrew Young

    d. Ron Brown

**24.** The brave child known as the "Bubble Boy" died at Houston's Children's Hospital in 1984 after a lifelong struggle against

    a. polio

    b. deficiency of the immune system

    c. cerebral palsy

    d. lupus

**25.** Merv Griffin, TV star and producer, entered the world of high finance during the 1980s. Who was his most serious big business opponent?

    a. Frank Lorenzo

    b. Ross Johnson

    **c.** Carl Icahn

    **d.** Donald Trump

**26.** What did Joan Quigley do for Nancy Reagan?

    **a.** She was her press secretary.

    **b.** She was her hairdresser.

    **c.** She was her astrologer.

    **d.** She was her masseuse.

**27.** When Chief Justice Warren Burger retired in 1986, who succeeded him to become the sixteenth chief justice of the United States?

    **a.** William Rehnquist

    **b.** Thurgood Marshall

    **c.** Harry A. Blackman

    **d.** Byron R. White

**28.** What Democrat did President Reagan appoint as ambassador to the United Nations in 1981?

    **a.** Jeane Kirkpatrick

    **b.** Elizabeth Dole

    **c.** Geraldine Ferraro

    **d.** Patricia Schroeder

**29.** In the early 1980s, which U.S. senator had a following among the New Right that was second in size only to that of President Reagan?

    **a.** Senator Strom Thurmond of South Carolina

    **b.** Senator Paul Laxalt of Nevada

    **c.** Senator Jesse Helms of North Carolina

    **d.** Senator Orrin Hatch of Utah

**30.** Baby Jessica McClure caught the nation's attention in 1987 when she was rescued from

    **a.** a pack of coyotes

    **b.** a shipwreck

    c. an abandoned well

    d. a fire

**31.** What leading opponent of apartheid was ostracized from the antiapartheid movement in 1989?

    a. Nelson Mandela

    b. Winnie Mandela

    c. P. W. Botha

    d. Desmond Tutu

**32.** Who is the media-conscious mayor whose popularity dimmed after Howard Beach and Black Monday?

    a. Tom Bradley

    b. Ed Koch

    c. Harold Washington

    d. Andrew Young

**33.** Whom did the Fox Television Network put on the air to compete for late-night viewers with Johnny Carson?

    a. Oprah Winfrey

    b. Joan Rivers

    c. Cristina Ferrare

    d. Maria Shriver

**34.** Where did Robin Givens file for divorce against her husband, Mike Tyson?

    a. Bernardsville, New Jersey

    b. Las Vegas, Nevada

    c. Los Angeles, California

    d. Cleveland, Ohio

**35.** In 1984, Pierre Trudeau resigned as prime minister of

    a. France

    b. Canada

    c. Switzerland

    d. Sweden

**36.** In May 1985, Sam and Pati Frustaci became the first U.S. couple to

   **a.** publicize bi-coastal marriage

   **b.** become the parents of septuplets

   **c.** become the parents of a test-tube baby

   **d.** travel in space together

**37.** What happened in the lives of Woody Allen and Mia Farrow during the 1980s?

   **a.** They both won Academy Awards.

   **b.** They married after many years of cohabitation.

   **c.** They became parents together for the first time.

   **d.** all of the above

**38.** What did Peter Holm seek in his divorce settlement with television actress Joan Collins?

   **a.** child custody

   **b.** 20 percent of her earnings during their marriage

   **c.** a role in "Dynasty"

   **d.** $1 million and $80,000 a month in temporary support

**39.** In 1981 the television personality whose trademark phrase was "And that's the way it is" retired. What was his name?

   **a.** Eric Severeid

   **b.** Jackie Gleason

   **c.** Walter Cronkite

   **d.** William ("Count") Basie

**40.** Which Nazi war criminal, hunted for forty years, was finally declared dead in June 1985?

   **a.** Adolf Eichmann

   **b.** Klaus Barbie

   **c.** Josef Mengele

   **d.** Rudolf Hess

# TEST 1: *Explanatory Answers*

1. **(b)** Susan Estrich became the first woman to manage a national campaign after Democratic candidate Michael Dukakis fired his manager, John Sasso, in the fall of 1987 for secretly releasing a videotape damaging to his fellow candidate Senator Joseph Biden. Estrich, a tenured professor at Harvard, had previously served as an adviser to former presidential candidates Ted Kennedy and Walter Mondale. However, when Dukakis's ratings in the polls fell just before the 1988 election, the candidate rehired John Sasso. Critics said that Estrich had not effectively countered George Bush's negative portrayals of Dukakis, ran a chaotic organization, and overall had "lousy political antennae."

2. **(a)** FBI agents allege that John Gotti became the boss of the Gambino family, one of five New York Mafia organizations, when he arranged the 1985 murder of Paul Castellano outside Sparks Steak House in Manhattan. Nicknamed "the Dapper Don" for his monogrammed Gucci socks and $2000 suits, Gotti has twice beaten state and federal indictments. The most publicized trial occurred in 1987 when a Brooklyn jury acquitted him of racketeering, a verdict that stunned federal prosecutors. Gotti allegedly heads a crime ring that engages in loan sharking, gambling, and extortion in the garment and construction industries. After posting bail in February 1989 for his third arrest—this time for plotting to shoot a union leader—Gotti gave detectives 3-to-1 odds that he would beat the rap again.

3. **(b)** Harvard MBA Mary Cunningham reluctantly left her position in strategic planning at the Bendix Corporation, a manufacturing and natural resources company, when the Bendix board of directors raised a brouhaha over her close relationship with her boss, married Chairman William Agee, age forty-three. The twenty-nine-year-old Cunningham, also married, insisted it was friendship, not romance, and resigned under pressure. She chronicled the ouster in her 1984 book, *Power Play*. Within six months of leaving Bendix, Cunningham had a top corporate position at Joseph Seagram & Sons, Inc. She and William Agee subsequently divorced their respective spouses, married, formed Semper Enterprises—a venture capital consulting firm—and had two children. In

1986 Cunningham quit the corporate world to establish the Nurturing Network, an agency that combats abortion by providing support and resources to unwed mothers.

**4. (b)** Dr. C. Everett Koop, unlike most of his predecessors, was more than a figurehead as surgeon general of the United States. He is credited with helping to change Americans' attitudes toward smoking and with educating the public about AIDS. In his ground-breaking 1986 AIDS report he called for humane treatment of AIDS victims, early AIDS sex education, and the use of condoms to prevent the spread of the disease. He resigned as surgeon general in 1989 after eight years of service.

**5. (c)** Baby M, so named in court papers, was the subject of a custody case between her natural mother, Mary Beth Whitehead, and William and Elizabeth Stern. The Sterns, a New Jersey couple in their early forties, had legally contracted with Whitehead in 1985 to conceive the child for them through artificial insemination, with William Stern as the biological father. When the baby was born in 1986, the Sterns named her Melissa. Whitehead, married and the mother of two other children, claimed that the overwhelming experience of childbirth changed her mind about parting with the baby she named Sara. Whitehead refused the $10,000 surrogate fee from the Sterns, and the adults went to court. When the legal battles ended in 1988, the Sterns won custody of Baby M, but Whitehead was given generous visitation rights.

**6. (d)** Divorce attorney Marvin Mitchelson had a plateful of trouble in the 1980s, including charges of rape and professional misconduct. In addition, he was labeled an "appeals nuisance." In 1985 two of his former clients charged him with rape, and although the criminal investigation was dropped for lack of evidence, the two women sued Mitchelson in civil court and won a $56,000 judgment. The state bar of California charged Mitchelson with a number of professional offenses, including billing outrageous fees and keeping unearned advance payments that should have been returned to clients. His pocketbook, as well as his reputation, was hit when the California courts fined him $40,000 for clogging up the court system with frivolous appeals.

7. **(c)** In a tense contest that lasted two months, Gary Kasparov of the Soviet Union defeated Anatoli Karpov to win the championship of the World Chess Federation and become the sport's youngest champion. Karpov, a fellow Soviet superstar, had held the title for ten years.

8. **(d)** In examining Quayle's background the news media charged that the draft-eligible Quayle had used family influence to enter the Indiana National Guard ahead of other young men, effectively avoiding active duty. Although Quayle finally admitted that he had personally sought the support of a retired National Guard general who had worked for his grandfather, he denied that he had broken any rules to get into the National Guard. The Republicans diffused the controversy by attacking the press for implying that National Guard service was unpatriotic. Regarding the other charges from the press, Quayle had no objection. He acknowledged a low grade-point average in college but joked that President Franklin D. Roosevelt had not been an academic genius. And Quayle had no problem with being compared to Robert Redford; he had himself referred to the resemblance in campaign literature.

9. **(c)** Jesse Jackson has long campaigned for civil and economic rights and against drugs, but he has not held an elected office. A native of South Carolina, Jackson left the Chicago Theological Seminary to work for Dr. Martin Luther King, Jr., as the director of Operation Breadbasket, the economic arm of the Southern Christian Leadership Conference. In 1972, four years after King's assassination, Jackson formed his own organization, PUSH (People United to Serve Humanity), which promotes economic independence among minorities. PUSH also sponsors an anti-drug program for inner-city students. Jackson's 1988 run for the Democratic presidential nomination was both impressive and well executed. Among a large field of candidates Jackson finished as the runner-up in the contest. At the Democratic National Convention in July he received 1219 votes to Dukakis's 2876.

10. **(c)** Karen Silkwood, who died in an automobile accident in 1974, gained posthumous fame with the release of the movie *Silkwood*, starring Meryl Streep. Silkwood had been an employee at a Kerr-McGee plant that processed nuclear fuel rods. On the night of her death she was driving to meet a *New York*

*Times* reporter, allegedly with company records in hand, to discuss her belief that the plant was contaminated with plutonium. A ten-year court battle followed in which Silkwood's heirs sought compensation from Kerr-McGee for plutonium contamination that Silkwood had suffered. A jury found in the heirs' favor, but Kerr-McGee won two rulings on appeal. In 1986 Kerr-McGee, admitting no guilt, agreed to pay Silkwood's estate $1.38 million; more than half of the settlement went to legal fees.

11. **(d)** Sally Ride became the first American woman in space in June 1983 on the first of her two missions aboard the *Challenger* spaceship. After the *Challenger* exploded on its tenth mission, on January 28, 1986—resulting in the deaths of all seven crew members—she served as the only astronaut on the president's investigative commission. When the hearings ended, NASA appointed her to head a major study to identify long-range goals for the space agency. In May 1987, Ride announced that she was resigning from NASA to take a fellowship at the Center for International Security and Arms Control at Stanford, the university at which she had earned her PhD in x-ray astrophysics.

12. **(c)** When Harold Washington, Chicago's first black mayor, died in office in 1987, black Alderman Eugene Sawyer became acting mayor until elections could be held. Richard M. Daley defeated Sawyer in the primary and went on to win the general election against Republican Edward R. Vrdolyak and black Alderman Timothy C. Evans. Richard M. Daley is the son of former mayor Richard J. Daley, last of the big city political bosses who ruled Chicago from 1955 to 1976.

13. **(b)** When newscaster Christine Craft was demoted from her job as anchor at KMBC-TV in Kansas City, Missouri, she filed suit against her employer, Metromedia, for sex discrimination. Craft alleged that her news director had said she could no longer appear on the air because she was "too old, too unattractive, and did not defer to men." Metromedia denied the charges, and a legal tangle ensued. In two trials in Kansas City, juries ruled in her favor, but two Reagan-appointed judges overruled the verdicts and monetary awards. Finally the case was submitted to the Supreme Court. The "court of last resort," however, did not agree to hear the case.

**14. (a)** Terry Anderson, chief correspondent for the Associated Press in the Middle East, was taken hostage in West Beirut on March 16, 1985. His captors belong to Hizballah, the Shi'ite Muslim fundamentalist group that is reportedly financed by Iran. The terrorists kidnapped Anderson and other Westerners in hopes of trading them for seventeen of their comrades imprisoned in Kuwait. During Anderson's imprisonment his father and brother have died in the United States, and his second daughter, Sulome, has been born. On a videotape made in October 1988, Anderson said to his family, "Kiss my daughters. Keep your spirits up, and I will try to do the same. One day soon, God willing, this will end."

**15. (d)** "The Refrigerator" is William Perry, defensive tackle for the Chicago Bears football team. "The Microwave," Vinnie Johnson, plays guard on the Detroit Pistons basketball team, and "Oil Can" (Dennis) Boyd pitches for the Boston Red Sox.

**16. (c)** In 1982, Samantha Smith of Manchester, Maine, wrote a peace plea to then-Soviet leader Yuri Andropov. She was hailed as a peacemaker and ambassador of goodwill by both Americans and Soviets. In 1985, on the way home from filming the "Lime Street" television series with Robert Wagner in London, Smith's plane crashed half a mile from her hometown airport. The author of the book *Journey to the Soviet Union* was thirteen when she died.

**17. (c)** President Arias of Costa Rica received the Nobel Prize for writing the peace plan that was signed by five Central American presidents in Guatemala City in the summer of 1987. Arias, oblivious to the possibility of winning, was at a weekend retreat without telephone or television when the announcement was made. The Reagan administration was equally surprised—but less joyful—at the announcement because the Arias plan did not call for the Sandinistas to negotiate a cease-fire directly with the *contra* rebels. In addition, it did not call for the withdrawal of Soviet and Cuban advisors from Nicaragua—two conditions that Reagan believed were essential to a peace settlement in the region.

**18. (c)** Bernhard Goetz, the so-called Subway Vigilante, claimed he shot four youths on the New York subway because they were about to rob him. No one was killed, but one of the young men remains paralyzed and brain damaged from the shooting.

Goetz was tried and acquitted for attempted murder but was convicted of illegal gun possession and sentenced to one year in prison.

**19. (b)** In 1988 the Pakistan People's Party won the country's democratic election, and thirty-five-year-old Benazir Bhutto, educated at Harvard and Oxford, became prime minister. Her victory came after she had spent seven years in jail, exile, or detention as ordered by the autocratic regime of President Mohammed Zia ul-Haq. Zia, backed by the military, had ousted Bhutto's father, Prime Minister Zulfikar Ali Bhutto, in 1977 and authorized his execution two years later. Zia died in a plane crash on August 12, 1988, three months before Benazir Bhutto's triumph.

**20. (b)** Charles Dederich, founder of the Synanon Foundation, and two of his "Imperial Marines" at the drug rehabilitation center admitted they had placed a $4\frac{1}{2}$-foot diamondback rattle-snake in the mailbox of Los Angeles lawyer Paul Morantz. Morantz was bitten in the thumb by the deadly snake as he reached for his mail. A neighbor saved his life by quickly applying a tourniquet. The murder attempt happened just three weeks after Morantz won a $300,000 settlement against Synanon for holding a woman captive in the 1970s.

**21. (c)** Kitty Dukakis has suffered from cross-addiction—a dependency on more than one drug, which can occur sequentially or simultaneously. Early in Michael Dukakis's presidential campaign Kitty Dukakis talked publicly about her twenty-six-year reliance on diet pills, an addiction she overcame in 1982. In the weeks following her husband's defeat in November 1988 she was drinking alarming amounts of alcohol and decided to enter a private clinic in Newport, Rhode Island, for treatment. Researchers estimate that cross-dependency affects between 40 and 70 percent of people who enter drug treatment programs.

**22. (c)** Bhagwan Shree Rajneesh was arrested for overstaying a temporary 1981 visa and for arranging sham marriages so that some of his Indian devotees could remain in the United States. His arrest ended a four-year investigation into alleged violations of immigration laws at the bhagwan's 64,000-acre ranch in Antelope, Oregon. At the retreat, where he housed his fleet of ninety-three Rolls-Royces, the "swami of sex" encouraged his followers to "be in the moment" and practice free love, using condoms and gloves. The bhagwan faced the enmity of his conservative Oregon neighbors and troubles with his gun-toting secretary, Ma Anand Sheela, who fled to West Germany just before the bhagwan's arrest in March 1985. Despite asserting his innocence to the immigration authorities, the bhagwan pleaded guilty and returned home to Poona, India.

**23. (d)** Washington lawyer Ron Brown was appointed national chairman of the Democratic party in 1989, the first black to hold the position for either the Democrats or Republicans. Raised in Harlem, Brown graduated from Middlebury College, was an army officer in Korea and Germany, and has been a leader of the National Urban League. His appointment was backed by Senator Edward Kennedy, the AFL-CIO, and the Reverend Jesse Jackson, among others.

**24. (b)** Although Americans never knew David's last name, they did know about his life, spent inside a germ-free plastic bubble at the Children's Hospital in Houston and a series of bubbles in his home. A victim of immunodeficiency, David lived to be twelve years old, longer than any other human being without a functioning immune system. A straight-A student, David ventured outdoors only once—in 1977, when NASA gave him a specially designed "space" suit. David and his family decided to chance a risky bone marrow transplant operation in 1984, and the "Bubble Boy" died two weeks later.

**25. (d)** Television producer Merv Griffin acquired a number of properties in the 1980s, but he fought a major battle to buy Resorts International, Inc.—a hotel and casino company based in Atlantic City, New Jersey—from Donald Trump. Griffin successfully derailed Trump's attempt to take the company private and won a bidding war against Trump with the stockholders. Griffin, who made a fortune on the game show "Wheel of Fortune," also owns the Beverly Hilton Hotel, several radio stations, and 157 acres of undeveloped land in Beverly Hills.

**26. (c)** In his 1988 book, *For the Record*, White House Chief of Staff Donald Regan wrote that the First Lady frequently consulted an astrologer to determine the timing of the president's activities. The press identified Mrs. Reagan's astrologer as Joan Quigley, a San Francisco socialite in her sixties. Although Mrs. Quigley admitted she had cast astrological charts for Mrs. Reagan, the president adamantly assured the public that astrology had never played a part in determining U.S. policy. Mrs. Quigley no longer forecasts the stars for the Reagans, but the public can buy her astrological advice on a series of twelve cassettes.

**27.** **(a)** When Warren Burger stepped down after seventeen years as chief justice, President Reagan picked William Rehnquist to assume the powerful position. Rehnquist, known for his conservative ideology, has served on the court since 1969.

**28.** **(a)** Jeane Kirkpatrick served as ambassador to the United Nations during President Reagan's first term in office. Although a lifelong Democrat, she was chosen by Reagan because of her tough-minded views on foreign policy and her belief that authoritarian regimes were preferable to Communist ones. Kirkpatrick switched to the Republican party in 1985, fueling speculation that she would seek national elective office or that she sought a cabinet appointment. Instead, she returned to her previous position as a Fellow at the American Enterprise Institute, pursued teaching at Georgetown University, and started a syndicated weekly newspaper column.

**29.** **(c)** In terms of campaign funds raised, Senator Jesse Helms of North Carolina was second only to Ronald Reagan as a favorite of the New Right during the early 1980s. In 1970 Helms left the Democratic party to run as a Republican and won a North Carolina seat in the U.S. Senate. Throughout the 1970s the former Baptist deacon introduced numerous bills to prohibit abortion, sex education, busing, and federal aid to refugees from abroad. He pushed these and other conservative causes in a garrulous fashion that did not endear him to fellow senators but did win him a large popular following.

**30.** **(c)** In October 1987 eighteen-month-old Jessica McClure fell down a narrow abandoned well in Midland, Texas, and became trapped 22 feet underground in a 12-inch-wide cavity. Her parents and millions of Americans followed the rescue effort that took $2\frac{1}{2}$ days to free the little girl. Using a high-pressure hydraulic drill, rescuers made an adult-size shaft alongside the well. Two paramedics descended into the shaft, placed a balloon under the child to keep her from slipping deeper into the well, secured her on a board, and pulled her to safety. Baby Jessica survived the ordeal with no major injuries.

**31. (b)** The leaders of South Africa's antiapartheid movement publicly denounced Winnie Mandela when she was implicated in a police investigation of three murders that involved her teenage bodyguards, the so-called Mandela United Football Club. In 1986, Mandela had been hailed as a South African heroine for defying a government ban to return to her home in Soweto. Over the next three years, however, her Soweto neighbors criticized her for encouraging violence and accused her street-tough bodyguards of criminal acts. Winnie Mandela is the wife of jailed African National Congress (ANC) leader Nelson Mandela and has been prominent in the antiapartheid movement throughout his twenty-seven-year imprisonment.

**32. (b)** Ed Koch enjoyed two successive terms as mayor of New York City between 1977 and 1985 and easily won election to his third term in 1985. Koch was credited with helping rescue the Big Apple from near bankruptcy in the mid-70s by revitalizing the financial and business services industries. However, his honeymoon with his constituency ended after his 1985 reelection with a barrage of investigations, indictments, and convictions against members of his administration. The charges ranged from bribery and perjury to extortion and conspiracy. Then, in December 1986, three blacks were brutally assaulted by a gang of whites in Howard Beach (in the borough of Queens), drawing the nation's attention to the city's mounting racial tension. On October 19, 1987, the stock market crash sent New York's healthiest industry reeling. Koch's problems were further compounded by a backlash against his support of big real estate developers as citizens complained of high rents and cramped quarters.

**33. (b)** On May 6, 1986, Fox Broadcasting Network announced that Joan Rivers would star in a late-night talk show that would compete with Johnny Carson's "Tonight Show." Rivers had been a permanent guest host of Carson's show since 1983 and admitted she owed much of her television success to Carson. Carson was not amused. He fired Rivers and refused to speak to her. "The Late Show Starring Joan Rivers" had its debut on October 9, 1986, but didn't prove to be serious competition for Carson. Rivers left the show after the May 15,

1987, telecast. The title of the show was changed, and a number of different hosts took over on a rotating basis.

**34. (c)** In the fall of 1988, Robin Givens filed for divorce in Los Angeles, although her home with heavyweight champion Mike Tyson during their one-year marriage had been in Bernardsville, New Jersey. Tyson supporters alleged that Givens, a star of ABC's "Head of the Class," was seeking to establish residency in California because it is a community-property state, where divorcing spouses split earnings fifty-fifty. Givens—who had described Tyson as a "dangerous manic-depressive" in the couple's much-publicized television interview with Barbara Walters—claimed she was physically abused by the champ. Tyson countered that the twenty-four-year-old actress and her young-looking mother had plotted the marriage and divorce in order to steal his money.

**35. (b)** Pierre Trudeau served as prime minister of Canada for sixteen years, the longest tenure of any contemporary Western leader. He resigned just before a national election in 1984 when his personal popularity had dimmed and his Liberal Party had fallen behind in the polls. As prime minister, Trudeau helped to reconcile some long-standing divisions between Canada's anglophone majority and the French-descended minority concentrated in Quebec. He also led the initiative in Parliament to revamp the constitution and add a charter of civil rights. The son of a millionaire, Trudeau didn't alter his flamboyant life-style during his first years as prime minister, driving sports cars and going out to discotheques. The country was shocked by his marriage to twenty-two-year-old Margaret Sinclair and years later by the couple's much-publicized divorce.

**36. (b)** Sam and Pati Frustaci set the record for multiple births in the United States in May 1985. Mrs. Frustaci, a high school English teacher, gave birth to seven children—one who was stillborn, three who subsequently died in the hospital, and two boys and a girl who survived. In addition to the problems of caring for three high-risk newborns and their one-year-old son, the couple faced more than $1 million in hospital bills. The three surviving septuplets suffer from mild cerebral palsy, eyesight problems, and chronic lung disorder.

**37.** **(c)** Woody Allen and Mia Farrow became the parents of a baby boy, Satchel—the first for Allen at age fifty-two and Farrow's fourth biological child at age forty-two. Farrow also has five adopted children. Allen said of their new baby, "The baby is fine. The only problem is, he looks like Edward G. Robinson."

**38.** **(d)** In 1987 "Dynasty" star Joan Collins filed for divorce from her fourth husband, forty-year-old Peter Holm, who had been a Swedish pop star. Holm picketed their former home in his bid for a hefty settlement—about $1 million plus $80,000 a month to cover his living expenses temporarily. The fifty-four-year-old Collins stated in court that their prenuptial agreement entitled him to only 20 percent of her earnings during their thirteen-month marriage. Represented by palimony lawyer Marvin Mitchelson, Collins won her case when the attorney produced an attractive twenty-three-year-old witness who testified she had been Holm's lover during his marriage to Collins.

**39.** **(c)** Walter Cronkite ended his last broadcast on the "CBS Evening News" in March 1981 with his familiar sign-off: "And that's the way it is." A Midwesterner—who, like Ronald Reagan, had early broadcast training as a radio baseball announcer— Walter Cronkite established an enviable credibility rating with the American public. Voted the "most trusted man in America" in many public opinion polls, Cronkite anchored the CBS nightly news for nearly twenty years. Toward the end of his career he was watched by 18.5 million Americans each night. When he retired at the age of sixty-four, Cronkite was succeeded by Dan Rather.

**40.** **(c)** A doctor at Auschwitz, Mengele presided over the selection process whereby Jews were either sent to the gas chambers or became slave laborers. For this and the medical experiments he conducted on prisoners, Mengele was called "the angel of death" and "the most hated man in the world." In 1985 a skeleton exhumed from a graveyard in São Paulo, Brazil, was reported to be Mengele. After a long investigation by medical experts it was concluded that the skeleton was Mengele and that he had probably drowned on a beach in São Paulo in 1979.

AP/Wide World Photos

# TEST 2

# *U.S. Events*

*America is back, standing tall.*

*—RONALD REAGAN*

1. The 1980 U.S. Census revealed that
   a. the traditional family, consisting of father, mother, and one or more children, accounted for less than one third of all U.S. households
   b. the median age of the U.S. population was about thirty
   c. the total U.S. population was 226,504,825
   d. all of the above

2. In April 1980 a secret U.S. military effort to rescue American hostages held prisoner in the U.S. embassy in Teheran failed because
   a. the Iranian government had advance notice of the raid
   b. U.S. helicopters developed mechanical problems
   c. the Soviet Union came to the aid of Iran
   d. the hostages had been moved out of the embassy

3. During a six-month period in 1980 the United States received more than 125,000 refugees from which country?
   a. Haiti
   b. Cuba
   c. Nicaragua
   d. El Salvador

4. Who was the Republican who ran as an independent in the 1980 Carter–Reagan presidential election?
   a. Howard Baker
   b. John Connally
   c. Robert Dole
   d. John Anderson

5. On May 18, 1980, Mt. St. Helens erupted in a tremendous explosion that created a 2-mile-wide crater. In what state is this volcano located?
   a. Alaska
   b. Washington

   **c.** Hawaii

   **d.** Oregon

**6.** What environmental peril threatened California's fruit and vegetable crops in 1981?

   **a.** drought conditions

   **b.** a vast swarm of locusts

   **c.** the Mediterranean fruit fly

   **d.** unseasonably cold weather

**7.** The U.S. spacecraft *Columbia,* which made its first flight in 1981, was notable because it

   **a.** was the first to repair a damaged satellite

   **b.** was the first space shuttle

   **c.** had the first black astronaut aboard

   **d.** provided the closest look ever at the Northern Lights

**8.** The oldest person ever to assume the U.S. presidency, Ronald Reagan was how old when he was sworn in on January 20, 1981?

   **a.** sixty years old

   **b.** sixty-two years old

   **c.** sixty-five years old

   **d.** sixty-nine years old

**9.** What group of federal employees went on strike in 1981, precipitating a dramatic showdown with President Ronald Reagan?

   **a.** post office workers

   **b.** railroad workers

   **c.** air traffic controllers

   **d.** FBI agents

**10.** In 1981 twenty-five-year old John Hinckley, Jr., shot President Ronald Reagan because

   **a.** he wanted to impress a movie actress

   **b.** God told him to do it

   c. he disagreed with the President's policies

   d. for no apparent reason

11. A massive criminal investigation effort was focused on Atlanta, Georgia, in 1981 following the murders of

   a. police officers

   b. black children

   c. prostitutes

   d. homosexuals

12. Seven people in the Chicago area died in 1982 as a result of poison introduced into which over-the-counter medicine?

   a. Tylenol

   b. Contac

   c. Anacin

   d. Excedrin

13. The largest public demonstration/protest/rally of the decade occurred in 1982 and concerned

   a. abortion

   b. disarmament

   c. racial equality

   d. budgetary cuts in social programs

14. Identified by the U.S. government in 1983 as the nation's top medical priority, AIDS (acquired immune deficiency syndrome) can be contracted by

   a. sexual contact

   b. sharing of needles among drug users

   c. blood transfusions

   d. all of the above

15. *A Nation at Risk*, a 1983 report on the quality of U.S. education, recommended

   a. longer school days

   b. merit pay for teachers

   c. higher admission standards for colleges

   d. all of the above

**16.** What country did the United States invade in 1983?

   a. Vietnam

   b. Grenada

   c. Guinea

   d. the Falkland Islands

**17.** In 1983 the U.S. government offered to buy the town of Times Beach, Missouri, which had been contaminated by

   a. radiation from nuclear weapons testing in the 1940s

   b. dioxin in the soil

   c. radiation from a nuclear power plant accident

   d. poisonous gas leaking from a nearby chemical plant

**18.** U.S. financial aid poured into Nicaragua and El Salvador in the 1980s to support

   a. the ruling government in each country

   b. rebel forces in each country

   c. the government in El Salvador, rebels in Nicaragua

   d. the government in Nicaragua, rebels in El Salvador

**19.** In President Ronald Reagan's landslide reelection in 1984 he lost only one state, the home state of his opponent, Walter Mondale, which was

   a. North Dakota

   b. South Dakota

   c. Wisconsin

   d. Minnesota

**20.** In 1985 two libel trials came to an end: former Israeli defense minister Ariel Sharon *vs. Time* magazine and General William C. Westmoreland *vs.* CBS. What were the outcomes?

   a. Both Sharon and Westmoreland won.

   b. Both Sharon and Westmoreland lost.

    c. Sharon lost; Westmoreland dropped his suit.

    d. Westmoreland lost; Sharon dropped his suit.

**21.** In 1986 the World Court ruled against the United States in a case involving Nicaragua because the United States

    a. aided in mining Nicaraguan ports

    b. held Nicaraguan officials as hostages

    c. imposed a blockade against Nicaragua

    d. shot down two Nicaraguan airplanes

**22.** The bombing of a house occupied by a radical group called MOVE led to a fire that destroyed sixty-one homes in the city of

    a. Los Angeles

    b. Detroit

    c. Philadelphia

    d. New York

**23.** One of the seven astronauts killed in the explosion of the space shuttle *Challenger* was Sharon Christa McAuliffe, who was

    a. a schoolteacher

    b. a navy pilot

    c. an engineer

    d. a nurse

**24.** The Immigration Reform and Control Act of 1986 was intended to

    a. prohibit employers from hiring illegal alien workers

    b. provide legal status to illegal aliens residing in the United States prior to 1982

    c. regulate the flow of immigrants into the United States

    d. all of the above

**25.** In May 1987 thirty-seven American sailors on board the USS *Stark* died when the ship was accidentally attacked in the Persian Gulf by a warplane from

a. Iraq

b. Iran

c. Lebanon

d. the Soviet Union

**26.** At the end of the 1980s the number of homeless people in the United States was estimated to be as high as

a. 10 million

b. 3 million

c. 250,000

d. 50,000

**27.** In 1987 Judge Douglas Ginsburg asked that his nomination to the U.S. Supreme Court be withdrawn when it was discovered that

a. he was in poor health

b. he owed back income taxes

c. he had smoked marijuana

d. he was an alcoholic

**28.** A 1987 report on the Iran-*contra* affair, issued by a joint Senate–House investigating committee, said that President Ronald Reagan

a. did not know about the diversion of funds to the *contras*

b. did know about the diversion of funds to the *contras* and approved it

c. knew about the diversion of funds but did not approve it

d. should bear the ultimate responsibility for the wrongdoings of his staff

**29.** In December 1987 President Ronald Reagan and Soviet leader Mikhail Gorbachev signed a historic arms control treaty that eliminated

    **a.** short-range nuclear weapons

    **b.** intermediate-range nuclear weapons

    **c.** long-range nuclear weapons

    **d.** some items in all of the above categories

**30.** Which foreign government leader was indicted in the United States in 1988 for drug trafficking?

    **a.** Fidel Castro of Cuba

    **b.** Manuel Noriega of Panama

    **c.** Muammar el-Qaddafi of Libya

    **d.** Roberto d'Aubuisson of El Salvador

**31.** In 1988 Congress enacted a new Medicare supplement called the Catastrophic Care Act, which provided for

    **a.** expanded medical coverage for the elderly and disabled

    **b.** increased premiums to be paid by Medicare beneficiaries

    **c.** limitations on Medicare patients' out-of-pocket expenses for hospitalization and doctor bills

    **d.** all of the above

**32.** In 1988 forest fires devastated over a million acres of which national forest?

    **a.** Denali National Park

    **b.** Yellowstone National Park

    **c.** Bryce Canyon National Park

    **d.** Yosemite National Park

**33.** At the end of the 1980s the military draft had been

    **a.** expanded to include women

    **b.** discontinued in favor of an all-volunteer force

    **c.** turned into a lottery system inducting men eighteen years of age and older into military service or alternative public service programs

    **d.** modified to require all men at age eighteen to register for a draft in case of national emergency

**34.** In 1988 Congress approved financial payments to sixty thousand Japanese-Americans to compensate for

    **a.** their internment in U.S. detention camps during World War II

    **b.** the years of discrimination in hiring that they had suffered

    **c.** Asian exclusion provisions in U.S. immigration laws during the 1930s

    **d.** all of the above

**35.** On July 3, 1988, 290 people were killed when the *Vincennes*, a U.S. Navy warship, mistakenly shot down a commercial airliner belonging to

    **a.** Iran

    **b.** Iraq

    **c.** Lebanon

    **d.** South Korea

**36.** On December 21, 1988, a bomb smuggled onto Pan Am flight 103 exploded over Lockerbie, Scotland, killing everyone aboard. The bomb was hidden in a

    **a.** briefcase

    **b.** video camera

    **c.** child's toy

    **d.** radio cassette player

**37.** The largest oil spill in U.S. history happened on March 24, 1989, and was caused by an oil tanker owned by

    **a.** Exxon

    **b.** Mobil

    **c.** Texaco

    **d.** Chevron

**38.** Which of the following Supreme Court justices was not appointed during the 1980s?

a. Sandra Day O'Connor

b. Antonin Scalia

c. Anthony M. Kennedy

d. John Paul Stevens

**39.** At the end of the decade the federal poverty line for an American family of four was equal to an annual income of

a. $11,611

b. $12,228

c. $13,982

d. $14,695

**40.** At the end of the 1980s which political party or parties controlled each house of the U.S. Congress?

a. Democrats controlled both houses of Congress.

b. Republicans controlled both houses of Congress.

c. Democrats controlled the Senate; Republicans, the House.

d. Republicans controlled the Senate; Democrats, the House.

# TEST 2: Explanatory Answers

1. **(d)** The 1980 Census was the largest in scope of all U.S. Census reports and took nine years to plan. When its final figures were released on December 31, 1980, after nine months of data processing, the figures not only tallied the total number of Americans but also reflected a wide variety of changes in American society. The 1980 Census was not only historic but also controversial. It aimed to be the most accurate census ever taken, but a number of cities, including Detroit, New York, Philadelphia, and Atlanta, claimed they were undercounted. Because congressional representation and federal financial aid are both dependent on Census figures, these cities filed suit against the Census Bureau.

2. **(b)** On April 25, 1980, six U.S. C-130 transport planes and eight RH-53 helicopters attempted a dramatic rescue mission to free fifty-three American hostages held in the U.S. embassy in Teheran. In the early stages of the secret mission three of the helicopters developed mechanical problems, and two of them never reached the refueling rendezvous point, "Desert One," 250 miles outside Teheran. The third crippled chopper made it to the desert landing but was rendered useless by the failure of its hydraulic system. Because only five helicopters remained to continue on to Teheran (plans called for a minimum of six), the mission had to be aborted. During the subsequent withdrawal from the desert one of the helicopters collided with one of the transport planes, causing an explosion that killed eight American servicemen.

3. **(b)** The mass exodus to the United States commenced when Fidel Castro opened up the Cuban port of Mariel and granted exit visas to anyone wishing to leave the country. That decision, coupled with President Jimmy Carter's "open arms" policy, resulted in a remarkable "sealift" that carried the Cubans into Florida, many of them on makeshift boats called the "ragtag regatta." When it was discovered that 2746 of the immigrants were criminals or mentally ill, the United States began negotiations with Cuba to return the "excludables." In 1984 the two countries reached an agreement, and a year later the first group of excludables was sent back to Cuba.

4. **(d)** A moderate Republican, ten-term congressman John Anderson abandoned the race for his party's nomination in 1980

to run for the U.S. presidency as an independent. Called "the thinking man's candidate," Anderson was a nontraditional campaigner whose eclectic ideas appealed to both Democrats and Republicans. In the final balloting he failed to capture any electoral votes but did win seven percent of the popular vote.

5. **(b)** The volcano, situated in southwestern Washington, erupted in a blast estimated to be five hundred times more powerful than the atomic blast that destroyed Hiroshima in 1945. The explosion literally blew the top off of Mount St. Helens, reducing its height by 1300 feet. The shock waves leveled 44,000 acres of trees, and volcanic ash 7 inches deep covered areas of Washington, Idaho, and Montana for days. The damage was estimated at $2.7 billion, and thirty-four persons were reported dead. The volcano erupted twice more within a month's time.

6. **(c)** The Mediterranean fruit fly, or "Medfly," a tiny pest about the size of a grain of rice, infested the lush orchards and farmlands throughout California, which grows about 40 percent of U.S. produce. Governor Jerry Brown resisted aerial spraying of the pesticide Malathion because he did not want Californians exposed to a chemical that was suspected of causing cancer and birth defects. However, the Reagan administration, concerned about the collapse of the State's $14-billion-a-year agricultural industry, threatened a nationwide quarantine of California produce unless Brown approved aerial spraying. When ground war techniques failed to eradicate the Medfly, Brown reluctantly allowed helicopters to spray Malathion.

7. **(b)** *Columbia* was the first space shuttle developed by NASA. Unlike previous space vehicles, a space shuttle is a commuter space transportation system capable of being flown back to earth and relaunched. Astronauts Robert L. Crippen and John W. Young manned *Columbia's* first flight in 1981. They made thirty-six orbits around the earth in $54\frac{1}{2}$ hours at speeds of up to 17,000 mph. *Columbia* was flown back to earth and later relaunched seven times.

8. **(d)** The fortieth president of the United States, Ronald Reagan at age sixty-nine was one year older than the next oldest man ever to assume the office—William Henry Harrison, who was

inaugurated in 1841. When elected for a second term in 1984, Reagan was seventy-three.

9. **(c)** On August 3, 1981, more than thirteen thousand air traffic controllers walked off the job in a dispute over wages, length of the work week, and retirement issues. Claiming that the walkout was illegal because federal employees are bound by a no-strike oath, President Ronald Reagan said the strikers would be fired if they did not return to work. Five leaders of the controllers' union, the Professional Air Traffic Controllers Organization (PATCO), were hauled off to jail, and the federal government levied fines of up to $1 million a day against the union. Although some air traffic controllers did return to work, approximately 11,500 lost their jobs permanently.

10. **(a)** Hinckley became obsessed with love for actress Jody Foster, whom he first saw in *Taxi Driver*, a movie about a loner who tries to shoot a presidential candidate. On March 31, 1981, Hinckley fired a shower of bullets from a 22-caliber handgun and wounded Reagan as well as presidential press secretary James Brady, Secret Service agent Timothy McCarthy, and police officer Thomas Delahanty. Awaiting trial, Hinckley wrote the following (complete with errors in spelling and date) to a correspondent for *Time* magazine: "The most important thing in my life is Jodie Foster's love. . . . We are a historical couple, like Napoleon and Josephine, and a romantic couple like Romeo and Juliet. . . . Of course, on March 30, I made my love known to her in my own unique way. . . ." On June 21, 1982, Hinckley was found not guilty by reason of insanity on thirteen charges related to the shootings and was subsequently committed to an institution for an indefinite period of time.

11. **(b)** Twenty-eight black children and young adults had been murdered in the Atlanta area by the time police arrested Wayne Williams, a twenty-three-year-old black photographer and talent promoter. The deaths, which occurred over a period of twenty-two months, terrorized the city and prompted one of the most extensive police investigations in U.S. history. Although Williams was suspected of killing most, if not all, of the young blacks, he was charged with only two counts of murder. On February 27, 1982, he was convicted on both counts and sentenced to two consecutive life terms in prison.

**12. (a)** In early October 1982, seven people died after taking Tylenol capsules that someone had tampered with by lacing them with cyanide. As a result, Johnson & Johnson, the makers of Tylenol, instituted a nationwide recall of the product, an action that cost the company $50 million. Copycat poisoners sprang up across the country, and the Food and Drug Administration counted 270 incidents of suspected product-tampering—from rat poison in pain relievers to hydrochloric acid in eye drops—in the month following the Chicago incidents. The Chicago murders have never been solved.

**13. (b)** Approximately 600,000 demonstrators marched through the streets of New York City on June 12, 1982, to protest the proliferation of nuclear weapons. The enormous demonstration was planned to coincide with the United Nations' five-week Second Special Session on Disarmament. Singing "All we are saying is give peace a chance," the crowd ended up in Central Park for an afternoon of speeches and song; there were no arrests. It was the largest rally not only of the 1980s, but of all U.S. history.

**14. (d)** An estimated ninety thousand Americans have contracted AIDS since the early 1980s, and approximately forty-five thousand have died. Of those who have been infected, 66 percent are male homosexuals, 16–17 percent are intravenous-drug abusers, about 8 percent are both male homosexuals and intravenous-drug abusers, 1 percent were infected by blood transfusions, 1–2 percent are hemophiliacs, and 4 percent were infected by heterosexual transmission. It is estimated that more than 270,000 Americans will have been stricken with the disease by 1991.

**15. (d)** The thirty-six-page report by the National Commission on Excellence in Education set off calls for wide-ranging educational reform. Highly critical of the quality of the U.S. educational system, *A Nation at Risk* stated that American students were far behind their counterparts in other industrialized nations in academic skills. The report called for longer school days and years, merit pay for teachers, and higher admission standards for colleges. In addition, it recommended more homework and a basic core curriculum for all high school students. According to the report, "If an unfriendly foreign power had attempted to impose on America the mediocre educational performance that exists today, we might well have viewed it as an act of war."

**16.** **(b)** On October 25, 1983, a seven-nation assault force led by U.S. Marines and Army Rangers invaded and occupied the Caribbean nation of Grenada. The U.S. government said it had taken military action to protect the lives of one thousand Americans who were trapped on the island following a left-wing military coup. Further, U.S. representatives said they had been asked to intervene by the members of the Organization of Eastern Caribbean States, who were fearful of a Soviet–Cuban military buildup on Grenada. Approximately 400 soldiers from Antigua, Barbados, Dominica, Jamaica, St. Lucia, and St. Vincent joined the 1900 U.S. troops in the successful mission. Before the fighting ended, the U.S. force had grown to more than 6000 men. Twenty-four Cubans were reportedly killed and 59 wounded; 18 Americans were killed and 116 wounded. Despite President Ronald Reagan's claim that the mission was a rescue, not an invasion, the UN General Assembly voted to denounce the action as a "flagrant violation of international law."

**17.** **(b)** Following a flood caused by the overflowing Meramec River, the Environmental Protection Agency found hazardous levels of dioxin in the soil beneath Times Beach. The source of the contamination was traced to the early 1970s, when the town had contracted to have oil spread on 10 miles of unpaved road as a means of controlling dust. However, residents were unaware that the person spreading the oil had mixed it with dioxin waste sludge from a nearby chemical plant. The federal government agreed to buy out all of the home- and business owners in Times Beach (population, 2400), representing the first federal purchase of a polluted city in U.S. history. Residents who moved were paid between $8800 and $98,900 for their homes. Today Times Beach is a ghost town.

**18.** **(c)** In 1984 the United States began providing $1.5 million a day to the government of El Salvador to back the centrist Christian Democratic party of President José Napoleon Duarte against militant Marxist rebels. In Nicaragua it has been U.S. policy to financially support the *contras*, guerrilla rebels who oppose Nicaragua's Marxist Sandinista government. These efforts, however, have done little to foster peace, democracy, or economic stability in either country. By the end of the 1980s, U.S. foreign policy toward both Central American countries began to change, precipitated in part by a change in government in El Salvador and the anticipated disbanding of the *contras* as a fighting force.

**19.** **(d)** Ronald Reagan captured 525 electoral votes and 59 percent of the popular vote as opposed to Mondale's 13 electoral votes and 41 percent of the popular vote. In addition to carrying the state of Minnesota, Mondale also won the District of Columbia.

**20.** **(c)** Sharon's $50 million libel suit charged that *Time* had published a false and defamatory article (cover story of February 21, 1983) characterizing Sharon as having encouraged the 1982 massacre of hundreds of Palestinians in the Sabra and Shatila refugee camps in West Beirut. A federal court jury ruled against Sharon. However, the jury reprimanded the *Time* correspondent for acting negligently and carelessly in writing his story. Westmoreland's $120 million libel suit charged that a CBS broadcast ("The Uncounted Enemy: A Vietnam Deception") had characterized Westmoreland as having conspired to deceive the government and the public regarding growing Viet Cong troop strength. After eighteen weeks of testimony, Westmoreland and CBS reached an out-of-court settlement.

**21.** **(a)** In 1984 eight ships from six nations were damaged by mines planted in the waters of Nicaraguan ports by the *contras*, the U.S.-backed Nicaraguan rebels. When it was learned that the CIA had directed and supervised the mining of the ports, both the U.S. Senate and the House of Representatives passed resolutions condemning the actions of the Reagan administration. The Nicaraguan government took its complaint to the World Court at The Hague, the judicial arm of the United Nations that settles disputes between nations. Before the case was heard, the United States said it would not take part in the proceedings and declared itself exempt from the court's jurisdiction. The court eventually ruled against the United States, saying that the Reagan administration had broken international law and violated Nicaraguan sovereignty by aiding the *contras* in mining the ports.

**22.** **(c)** On May 13, 1985, residents of the City of Brotherly Love watched in amazement and horror as a police evacuation operation turned a neighborhood on Osage Avenue into a towering inferno. The catastrophic day was a result of local government and police confrontations with a radical cult group called MOVE, whose members occupied a two-story house in West Philadelphia. After cordoning off a five-block area and evacuating residents, police ordered MOVE members to leave their house; police had arrest warrants for four of the members. After repeated attempts to flush out MOVE members failed, police dropped a bomb on the house and the explosion set off a fire that spread to surrounding homes. Six MOVE members were killed, along with five of their children. In addition, sixty-one houses were burned down, leaving three hundred people homeless.

**23.** **(a)** Sharon Christa McAuliffe was a schoolteacher and the first private citizen chosen to go into space. She was picked from among eleven thousand applicants who took part in NASA's program that selected a teacher to give two lessons from space while students watched on television. Born on September 2, 1948, McAuliffe was the wife of Ed McAuliffe and the mother of two children.

**24.** **(d)** Signed into law on November 6, 1986, the Immigration Reform and Control Act took steps to provide a realistic solution to the problem of uncontrolled illegal immigration into the United States, primarily from Mexico. Noncitizens living illegally in the United States prior to 1982 were offered amnesty and temporary legal status, with an opportunity to begin the process of obtaining permanent residency and eventually becoming U.S. citizens. Employers were affected by the new law's provision, with fines of $250 to $10,000 for hiring undocumented illegal alien workers. They were also made responsible for ascertaining the legal citizenship or residency of all employees.

**25.** **(a)** The attack on the *Stark* came as a shock to U.S. government officials because Iraq was considered a "friendly" nation. At the time, Iran and Iraq had been at war for six years, and both had frequently attacked ships, usually oil tankers, in the Persian Gulf. The *Stark*, however, was 40 miles away from any known Iraqi attack. The tragedy was compounded by the fact that a single Iraqi fighter plane and two missiles could wreak such havoc on a modern navy frigate. In subsequent investigations the government of Iraq stated that the incident was an "unintentional accident" and that the pilot mistook the American vessel for an Iranian tanker. In 1989 Iraq agreed to pay $27.3 million in compensation to the families of the thirty-seven crew members who were killed.

**26. (b)** During the 1980s homelessness in America increased to levels not seen since the Great Depression of the 1930s. Many factors contributed, including housing shortages, unemployment, and drug and alcohol abuse. Nearly one quarter of the 1980s homeless population were employed, and over one third were families with children—also the fastest-growing segment of the homeless population. In 1987 Congress passed the McKinney Homeless Assistance Act, which provided about $1 billion in aid, primarily for emergency shelters and counseling services. In 1988 the General Accounting Office of the federal government took the unprecedented step of advising President-elect George Bush to allocate $20 billion to renovate public housing to offset the crisis.

**27. (c)** Only nine days after President Ronald Reagan chose Judge Douglas Ginsburg to fill a Supreme Court vacancy, the nomination went up in smoke. The furor was caused by Ginsburg's admission that on a few occasions, as a college student and as a law professor, he had smoked marijuana. That announcement turned out to be a surprise as well as a political bombshell for the president, who was leading a vigorous campaign against drugs. Even though several national polls showed that the majority of Americans did not think that Ginsburg's use of marijuana should disqualify him, Reagan officials asked him to bow out, and he did so on November 7, 1987. It was the president's second failure in one month to fill the vacancy on the high bench; earlier the Senate had rejected the nomination of Judge Robert H. Bork. This seat was finally filled with the appointment of Anthony M. Kennedy.

**28. (d)** The 690-page report was highly critical of the president and his administration regarding the sale of U.S. arms to Iran and the diversion of profits from those sales to aid the *contras*. Although the president did authorize arms shipments to Iran to help the hostages, the report stated that there was no evidence to contradict Reagan's claim that he knew nothing about the funds that were secretly transferred to the *contras*. However, the report concluded that the president, as chief executive of the United States, had a constitutional obligation to execute the laws of the nation and thus had the "ultimate responsibility" for the actions of his staff.

**29. (b)** The two superpowers began negotiating to reduce these weapons in 1980, and on December 8, 1987, a historic treaty—the INF (Intermediate-Range Nuclear Forces) treaty—was signed by Ronald Reagan and Mikhail Gorbachev. It called for the dismantling of all 1752 U.S. and 859 Soviet missiles with a range of between 300 and 3400 miles. In addition, the treaty called for an unprecedented on-site inspection of missile bases and for verification of the systematic destruction of specific missiles.

**30. (b)** General Manuel Antonio Noriega, head of Panama's armed forces since 1983 and the effective ruler of the country, was indicted by federal grand juries in Miami and Tampa, Florida. Charged with protecting and helping international drug traffickers, Noriega was also accused of laundering drug profits through Panamanian banks. It was alleged that he received millions of dollars in payoffs from the Medellin drug cartel, which has been linked to 80 percent of the cocaine smuggled into the United States. Noriega denied the charges and ignored the indictments.

**31. (d)** Signed into law on July 1, 1988, the Catastrophic Care Act actually went into effect in 1989, with other provisions to become effective in 1990 and 1991. It was the largest expansion of the Medicare program in its twenty-three-year history. The new law was designed to protect 33 million elderly (sixty-five and older) and disabled Americans from the financial devastation that can result from serious illness. The law placed limits on patients' out-of-pocket expenses for in-patient hospital expenses, doctors' charges, and prescription drug costs and extended benefits for time spent in nursing homes. The cost of the entire program was to be financed by the recipients in the form of a monthly premium deducted from social security income. For the 40 percent of Medicare recipients with enough income to pay federal taxes, an income tax surcharge was also to be levied. The law was criticized for failing to provide adequate coverage for long-term nursing home expenses, which constitute the largest single medical expense for Americans over sixty-five.

**32. (b)** The summer of 1988 was uncommonly dry, and in Yellowstone National Park drought conditions were the worst in over one hundred years. Eleven major fires erupted that summer, all initially believed to be caused by lightning. (Subsequent investigations found that three had been started by campers.) The fires were not put out because of the National Park Service's "free burn" policy of noninterference with naturally occurring forest fires, a policy in effect since 1972. However, the fires soon became uncontrollable infernos, and twenty-five thousand firefighters were brought in to suppress the blazes. The firefighting efforts did little to contain the fires, and the park was closed for the first time in 116 years. In early September rain and snow finally doused the fires. Nearly 1 million of the park's 2.2 million acres had been seared. In 1989 the Bush administration revised federal firefighting policy, restricting the number of national forest fires that will be allowed to burn uncontested, but the let-burn policy was reaffirmed. Environmentalists contend that wildfires have ecological benefits because they clear away dead timber and overgrowth and rejuvenate forests by promoting the growth of plants and shrubs.

**33. (d)** In 1980 Congress reinstated a "standby" draft, which had been originally instituted in 1973 and discontinued in 1975. The new law was challenged in many lawsuits, but on July 25, 1981, the U.S. Supreme Court ruled it to be constitutional. It upheld the requirement that all men, upon reaching age eighteen, be required to register with the Selective Service System. This draft did not actually induct anyone into the armed forces but instead provided a list of eligible potential inductees for the armed forces in case of emergency. The U.S. military forces remain manned by an all-volunteer, paid body of Americans.

**34. (a)** After the Japanese attacked Pearl Harbor in 1941, approximately 112,000 Japanese living in the United States (mostly in California) were rounded up and transported to ten internment camps for the duration of World War II. Most of them were American citizens, and not a single person was accused of espionage or sabotage. Imprisoned solely because of their race, many Japanese lost everything, and the federal commission on Wartime Relocation and Internment of Civilians estimated that collectively the Japanese-Americans lost the present-day equivalent of $2 billion in property and income.

In addition, the Commission in 1983 recommended that the U.S. government pay $20,000 to each of the sixty thousand surviving Japanese-Americans who had lived in the camps. The money would serve as an "act of national apology." On August 10, 1988, President Reagan signed a redress bill into law, authorizing the $20,000 payments, which lawmakers pledged would be totally paid by 1998.

**35. (a)** Gunfire had already been exchanged by the USS *Vincennes* (patrolling the waters of the Persian Gulf) and Iranian gunboats when radar aboard the U.S. Navy warship indicated a plane on course toward the *Vincennes*. Believing the aircraft to be an Iranian military plane, the captain of the *Vincennes* issued seven warnings to the plane, and upon receiving no response, he ordered his crew to fire two missiles at it. The plane turned out to be a commercial Iranian airliner, and all 290 people aboard were killed. The Iranian government called the incident "a barbaric massacre." President Reagan apologized to Iran for the tragic accident.

**36. (d)** British investigators determined that a bomb hidden in a radio cassette player caused the explosion aboard Flight 103 as it flew from London to New York. The disaster took the lives of all 259 people on board as well as 11 people on the ground. Although authorities later admitted having received advance warning of a bomb threat, they had decided it was a hoax and thus did not make the threat public prior to the departure of Flight 103. The perpetrators of the crime have not been identified.

**37. (a)** The oil tanker *Valdez*, owned by Exxon, ran into a reef and spilled over 11 million gallons of oil into Prince William Sound. The oil covered more than 9600 square miles of southern Alaska coastal waters, and the cost of cleanup was estimated at at least several hundred million dollars. Not only was the spill the largest in U.S. history, but it was the worst in terms of ecological damage. Although the extent of the damage will not be known for years, thousands of birds and otters died as a result of the spill, and commercial fishing in the area was sharply curtailed. Blood alcohol tests taken ten hours after the incident revealed that the tanker's captain was intoxicated at the time he turned over command of the vessel to an unqualified third mate.

**38.** **(d)** Appointed in 1975 by President Gerald R. Ford, John Paul Stevens of Illinois is generally believed to maintain a centrist position on the high court. O'Connor, Scalia, and Kennedy were appointed in 1981, 1986, and 1988, respectively.

**39.** **(a)** At the end of the decade approximately 32.5 million Americans lived in poverty. Although the $11,611 does not include the value of food stamps, housing subsidies, and health care, nonetheless the numbers have been considered a national disgrace. A majority of the poor are white and live outside the central cities; however, one out of every four residents of New York City lives below the federal poverty line. The growing problem has led to a new definition of the poor: "the underclass," those who have been virtually disenfranchised from all institutions in society.

**40.** **(a)** Democrats held majorities in both houses of the 101st Congress, the last Congress to be elected in the 1980s. Democratic control continued through the end of the decade, despite a few changes following special elections held to fill vacancies. In September 1989, of the one hundred Senate seats, Democrats held fifty-five to the Republicans' forty-five. Of the 435 House seats, Democrats held 257 seats, and Republicans held 176 (2 were vacant).

UPI/Bettmann Newsphotos

## TEST 3

# *World Events*

*The caravan of democracy will go forward. . . Nobody can stop it.*

*—BENAZIR BHUTTO*

43

1. Who were the Gang of Four?

   a. four Japanese businessmen arrested for insider trading

   b. four Austrian vintners charged with adulterating white wine

   c. four ultraleftist Chinese political figures accused of crimes against the state

   d. four Eastern European countries seeking freedom from Soviet domination

2. Which two Middle Eastern countries were at war with each other throughout most of the 1980s?

   a. Israel and Egypt

   b. Syria and Egypt

   c. Israel and Iraq

   d. Iran and Iraq

3. Indira Gandhi, prime minister of India, was assassinated in 1984. Who did it?

   a. her own Sikh guards

   b. an unknown Muslim terrorist

   c. a Pakistani agent

   d. a Soviet counterspy

4. What country was Great Britain's opponent in the Falklands War of 1982?

   a. Peru

   b. Argentina

   c. Nicaragua

   d. Costa Rica

5. On October 23, 1983, 241 Americans were killed in an attack on U.S. Marine Corps headquarters in Beirut, Lebanon. How?

   a. A suicide terrorist drove a truck loaded with TNT into the headquarters.

    **b.** A kitchen worker with PLO ties laced the marines' food with poison.

    **c.** A bomb was placed under the hood of a general's car.

    **d.** Three snipers pumped bullets into the headquarters from a building across the way.

**6.** What was the trend in the *rate* of world population growth in the period from 1974 to 1984?

    **a.** It rose slightly.

    **b.** It fell slightly.

    **c.** It rose steeply.

    **d.** It remained even.

**7.** Which of the following female national leaders both first took office in the 1980s?

    **a.** Corazon Aquino and Margaret Thatcher

    **b.** Indira Gandhi and Benazir Bhutto

    **c.** Imelda Marcos and Margaret Thatcher

    **d.** Corazon Aquino and Benazir Bhutto

**8.** On April 28, 1986, a massive nuclear disaster occurred. Where?

    **a.** Doncaster, England

    **b.** Chernobyl, the Soviet Union

    **c.** Three Mile Island, Pennsylvania

    **d.** Bhopal, India

**9.** An international treaty on the environment was signed into being in 1987. It was designed to

    **a.** protect endangered species

    **b.** protect Antarctica

    **c.** protect the ozone layer

    **d.** protect the Brazilian rain forest

**10.** Salman Rushdie's 1989 novel *The Satanic Verses* caused an international uproar because Muslims claimed it

   **a.** criticized the Ayatollah Khomeini

   **b.** advocated freedom for women

   **c.** blasphemed the Prophet Muhammad

   **d.** ridiculed Arab terrorism

**11.** In the 1980s the Soviet Union's Red Army fought in a war for the first time since World War II. Where?

   **a.** Pakistan

   **b.** Lebanon

   **c.** Kampuchea

   **d.** Afghanistan

**12.** Why did U.S. planes attack Libya in April 1986?

   **a.** Evidence linked that country to a terrorist bombing on April 5 of a discotheque in West Berlin.

   **b.** Libyan leader Muammar el-Qaddafi had ordered an attack on a U.S. destroyer.

   **c.** It was an accident.

   **d.** Negotiations about territorial waters had broken down.

**13.** Mikhail S. Gorbachev became leader of the Soviet Union in March 1985. Whom did he replace?

   **a.** Leonid Brezhnev

   **b.** Yuri Andropov

   **c.** Nikita Krushchev

   **d.** Konstantin U. Chernenko

**14.** In October 1984 the Chinese government implemented major economic reforms that

   **a.** abolished collective farms

   **b.** allowed urban factory managers some freedom from state control

   **c.** freed exporters from government interference

   **d.** ended the practice of centralized economic planning

**15.** On September 1, 1983, the Soviet Union shot down a foreign civilian airliner. From what country was it?

    **a.** Iran

    **b.** France

    **c.** the United States

    **d.** South Korea

**16.** On December 19, 1984, Britain agreed to cede control of Hong Kong in 1997. What was scheduled to happen to it?

    **a.** It would revert to Chinese control.

    **b.** It would become independent.

    **c.** It would come under Japanese rule.

    **d.** It would be taken over by Singapore.

**17.** Klaus Barbie, a Nazi war criminal, was arrested in 1983 and sentenced to life in prison in 1987. What had been his wartime nickname?

    **a.** "the killer of Auschwitz"

    **b.** "the butcher of Lyon"

    **c.** "the scourge of Paris"

    **d.** "the devil of Berlin"

**18.** On August 4, 1983, Bettino Craxi was sworn in as Italy's premier. He was

    **a.** the first Italian Socialist premier

    **b.** the first Italian premier born in Naples

    **c.** the first Italian Protestant premier

    **d.** the first Italian coalition premier

**19.** One of the most striking social trends in Europe is the dramatic increase in immigrants from the Third World. What percentage of the population of Western Europe is of non-European descent?

    **a.** 4 percent

    **b.** 10 percent

    c. 14 percent

    d. 19 percent

**20.** In 1987, after very lengthy disputes, Canadians reached agreement over the constitutional status of the French-speaking province of Quebec. What was the agreement?

    a. Quebec was granted total autonomy from the rest of Canada.

    b. Quebec was given sovereignty over the English-speaking Maritime Provinces.

    c. Quebec was given double representation in the Canadian parliament.

    d. Quebec was designated in the constitution as a "distinct society."

**21.** In 1989, Prince Norodom Sihanouk agreed to return to Cambodia as head of state even if he had to abandon which of his allies?

    a. South Vietnam

    b. Taiwan

    c. the Khmer Rouge

    d. the Vatican

**22.** In 1989 which two countries held their first summit meeting in thirty years?

    a. China and the Soviet Union

    b. China and the United States

    c. Japan and China

    d. the Soviet Union and the United States

**23.** Britons protested NATO's plan to deploy Pershing II and cruise missiles in Europe in April 1983. What happened in the biggest demonstration of this campaign?

    a. People formed a 14-mile-long human chain.

    b. People lay down in front of U.S. military vehicles.

    c. People picketed the U.S. embassy.

    d. People went on hunger strikes.

**24.** In Sri Lanka, war was fought for four years between
   a. native Sri Lankans and foreigners
   b. Sri Lanka and India
   c. Tamils and Sinhalese
   d. Hindus and Muslims

**25.** Which of the following heads of state deposed in the 1980s had been in power longest?
   a. Milton Obote
   b. Alfredo Stroessner
   c. Jean-Claude Duvalier
   d. Ferdinand Marcos

**26.** The Contadora Group of countries tried but failed to achieve a negotiated settlement to the fighting in Central America during the 1980s. Which of the following countries was *not* a member of the group?
   a. Colombia
   b. Mexico
   c. Venezuela
   d. Nicaragua

**27.** In September 1986, in response to several acts of terrorism, one European nation began to require visas from all foreign visitors except those from European Community countries and Switzerland. What country was it?
   a. West Germany
   b. Great Britain
   c. France
   d. Italy

**28.** What is Europe's "Green wave"?
   a. environmentalist political parties
   b. agricultural reform for autonomy in food production
   c. algae blooms that are poisoning the lakes

    **d.** pro-Irish sympathy among Continental political parties

**29.** In April 1989, Soviet police brutally crushed a rally in Tbilisi, Georgia. What was the focus of the rally?

    **a.** abortion rights

    **b.** freedom for dissident intellectuals

    **c.** a call for restoration of the czar

    **d.** Georgian nationalism

**30.** In the spring of 1989 a series of demonstrations in favor of democracy took place in China. What group led these protests?

    **a.** university students

    **b.** old Maoists

    **c.** peasant farmers

    **d.** American agents

**31.** On April 26, 1985, the Soviet Union and its Eastern-bloc allies renewed the Warsaw Pact made thirty years earlier. Which of the following Eastern European Communist countries was *not* involved?

    **a.** Yugoslavia

    **b.** Poland

    **c.** Hungary

    **d.** Rumania

**32.** The Pentagon claimed that at least nine nations were developing biological weapons during the 1980s. Which of the following was *not* one of them?

    **a.** Iraq

    **b.** India

    **c.** the Soviet Union

    **d.** Taiwan

**33.** Apart from the world's five "official" nuclear powers, which other countries are thought to have developed nuclear weapons in secret?

   **a.** South Africa, Pakistan, India, Israel

   **b.** France, India, Libya, Iraq

   **c.** North Korea, China, India, Iran

   **d.** Brazil, France, South Africa, Israel

**34.** What of the following was *not* one of the Soviet political reforms introduced under Gorbachev?

   **a.** contested elections

   **b.** a multiparty system

   **c.** codified individual rights

   **d.** unopposed candidates

**35.** When first legalized in the early 1980s, the Polish group called Solidarity was

   **a.** the only independent trade union in the Soviet bloc

   **b.** a political party challenging Marxist orthodoxy

   **c.** a peasants' organization demanding land reform

   **d.** none of the above

**36.** Which of the following relaxations of apartheid—South Africa's government policy of racial segregation—did *not* occur in the 1980s?

   **a.** representation of people of mixed race ("coloureds") in the government

   **b.** the lifting of the "pass" laws

   **c.** representation of Asians in the government

   **d.** representation of blacks in the government

**37.** On January 29, 1986, Yoweri Museveni took the oath of office as president of what African country?

   **a.** Uganda

   **b.** Tanzania

    c. Lesotho

    d. Ethiopia

**38.** In 1986 Great Britain and France announced plans for a joint project to be completed in 1993. What was it?

    a. a tunnel underneath the English Channel

    b. a new jet plane to rival the Concorde

    c. a nuclear fusion laboratory

    d. a giant French-English nuclear supercollider

**39.** Which of the following leaders was *not* assassinated when an attempt on his life was made in the 1980s?

    a. Lebanese prime minister Rashid Karami (1987)

    b. Swedish premier Olof Palme (1986)

    c. Bangladesh president Ziaur Rahman (1981)

    d. Chilean president Augusto Pinochet Ugarte (1986)

**40.** On November 5, 1987, Habib Bourguiba ended thirty years of rule over what country?

    a. Tunisia

    b. Nigeria

    c. Saudi Arabia

    d. Ethiopia

# TEST 3: *Explanatory Answers*

**1. (c)** Among ten people tried by the Chinese government for crimes against the state in 1980 were the so-called Gang of Four, led by Jiang Qing, the widow of Chinese Communist party chairman Mao Zedong. Challenging the court to sentence her to death "in front of one million people in Tiananmen Square" in Beijing, she said she was innocent of any crime because she did only what her husband ordered her to do. On January 25, 1981, a Beijing court sentenced her to death, but in 1983 the sentence was commuted to life imprisonment.

**2. (d)** The war, which began in 1980, escalated in February 1984 when Iraq bombed nonmilitary targets and Iran retaliated by attacking Iraqi cities. Threats concerning oil shipments exacerbated the situation, and in March, Iran accused Iraq of using chemical weapons. U.S. officials confirmed the accusation, citing evidence showing that the Iraqis had unleashed mustard gas, outlawed by the Geneva Conventions in 1925.

**3. (a)** Indira Gandhi, the dominant political figure of India for nearly two decades, was assassinated on October 31, 1984. She was shot down in the garden of her New Delhi home by two Sikh extremists who were members of her own security guard. Earlier in the year Indira Gandhi had ordered a raid on the Sikhs' holiest temple, in which six hundred died. The attack was meant to quell militants' demands for independence for the Punjab, where Sikhs make up more than 60 percent of the population. The night before her assassination she said, "Our search was for peace, and I think we were right." On the day of Indira's assassination the cabinet unanimously elected her son, Rajiv Gandhi, prime minister. Two months later, in national elections, the Indian people overwhelmingly gave Rajiv their vote.

**4. (b)** Though the Falkland Islands are only about 240 miles (400 km) off the coast of South America and are claimed by Argentina, they remain a British colony partly because the 1800 inhabitants, of British stock, want to stay British. In the spring of 1982 Argentina tried to capture the islands. After a mid-March landing on another British South Atlantic island, on April 2, 1982, a force of several thousand Argentine soldiers invaded the Falklands themselves, which they call the

Malvinas, easily defeating a British force of only eighty-four soldiers. On April 3, British prime minister Margaret Thatcher told Parliament that a large naval task force had steamed off to challenge the interlopers, and she also froze about $1.2 billion of Argentine assets in Britain. On May 2 the Argentine cruiser *General Belgrano* was sunk by the British; 321 died. On May 4 the Argentines sank the British destroyer *Sheffield*, killing twenty. The European Community countries declared sanctions against Argentina, and the United States declared its support for Great Britain. On May 21 the British landed on East Falkland Island, and less than a month later, on June 15, the Argentines surrendered. Two days later, Lieutenant General Leopoldo Galtieri resigned as president of Argentina, member of the ruling junta, and commander-in-chief of the army. The economy of the Falklands is based on agriculture, with sheep-raising the main occupation, but there may be oil deposits offshore.

5. **(a)** The terrorist drove a TNT-laden truck into U.S. Marine Corps headquarters at Beirut (Lebanon) International Airport, and 241 Americans died, most of them marines. Almost at the same time another truck loaded with explosives ran into a French paratrooper barracks; fifty-eight died. In an earlier incident, on April 18, the U.S. embassy in Beirut was almost completely destroyed by what appeared to be a car bomb. Seventeen Americans were among the sixty-three people killed. Evidence pointed to Iran as the responsible party. The marines withdrew from Lebanon in 1984.

6. **(b)** On August 6, 1984, a United Nations international conference met in Mexico City, with 149 nations represented. Figures were released showing that the annual rate of world population growth fell from 2 percent in 1974 to 1.7 percent in 1984. However, despite this overall drop, up to 90 percent of future growth was expected to occur in the Third World. Fearing that the difference in population growth rates between developed and underdeveloped countries would cause an even greater disparity in quality of life, the United Nations requested help in family planning for the Third World. However, the United States said it would cut off aid to international population programs that practiced or advocated abortion.

7. **(d)** In 1986, Corazon Aquino, widow of the opposition leader Benigno Aquino, who had been assassinated in 1983, ran for

president of the Philippines. When election fraud made it appear that Marcos had been reelected, Aquino led a protest. Following massive demonstrations and an armed forces mutiny in her favor, she was declared president, the first woman to win this honor in the Philippines. She said, "The long agony is over. A new life starts for our country." Marcos fled to Hawaii. Benazir Bhutto, daughter of Pakistan's President Zulfikar Ali Bhutto—hanged in 1979 for allegedly conspiring to murder a political opponent—came to power in Pakistan in 1988, two years after returning from self-imposed exile in Europe. She was the leader of the Pakistan People's Party and campaigned against General Mohammad Zia-ul-Haq, president of Pakistan. Prime Minister Margaret Thatcher of Great Britain, who won an unprecedented third term in the 1980s, began her first term in 1979. Indira Gandhi was prime minister of India from 1966 to 1984.

8. **(b)** The nuclear accident, which occurred at the Chernobyl power plant about 80 miles (130 km) north of Kiev in the Soviet Union, was first detected in Sweden, 800 miles away, when a radiation alarm went off there. Twelve hours later the Soviets belatedly admitted to the accident, which released more radiation than the World War II nuclear bombings of Hiroshima and Nagasaki. About 135,000 people were evacuated from the area around Chernobyl. Though the Soviets tried to contain the damage, a radioactive cloud drifted over a large part of the world. Abnormally high levels of radioactivity in the atmosphere were detected in several parts of Europe. Only thirty-one people died in the reactor fire, but the effects of the accident will probably eventually kill at least four thousand people.

9. **(c)** On September 16, 1987, an international conference was held in Montreal to discuss restriction of the use of chemicals that were destroying the ozone layer in Earth's atmosphere that protects terrestrial life by blocking out certain dangerous ultraviolet rays. The agreement hammered out was eventually ratified by thirty-eight nations. The chemicals that destroy the ozone are CFCs (used in refrigeration, air conditioning, cleaning computer chips, and the manufacture of foam products) and halons (used in fire suppressants). One CFC molecule destroys more than 100,000 ozone molecules. The dangers in ozone depletion include eye damage, skin cancer, and injury

to the immune system. In spite of the agreement and other even more stringent actions by individual nations, the damage to the ozone layer cannot be reversed for at least 100 years—the life of various CFCs lasts from 75 to 120 years. Before 1935 the ozone was free of CFCs. Since the 1970s concentrations have grown in the atmosphere by 5 to 7 percent per year, according to the Environmental Protection Agency.

10. **(c)** The novel, set in present-day London and featuring two Indian actors as its main characters, includes a dialogue about the Prophet Muhammad that orthodox Muslims consider blasphemous. Publication of the book touched off mass riots in India and Pakistan in which six people were killed, and it provoked the Ayatollah Khomeini of Iran to put a price on the head of the forty-one-year-old Indian-born, British-educated author. The book was also hurriedly removed from some but not all bookstores and libraries before anyone had a chance to read it. (According to one review, *The Satanic Verses* is "an Arabian nights enchantment.") When returned to the shelves after mass protests, it spent more than 24 weeks on the *New York Times* best-seller lists.

11. **(d)** The Soviets invaded neighboring Afghanistan in December 1979 and withdrew in 1989. According to some estimates, the war killed more than 1 million Afghan civilians and twelve thousand to fifteen thousand Soviet soldiers. Imbued with village values and not afraid to die for them, the Afghans were difficult to suppress, so the Soviets carpet-bombed urban and farm areas, mined strategic sites, and killed civilians. Their withdrawal can be viewed as a defeat, frequently discussed as analogous to the United States' experience in Vietnam.

12. **(a)** President Ronald Reagan first imposed economic sanctions on Libya for its support of international terrorism. Then, in a surprise 11-minute attack, U.S. planes (F-111s) bombed Libyan military targets. Thirty-seven Libyans and two Americans were killed. After the bombing, Reagan said, "We have done what we had to do." Six weeks later, Muammar el-Qaddafi stated, "We are capable of striking and exhausting America. . . . We must be prepared to die." The attack was condemned by U.S. allies.

13. **(d)** Soviet head of state Leonid Brezhnev died in November 1982 and was succeeded by Yuri Andropov. On the death of

Andropov on February 9, 1984, Konstantin U. Chernenko, seventy-two, replaced him as head of the Communist party (February 13) and as chairman of the Presidium of the Supreme Soviet (April 11). When Chernenko died in March 1985, Mikhail Gorbachev took over. In an initial reaction, the Western press talked of his "smile offensive," with its "iron teeth."

**14. (b)** On October 20, 1985, the Central Committee of the Communist party in China implemented reforms in urban economic practices. The change gave great power to factory managers, who could now lease their facilities and run their businesses without government interference in employee and production matters. They were allowed to sell goods at a reasonable profit (with some limits). However, this did not mean a complete turn to capitalism. The Chinese government remained the owner of means of production and continued to control major industries like coal and steel. This followed the 1978 partial (and successful) abandonment of central planning in agriculture.

**15. (d)** A Soviet fighter plane shot down a South Korean airliner that had wandered off course on its way from Alaska to Seoul and into Soviet air space near Sakhalin Island. In the disaster, 269 people died. It was not until September 6, five days later, that the Soviets admitted responsibility. They claimed that the airliner was spying for the United States and had not responded to Soviet signals. Though President Reagan denied this, it was later revealed that a U.S. spy plane had been in the air space earlier. On September 21 the Soviets finally admitted that their pilot had made a mistake in identifying the Korean plane as a military reconaissance plane.

**16. (a)** The agreement signed by British prime minister Margaret Thatcher and Chinese premier Zhao Ziyang in Beijing guaranteed that Hong Kong would revert to China on July 1, 1997, the date that Britain's ninety-nine-year lease will expire. Nevertheless, Hong Kong's economy would be allowed to remain thoroughly capitalist, at least until 2047.

**17. (b)** Less than two weeks after his arrest in Bolivia on January 25, 1983, Barbie was extradited to France to stand trial in Lyon, where he was convicted of crimes against humanity and sentenced to life in prison on July 4, 1987. He was then seventy-three. As head of the Gestapo in German-occupied

Lyon between 1942 and 1944, he had ordered the deportation and torture of Jews and members of the French Resistance. After the war Barbie worked for the U.S. Army Counterintelligence Corps; in fact, U.S. authorities may have helped him escape to Bolivia.

**18. (a)** Bettino Craxi was the first Socialist premier of Italy. His five-party government was the forty-fourth since World War II. Craxi supported Italian ties to the United States and Western Europe and tried to cure Italy's severe unemployment and high inflation rate. His government fell on March 3, 1987.

**19. (a)** Of the 350 million Western Europeans only 4 percent are from minorities of non-European descent; in the United States, 20 percent of the population is considered minority. European minorities are concentrated in cities and compete with other Europeans for social services and jobs. Many are immigrants' children who, though born in Europe, are without the privileges of citizenship. Sixty percent of people of North African background living in France are French-born. In Britain 50 percent of nonwhites are native-born. In 1987 four nonwhites were voted into the House of Commons; one was the first black woman ever elected to Parliament.

**20. (d)** On May 1, 1987, Prime Minister Brian Mulroney announced that Quebec had finally agreed to sign the Canadian constitution, which would include a phrase designating Quebec as a "distinct society." The agreement also enhanced the rights of all provinces in matters such as immigration, changes to the constitution, and appointments to the Supreme Court.

**21. (c)** After a right-wing coup, the "mercurial" Prince Sihanouk ruled Cambodia from 1941 to 1970, through Japanese and French regimes, as king, prime minister, and head of state. In 1970, following a coup said to have been engineered by the CIA, he was ousted and went to live abroad. During his exile, Cambodia was ruled first by a right-wing government, then by the Communist Khmer Rouge—who in a 3½-year reign of terror killed 1 million people—and finally by the Vietnamese, who invaded in 1978 to evict the Khmer Rouge. The Vietnamese later agreed to withdraw in September 1989, and Sihanouk prepared to return as president of a coalition government including the Khmer Rouge as well as a right-wing group. On May 3, 1989, he stated that he would be head of state of

Cambodia even if it meant abandoning the Khmer Rouge, who, it was believed, would never accept the changes implemented under Premier Hun Sen; these included acceptance of the right to private property, a free-market economy, and Buddhism as the state religion. On August 28, 1989, during a 19-nation Paris meeting on the Cambodian question, Sihanouk resigned as his political party's president in order to put himslf on an equal footing with Premier Hun Sen. He continued to command the party's military forces. The Paris meeting ended without settling Cambodia's future.

**22.** **(a)** The last Soviet-Chinese summit had been in 1959. The issues of the 1989 summit included the Soviet invasion of Afghanistan and the Chinese perception that the Soviet Union had lapsed in ideological purity. However, the main focus was the 4500-mile Soviet-Chinese border, which has been of concern since Ghengis Khan's devastating invasion of Russia 750 years ago. Though the Soviets have 500,000 troops on the border, China has considerably more (number unknown); on the other hand, Soviet weapons are superior. Rapprochement between the two countries started in 1985 with Gorbachev's "new thinking" in foreign affairs. Both countries were motivated by the need to cut military spending in order to reform their economies. The four-day summit, held in Beijing, began May 15. The key Chinese figures in attendance were Deng Xiaoping, China's most powerful leader; Zhao Ziyang, general secretary of the Communist party; and Li Peng, China's premier. The Soviet visitors were Mikhail S. Gorbachev, head of government in the Soviet Union and general secretary of the Communist party; Eduard A. Shevardnadze, Soviet foreign minister; and Alexander N. Yakovlev, chairman of the party's international affairs commission.

**23.** **(a)** Tens of thousands of Britons formed a 14-mile-long human chain in protest. The line began at an air base at Greenham Common, went past a nuclear weapons research laboratory, and ended at an armaments factory at Burghfield.

**24.** **(c)** For four years ethnic Indian Tamils (who are mostly Hindus) and the majority Sinhalese (mostly Buddhists) fought against each other in Sri Lanka. Some Tamil extremists, intent on achieving independence, formed guerrilla groups and engaged in terrorist attacks. In response, the government sent troops to attack the guerrillas' bases. Civil war raged until, under a 1987 agreement between Sri Lanka and India, the Tamil areas received greater autonomy plus a peacekeeping force of Indian troops, and Tamil bases in India were closed. Later, however, there was more fighting, this time between Tamils and the Indian troops.

**25.** **(b)** Anti-Communist dictator Alfredo Stroessner, seventy-six, lost his power in Paraguay after a rule of thirty-four years, which began in a military coup in 1954. General Andrès Rodriguez, whose daughter was married to Stroessner's son, staged the rebellion in 1988. North Korea's Kim Il Sung was the only dictator who had held power longer. Obote was president of Uganda twice, from 1966 to 1971 and again from 1980 to 1985, for a total of ten years. Both times he was deposed in a military coup. Haiti's Duvalier had been in power for fifteen years when deposed in 1986. Marcos had been president of the Philippines for twenty-one years when he lost power and fled the islands in 1986.

**26.** **(d)** The members of the Contadora Group were Mexico, Panama, Colombia, and Venezuela. They were supported by Argentina, Peru, Brazil, and Paraguay. The group's efforts to achieve a settlement of the fighting between Nicaragua's Sandinista government and the *contra* rebels failed when the Sandinistas refused to sign any agreement until the United States stopped supporting the *contras*.

**27.** **(c)** In July a rash of terrorist acts culminated in the bombing of a Paris police headquarters annex, killing a police inspector and injuring more than twenty other people. The following September, five terrorist bombings took place within a ten-day period. The last, on September 17 outside Tati, a department store on the Rue de Rennes, killed five and wounded fifty-three. The total September toll: 8 killed and 162 wounded. Police and military personnel were given authority to search packages for explosives. The French government announced that all visitors to the country except those from other European Community countries and from Switzerland would have to obtain visas.

**28.** **(a)** There had been a "Green" party in West Germany championing environmentalist causes since the early 1970s, but in the 1980s the Green movement became an important force in many European nations. In the later years of the decade Europeans became intensely aware of their deteriorating environment: the Mediterranean was a virtual sewer, art was being destroyed by acid rain, and the air was polluted by auto exhaust. By the end of the 1980s there were more than three thousand Greens in lawmaking bodies in West Germany. In addition, throughout Europe the environmentalist cause was being taken up by the more traditional parties such as the British Conservatives and Italian Communists. Queen Beatrix of the Netherlands expressed alarm: "The Earth is slowly dying, and the inconceivable—the end of life itself—is actually becoming conceivable." Even Margaret Thatcher went Green with a powerful environmental speech in September 1988. But some others, like Stanley Clinton Davis, chairman of the environmental group Pollution of the Seas, were skeptical. "Green is the flavor of the month," he said. The cause has served to unite European countries because pollution is not confined within political borders. For example, eighteen nations pollute the Mediterranean Basin, and British-generated acid rain kills trees in German forests. The European Commission and European Parliament have voted to speed up implementation of auto-emission standards to reduce auto pollution in Common Market countries by 75 percent by 1993. In addition, Green Party candidates won significant victories in the European Parliament elections of June 1989.

**29. (d)** In 1988 and 1989, several peoples of the Soviet Union— Armenians, Ukrainians, Georgians, and others—openly expressed a desire for greater national autonomy. On April 9, 1989, police used force to halt a nationalist rally in Tbilisi, Georgia. In the ensuing melee twenty people were killed and three hundred more were wounded.

**30. (a)** On April 27, 1989, after a series of smaller demonstrations, more than fifty thousand student protesters and fifty thousand sympathizers marched through the streets of Beijing for twelve hours to demand democratic reforms, including freedom of the press, better treatment of intellectuals, and an end to government corruption. To press these demands, several hundred students then launched a hunger strike, camping out in the center of Beijing in Tiananmen Square. For several weeks, as support demonstrations grew and the government wavered, real change seemed possible. However, on the night of June 3–4 government troops opened fire on the demonstrators, killing an unknown number. The students and their supporters fled from Tiananmen Square, and many of their leaders were later arrested. After the massacre the chances for democracy in China seemed bleak.

**31.** **(a)** Though nominally Communist, Yugoslavia has never been a member of the Warsaw Pact. The pact, originally signed in 1955 and renewed for twenty years in 1985, enjoins its signers (the Soviet Union and its Eastern European allies) from joining any other coalition or alliance, and it includes guarantees of assistance in case of armed aggression.

**32.** **(b)** The countries identified as engaged in developing biological weapons were Iraq, the Soviet Union, China, North Korea, Taiwan, Egypt, Israel, Iran, and Syria. These weapons are designed to bring about deadly epidemics of diseases such as typhoid, cholera, and anthrax. In September 1988, Kurdish rebels accused the Iraqis of unleashing typhoid on them, but it appears that the accusation was not true. However, a document dated August 3, 1986, seized by Kurdish guerrillas, reveals that the Iraqi army has an inventory of "chemical and biological" materials. Iraq has used *chemical* weapons—against hundreds of Kurdish villages in 1988.

**33.** **(a)** The "nuclear club," or nations officially possessing atomic weapons, consists of the United States, the Soviet Union, Great Britain, France, and China. Nations known to have nuclear weapons technology and the ability to produce and deploy such weapons are South Africa, Pakistan, India, and Israel. Nations that are pursuing nuclear weapons technology include Brazil, Argentina, Libya, Iraq, and North Korea.

**34.** **(b)** Although Gorbachev's reforms did not include a multiparty system, they brought startling political changes to the Soviet Union. In April 1989, the citizenry voted in a real national election for the first time since 1917. The country's new political structure, a bold attempt at democratizing a creaky bureaucracy, includes a Congress of People's Deputies—made up of 1500 popular candidates and 750 candidates selected by public organizations—that selects 544 of its members for the Supreme Soviet, a new legislature. The Supreme Soviet shares authority with the Communist party hierarchy. The first election brought some surprises. Even some party hacks running unopposed lost because so many voters crossed out their names. Voters axed the mayors of Kiev and Moscow, the president and prime minister in Lithuania, and the KGB chief in Estonia. Boris Yeltsin, a populist who was kicked out of the Politburo in 1988, won 98 percent of the vote in the at-large Moscow district. When the Congress of People's Deputies did not select him for membership in the Supreme Soviet, Alexei I. Kazannik, a Siberian law professor, gave up his place so that Yeltsin could be seated.

**35.** **(a)** Solidarity began as an illegal workers' organization that led a strike at the Lenin Shipyards in Gdansk in August 1980. When the strike grew into a widespread workers' protest movement, government officials agreed to make Solidarity the only legal independent union in the Soviet Bloc. However, when the protests continued, on December 13, 1981, martial law was declared, Solidarity was suppressed, and its leader, Lech Walesa, was jailed. In the late 1980s, with the country's economic plight at an impasse, the government and Solidarity leaders opened talks. On April 5, 1989, Solidarity was again legalized. Following the election to parliament of numerous Solidarity candidates, in August 1989 Solidarity was invited to lead a new government—the first non-Communist-led government in Eastern Europe since the 1940s.

**36.** **(d)** Although blacks make up 10 percent of South Africa's population, they had no voice in the government. During the first half of the decade blacks led widespread protests against the harsh apartheid policies. In response, the government declared a state of emergency. In addition, concessions were made to other groups: "coloureds" (people of mixed race) were allowed to elect members of their own House of Representatives, and Asians were allowed to elect members to a House of Delegates. However, the whites-only House of Assembly had veto power over the other two houses. In April 1986 the government lifted the "pass" laws, onerous regulations limiting blacks' freedom to move about within the country.

**37.** **(a)** In December 1985, Museveni, leader of the National Resistance Army (NRA) and for five years an opponent of the government, signed a peace accord with General Tito Okello, chairman of the military council that had ruled Uganda since the overthrow of President Milton Obote in July 1985. On January 26, 1986, the NRA claimed that it had total control of Uganda after capturing the capital, Kampala. On January 29, Museveni took over the government as president and swore to restore democracy and uphold individual rights.

**38.** **(a)** The Channel Tunnel has been described as the largest European construction project of the century. Scheduled to open in 1993, the "chunnel" will consist of three tunnels—two for rail traffic and one service tunnel—that will carry up to four thousand vehicles per hour in each direction. A trip through the 30-mile-long route will take about half an hour.

**39.** **(d)** On September 7, 1986, while Pinochet's motorcade was crossing a bridge outside Santiago, it was attacked by explosives, rockets, and sniper fire. Five men in his escort were killed, and eleven were wounded. Manuel Rodriguez's Patriotic Front took credit for the attempt. Pinochet retaliated by suppressing the press and arresting several opponents. All of the other assassination attempts succeeded. Karami, ten times prime minister in thirty-two years, was murdered by a bomb explosion on a military helicopter taking him from Tripoli to Beirut less than a month after he tendered his resignation to President Amin Geyamel. Palme, a widely respected socialist and feminist, was shot on February 28, 1986, as he and his wife were coming home from the movies. Though police investigated, no suspect was formally charged until 1989. On July 27, 1989, longtime criminal Christer Pettersson was sentenced to life in prison for the assassination. On May 30, 1981, Rahman, who had been president of Bangladesh since 1977, was killed in his sleep in the city of Chittagong, probably on the orders of his political enemy, Major General Mohammad Abdul Manzoor, who, with some fellow officers, was arrested by the government on June 1.

**40.** **(a)** President-for-Life Habib Bourguiba was deposed by Prime Minister Zine al-Abidine Ben Ali, who said that the eighty-four-year-old was too senile to rule. Bourguiba had been president since Tunisia gained independence from France in 1956. The new ruler, who favored a multiparty system, expressed the need to change the constitution, which had been amended to allow a lifetime president.

AP/Wide World Photos

## TEST 4

# *Business and Economics*

*Economists are the failed priests of our generation.*

—*LOUIS RUKEYSER*

1. In the 1980s the take-home pay of CEOs (chief executive officers) skyrocketed. According to a 1988 *Business Week* list, the average CEO in America's top corporations took home $2 million that year. The executive highest on the list was

   a. John Sculley, chairman, Apple Computer

   b. William P. Stiritz, chairman, Ralston Purina

   c. Martin S. Davis, chairman, Gulf and Western

   d. Michael D. Eisner, chairman, Walt Disney

2. On October 22, 1986, President Reagan signed into law the Tax Reform Act of 1986. Which of the following did the far-reaching reform *not* include?

   a. elimination of deductions for sales tax

   b. elimination of deductions for interest on personal loans

   c. increase in standard deduction for single and joint filers

   d. increase in deduction for medical expenses and unreimbursed business expenses

3. NexT, Inc., is

   a. the new company started in 1988 by Apple Computer co-founder Steve Jobs

   b. the independent automobile company founded by John DeLorean

   c. Donald Trump's real estate development company

   d. a board game similar to Monopoly

4. The total wealth of *Fortune* magazine's 1988 list of billionaires equaled $320.6 billion in assets. Number one on the list of billionaires was

   a. Forrest E. Mars

   b. Tamesaburo Furukawa

   c. the Sultan of Brunei

   d. Queen Elizabeth II

**5.** What was the immediate cause of the stock market crash of 1987, according to the Presidential Task Force on Market Mechanisms?

　**a.** use of computerized program trading

　**b.** rising interest rates

　**c.** junk bond trading

　**d.** consumer failure to spend

**6.** The new chairman of the Federal Reserve Board, who took over after Paul Volcker resigned in 1987, was

　**a.** Donald Regan

　**b.** David Stockman

　**c.** Alan Greenspan

　**d.** David Rockefeller

**7.** What major U.S. oil company filed for bankruptcy in April 1987?

　**a.** Pennzoil

　**b.** Exxon

　**c.** Texaco

　**d.** Getty

**8.** Overriding President Reagan's veto, what did Congress do to act against apartheid in 1986?

　**a.** halt immigration from South Africa

　**b.** ban the purchase of Krugerrands in the United States

　**c.** ban the import of South African diamonds

　**d.** ban all new investments in South African businesses by U.S. citizens

**9.** What was the intent of the 1985 Gramm-Rudman Act?

　**a.** to control the federal budget deficit

　**b.** to give financial power to the states

　**c.** to reform the tax laws

　**d.** to establish free trade

TEST YOUR '80S CULTURAL LITERACY

**10.** What company filed for bankruptcy when its product—a device that sold for about $3—resulted in more than twelve thousand lawsuits?

    **a.** A. H. Robins

    **b.** Capitol Records

    **c.** R. J. Reynolds

    **d.** Walt Disney

**11.** Trump Tower, built in 1982, is

    **a.** the tallest building in Hong Kong

    **b.** an International-style office building in Chicago

    **c.** a famous New York skyscraper

    **d.** Merv Griffin's newest hilltop home

**12.** In 1985 the United States and what other country signed their first free-trade accord?

    **a.** Japan

    **b.** Israel

    **c.** the Soviet Union

    **d.** Canada

**13.** What industrial accident killed 3400 people in Bhopal, India, on December 3, 1984?

    **a.** a toxic gas leak

    **b.** a nuclear power plant meltdown

    **c.** an oil refinery explosion

    **d.** dioxin contamination in the drinking water

**14.** In June 1984 the U.S. Supreme Court voted in favor of job seniority rights by ruling that

    **a.** the retirement age would be raised to eighty-five

    **b.** seniority systems could not be sacrificed for affirmative action programs

    **c.** older workers must be rehired first after a layoff

    **d.** affirmative action programs would be dismantled

**15.** The amazing "Mac" was first shown to the American public in a historic commercial titled "1984," shown on television during the Super Bowl. The Mac was

   **a.** McDonald's new 1/2-pound hamburger

   **b.** American Motors' new jeep

   **c.** Apple's new computer

   **d.** Reebok's latest athletic shoe

**16.** In 1984 the Federal Communications Commission (FCC) raised the limit on

   **a.** the number of phones allowed in private homes

   **b.** the size of television screens that could be sold commercially

   **c.** the number of television stations an individual or company could own

   **d.** the permissible size of home satellite dishes

**17.** What was saved from financial crisis by a $4.5 billion U.S. government bailout in 1984?

   **a.** a Texas petroleum-drilling company

   **b.** an Illinois bank

   **c.** a Pennsylvania steel manufacturer

   **d.** a major automobile company

**18.** In 1984 the largest reported dollar amount in a libel suit settled out of court was paid by

   **a.** the *Wall Street Journal*

   **b.** the *National Enquirer*

   **c.** *The New York Times*

   **d.** *People* magazine

**19.** In 1983 what occurred to disrupt the successful system known as "Ma Bell"?

   **a.** Japanese competition

   **b.** a lawsuit by Alexander Graham Bell's great-great-great-granddaughter

c. the invention of fiber-optic cable

d. court-ordered divestiture

**20.** In January 1983 the Group of Ten agreed that the International Monetary Fund (IMF) should be increased from $7.1 billion to $19 billion. The Group of Ten is composed of

a. ten oil sheiks

b. ten Wall Street tycoons

c. ten members of the Trilateral Commission

d. ten industrial countries

**21.** As of 1989 the combined debt of Latin American countries reached $1.3 trillion. Heading the list of debtors was

a. Mexico

b. Chile

c. Brazil

d. Argentina

**22.** A description of the U.S. economic state at the beginning of 1982 would include

a. the worst economic slide since the Great Depression

b. high-ticket consumer spending

c. an unemployment rate at its lowest since World War II

d. a sharply rising rate of inflation

**23.** In 1982, $400 million in back pay was obtained under the Fair Labor Standards Act by

a. football players

b. postal workers

c. screen actors

d. garbage collectors

**24.** Johnson & Johnson was ordered to pay $10.5 million in damages to an individual who had suffered physical harm from the company's

    **a.** aspirin

    **b.** baby powder

    **c.** skin lotion

    **d.** tampons

**25.** The *Washington Post* was assessed $2.05 million in damages for libel in a case involving what major company?

    **a.** CBS

    **b.** Mobil Oil

    **c.** Bethlehem Steel

    **d.** Chrysler Motors

**26.** In September 1985 which of the following industrialized countries became a debtor nation for the first time since World War I?

    **a.** Japan

    **b.** West Germany

    **c.** Great Britain

    **d.** the United States

**27.** In 1981 a lawsuit concerning two Hollywood movie and TV studios threatened to affect the way millions of households watch television. The final court decision made it legal to

    **a.** build a home satellite dish

    **b.** erase TV commercials when using a home video cassette recorder (VCR)

    **c.** home-videotape R-rated movies

    **d.** use a home VCR to record copyrighted TV programs

**28.** In 1981, for the first time in history, the U.S. federal debt ceiling was raised to

    **a.** $150 million

    **b.** $25 billion

    c. $73 billion

    d. $1 trillion

**29.** In a surprise move in May 1981 a major trading partner announced that it would limit exports to the United States of one of its major products. The country and product were

    a. Hong Kong; textiles

    b. South Korea; TV sets

    c. Saudi Arabia; petroleum

    d. Japan; automobiles

**30.** Why did Nestlé Alimentana, S.A., form the Infant Formula Audit Commission in 1982?

    a. to monitor its marketing of infant formula in the Third World

    b. to create marketing plans for worldwide distribution of its baby formula

    c. to develop a new baby formula for the North American market

    d. to involve mothers in testing new flavored baby formulas

**31.** Who in President Reagan's cabinet became famous for outspoken criticism of Reagan's supply-side economics theory, calling it "a Trojan horse"?

    a. Budget Director David Stockman

    b. Press Secretary James Brady

    c. Secretary of the Treasury Donald Regan

    d. Secretary of State George Schultz

**32.** After years of negotiation, what two countries joined the European Economic Community in 1986?

    a. Ireland and Turkey

    b. France and Great Britain

    c. Hungary and Czechoslovakia

    d. Spain and Portugal

**33.** In January 1980 President Carter instituted an embargo against the Soviet Union in retaliation for the invasion of Afghanistan. The embargo covered

    **a.** high-technology products

    **b.** wheat

    **c.** Soviet fishing rights in U.S. waters

    **d.** all of the above

**34.** What brash businessman became an American folk hero and was even encouraged to run for president?

    **a.** Donald Trump

    **b.** Lee Iacocca

    **c.** H. Ross Perot

    **d.** Marvin Davis

**35.** What was the record high prime rate reached in December 1980?

    **a.** 7.5 percent

    **b.** 12 percent

    **c.** 17.5 percent

    **d.** 21.5 percent

**36.** What automobile company was saved from financial ruin through a bailout from the U.S. government in 1980?

    **a.** Chrysler

    **b.** Ford

    **c.** DeLorean

    **d.** Pontiac

**37.** Which of the following banks collapsed in the 1980s?

    **a.** Continental Illinois Bank

    **b.** Citibank

    **c.** Bank of America

    **d.** Chase Manhattan Bank

**38.** Investing in junk bonds became popular in the 1980s. Just what is a junk bond?

   **a.** a worthless bond

   **b.** a bond in a fly-by-night company

   **c.** a municipal bond in default

   **d.** high-risk, high-yield bonds

**39.** Why did so many savings and loan institutions fail in the 1980s?

   **a.** fraud

   **b.** bad management

   **c.** poor government supervision

   **d.** all of the above

**40.** A home equity loan, a type of financial arrangement that became hugely popular in the 1980s, is

   **a.** a loan made to pay only for house repairs

   **b.** a loan to the poor to pay for housing

   **c.** a second mortgage held by a relative

   **d.** a loan made on the value of a house

# TEST 4: Explanatory Answers

1. **(d)** Michael Eisner, chairman of the Walt Disney Corporation, topped the 1988 *Business Week* list of the twenty-five highest paid executives with $40.1 million in salary, bonuses, and stock options. Frank G. Wells, president of Walt Disney, was second on the list with $32.2 million. Recruited in 1984 to improve Disney's profit picture, both took smaller base salaries in exchange for bonuses and stock options. It was obviously a smart strategy. To compile the list, *Business Week* surveyed the two highest-paid executives at 354 companies and found that the average salary and bonus for CEOs was over $1 million and the average total compensation (including stock options and other payments) was over $2 million, 17 percent more than in 1987. The increase can be partly explained by the increase in U.S. corporate profits—up 32 percent from 1987 to 1988. Since 1960, the gap between the salaries paid corporate executives and those of ordinary people has widened enormously. For example, in 1960 the average CEO brought home eleven times more than a schoolteacher; in 1988 he brought home seventy-two times more. The huge salaries paid CEOs have not gone unnoticed by critics. Union leaders, for instance, have talked of "executive pig-out."

2. **(d)** Severely restricted were deductions for medical expenses, business expenses, union dues, retirement plans and tax preparation fees. The biggest winners were the working poor, 6 million of whom were cut altogether from the tax rolls. Though the top marginal tax rates were brought down to 28 percent from 70 percent in 1981 and 50 percent in 1982, the very rich did not see great change in their taxes because they had always found loopholes in the law. Tax brackets for individuals were 15 percent and 28 percent with a 5 percent surcharge for high-income taxpayers. (The old law provided for fourteen brackets.) Mortgage interest became deductible only on first and second homes, and consumer interest deductions were gradually phased out.

3. **(a)** In October 1988 college dropout Steven P. Jobs, who in his twenties co-founded the Apple Computer Corporation, unveiled his latest accomplishment, a new personal computer to be sold by his latest company, NexT, Inc. The computer, also called NexT, features a high-resolution monitor and can

record and play music with the fidelity of a compact disc. Instead of a floppy disk drive, it uses an erasable optical-disk drive with a phenomenal memory—enough to fill hundreds of books (100,000 pages of text). Originally designed for the higher-education market, the computer uses the Unix operating system and features sophisticated graphics and networking capabilities.

**4. (c)** The 1988 *Fortune* billionaires' club included 129 individuals and their families whose total assets could finance the U.S. defense budget for a year—while simultaneously wiping clean the national debts of Ecuador and Colombia. The richest man was the forty-two-year-old sultan of oil-rich Brunei (on the island of Borneo), who was worth $25 billion (or 25,000 times $1 million) and had two wives, a 1788-room palace, and two hundred polo ponies to spend it on. The richest American was eighty-four-year-old Forrest Mars, the candy maker and food mogul (Milky Way, Snickers, M&Ms, Kal Kan pet foods, Uncle Ben's Rice), worth $12.5 billion. Donald Trump, worth a paltry $1.3 billion, still made the list. The youngest was thirty-two-year-old Harvard dropout William H. Gates III, who made $20,000 in tenth grade with a computer program he developed to map Seattle traffic patterns and who was cofounder of Microsoft, a computer software company worth $1.4 billion. The oldest billionaire, worth $1.5 billion, was ninety-eight-year-old Tamesaburo Furukawa, chairman of Nippon Herald Films (a distributor of foreign films and owner of Japanese movie houses). The richest woman was sixty-two-year-old Queen Elizabeth II of Great Britain, with her own fortune of $8.7 billion, including real estate (for example, Balmoral Castle in Scotland), racehorses, jewelry, and art.

**5. (a)** On Monday ("Black Monday"), October 19, 1987, after a day of frantic trading on Wall Street in which 604 million shares changed hands, the Dow Jones Industrial Average fell 508.32 points to 1738.74, the biggest percentage decline since 1914. Stock portfolios lost an estimated $500 billion. Some of the blue chip stocks that suffered were IBM, General Motors, and Exxon. The immediate cause of the crash was the use by a few large investors of computerized program trading, in which computers automatically order buying or selling of a large volume of shares when specified circumstances occur. An SEC report of February 2, 1988, called for greater regulation, and on February 4 the New York Stock Exchange forbade the use of its electronic order system for program trading whenever there was a more than 50 percent fluctuation in the Dow Jones average in one day. Long-range causes included worries about U.S. international trade and federal budget deficits.

6. **(c)** Paul Volcker, one of the most powerful and respected men in the financial world, resigned as chairman of the U.S. Federal Reserve Board in June 1987. His replacement, Alan Greenspan, had been an economic adviser to President Nixon. Greenspan's economic philosophy is said to be based on laissez-faire capitalism with decreased government regulation, a return to the gold standard, and a balanced budget. He has admitted that the probability of these events occurring in the near future is slim.

7. **(c)** Texaco, Inc., the third largest oil company in the United States, filed for bankruptcy probably because of losses sustained in a lawsuit with the Pennzoil company. In the suit, Pennzoil claimed that Texaco had interfered with an agreement Pennzoil had with the Getty Oil Company. A Texas court decided in Penzoil's favor and awarded the company $10.53 billion in damages. A reorganization plan filed in federal bankruptcy court by Texaco included a $3 billion settlement with Pennzoil.

8. **(d)** The U.S. Senate and House of Representatives overrode the president's veto of sanctions imposed against South Africa because of that country's refusal to abandon racial separation. Along with the ban on new investments by U.S. citizens, Congress prohibited importation of South African coal, textiles, uranium, steel, and certain agricultural products. It also canceled landing rights of South African airlines at airports in the United States. Reagan denounced the sanctions, saying that they would not be as effective as U.S. efforts toward persuasion.

9. **(a)** The Balanced Budget and Emergency Deficit Control Act of 1985 (also known as the Gramm-Rudman-Hollings bill), intended to force Congress to meet annual targets for reducing the budget deficit, became a bit hollow by the end of the decade as Congress discovered "creative accounting" methods allowing it to spend money without appearing to do so. One example:

advancing the October 1 military payday by 24 hours permitted that expense to be dumped into the budget for the year before.

**10. (a)** A. H. Robins Company, the 119-year-old pharmaceutical firm, was inundated by lawsuits claiming injuries from its Dalkon Shield intrauterine birth control device (IUD), which was sold in the 1970s to an estimated 2.5 million women. The device was linked with sterility, infections, and even death. The company went into Chapter 11 bankruptcy in August 1985 facing claims of over $1.75 billion. In 1989 it was bought by American Home Products (birth control pills Lo-Ovral and Triphasil, Chef Boyardee canned goods, and Jiffy popcorn), and the company's creditors accepted a reorganization that included a $2.47 billion trust fund for the 195,000 women who filed claims that they had been injured.

**11. (c)** Trump Tower, a complex of shops, offices, and condominiums built on Manhattan's Fifth Avenue in 1982, is named for Donald Trump, the flamboyant real estate tycoon and billionaire. He and his partner, the Equitable Life Assurance Society, built the famous tower, with its rose marble shopping atrium, for a cost of about $190 million; the tower continues to pay Trump a $30 million yearly annuity for space that cost him $45 million. Trump Tower is next door to Tiffany, the jewelry store celebrated in the movie *Breakfast at Tiffany's*. Partly because of the spiffy address, the condos in Trump's tower sold for $700 a square foot, about double the amount charged for other high-priced apartments and condos in Manhattan.

**12. (b)** In March 1985 the United States and Israel agreed to eliminate tariffs within ten years. This accord, Israel's first free-trade agreement with any country, will help strengthen Israel's troubled economy.

**13. (a)** The storage tank at a Union Carbide plant in Bhopal, India, sprang a leak, releasing 45 tons of poison gas (methyl isocyanate, an ingredient for pesticide) that formed into a lethal cloud and spread quickly over the crowded city, killing 3400 people and injuring 200,000. Union Carbide had no advance plan for dealing with such a disaster. The Indian government charged the chief executive of the company, Warren Anderson, with murder and asked for $3.3 billion to settle claims. Although criminal charges were dropped, the

Indian Supreme Court ordered Union Carbide to pay $470 million in damages to the victims by March 23, 1989. In exchange the government of India dropped all charges against Anderson and the company, which claimed that the leak was caused by employee sabotage. Many Indians saw the settlement as a sellout by their government.

14. **(b)** The U.S. Supreme Court, in a 6-to-3 decision, upheld job seniority rights by ruling that a bona fide seniority system could not be ignored to preserve jobs of minorities who had been hired because of affirmative action programs. The case that prompted this decision was brought by white firefighters in Memphis, Tennessee, who were laid off when a federal judge ordered the city to increase its number of black firefighters.

15. **(c)** The "Mac," or Macintosh personal computer, the successor to the Apple, is a revolutionary product introduced in 1984 to be "user-friendly." It was developed by a team of engineers headed by Steve Jobs, who co-founded the Apple Computer Corporation when he was only in his twenties and left the company in 1985.

16. **(c)** In July 1984 the F.C.C. repealed a thirty-one-year-old law that restricted to seven the number of television stations an individual or a company could own. The new ruling increased the number to twelve. All restrictions will be removed by the year 1990.

17. **(b)** Continental Illinois National Bank and Trust Company of Chicago received the largest amount of federal support given to a private company up to that time—$4.5 billion—to rescue it from insolvency. The bank had billions of dollars in bad loans.

18. **(a)** The *Wall Street Journal*, owned by Dow Jones and Company, agreed to pay $800,000 to two former federal prosecutors who claimed the prestigious business newspaper had defamed them in 1979. The two prosecutors were suing for $5 million.

19. **(d)** On August 5, 1983, a U.S. district court issued a nine-page order approving the divestiture of American Telephone and Telegraph Company's twenty-two wholly-owned local phone companies. Effective January 1, 1984, the twenty-two companies were to be broken up into seven separate companies,

each serving a different region of the United States. These new firms have since become known as "Baby Bells." After divestiture, AT&T assets were $34 billion.

**20.** **(d)** The Group of Ten—the United States, Great Britain, Canada, Belgium, France, the Netherlands, Sweden, West Germany, Japan, and Italy—agreed in Paris in January 1983 that the IMF should be increased. The IMF granted loans to debtor nations that agreed to stabilize their economies by reducing budget deficits, inflation, wages, and consumption. This signaled other creditors of the possible greater solvency of the debtor nations, and they made their own private agreements concerning loans, such as extending due dates.

**21.** **(c)** In 1988 Brazil owed $115.2 billion, an almost 35 percent increase since 1982. The burden of just paying interest on the debt has caused the economy to slow down, resulting in huge losses of personal income. Mexico was close behind Brazil, with a $105 billion debt. However, world bankers have hope for Mexico because of its attempt to cut its deficits. Argentina was third on the list, with a debt of $58.4 billion, and Chile owed $19.5 billion. Why all this debt? Some of it can be blamed on northern (Yankee) bankers, but also responsible are deficits and inflation, fat bureaucracies, and poorly managed state enterprises.

**22.** **(a)** The recession of 1981 continued into 1982, qualifying as the worst economic slide since the Great Depression of the 1930s. The unemployment rate rose to over 10 percent, its highest level since 1940, when the average for the entire year was 14.6 percent. More than 11 million people were jobless, and almost 5 million Americans were collecting unemployment benefits—the highest number since 1935. Experts estimated that 1.6 million workers were "discouraged"—i.e., no longer looking for work—and therefore not included in the unemployment rate; in addition, 6.6 million people were working part-time though they wanted to work full-time. Thousands of companies went bankrupt.

**23.** **(b)** In a wage settlement approved on October 21, 1982, 800,000 postal workers won $400 million in back pay from the U.S. Postal Service for alleged violations of a federal wage law concerning minimum overtime, night shifts, and extra pay for Sundays and training time. The plaintiffs included the

Department of Labor. It was the largest settlement obtained up to that time under the Fair Labor Standards Act.

24. **(d)** A California jury awarded $10.5 million to Lynette West, who suffered toxic shock syndrome after using tampons manufactured by a division of Johnson & Johnson. She recovered from the illness after being hospitalized with nausea, kidney problems, a sharp drop in blood pressure, and other symptoms. Part of the reason for the large settlement is that the long-term effects of toxic shock syndrome are not known. The highest previous award in a similar case was $500,000 to the family of a woman who died.

25. **(b)** In 1982, Mobil Oil president William Tavoulareas was awarded $2 million in a libel suit against the *Washington Post*. Tavoulareas claimed that in 1979 the *Post* had printed stories about him and his business relationship with his son Peter that were libelous. The *Post* had alleged that Tavoulareas used money and influence to help a maritime company that Peter owned. Also, an article accused both father and son of having business dealings that violated Securities and Exchange Commission disclosure rules; the court ruled this accusation not libelous. Tavoulareas called the judgment, which came after twenty-one days, a vindication and a call for more responsible journalism. However, journalists saw it as a trend toward libel judgments against the press that would make controversial investigative reporting more difficult. In 1983 a federal judged voided the award because there was "insufficient evidence" that Tavoulareas had been injured by the articles.

26. **(d)** By 1985, U.S. ownership of foreign assets was $30 billion less than foreign ownership of U.S. assets. As protectionist sentiment rose drastically, more than two hundred bills designed to reduce foreign competition were brought up in Congress. An agreement between the Group of Five—the five major industrial countries (the United States, West Germany, Japan, the United Kingdom, and France)—helped to depreciate the dollar but only in the short term. By December the dollar had fallen 20 percent against the yen, 15 percent against the deutsche mark, and 10 percent against the pound sterling. The move did little to help lower the federal deficit because of increased defense spending and higher interest payments on the national debt.

27. **(d)** On October 19, 1981, a San Francisco federal appeals court ruled in favor of Universal and Disney and against the Sony Corporation (manufacturer of the Betamax VCR) and the Doyle Dane Bernbach advertising agency, making it illegal to use a home video recorder to tape copyrighted TV programs for noncommercial use and making users and makers of VCRs liable for damages. It was an important decision—in 1981 there were 3 million VCRs in U.S. homes. The basis for legal opposition to the VCR was copyright infringement. Later the Supreme Court overturned the decision, ruling that recording TV programs for later viewing constitutes "fair use" of copyright materials. (Once upon a time the movie industry also tried to get the television set outlawed as a competitive threat.) By November 1988, 62 percent of U.S. households were equipped with VCRs.

28. **(d)** The new $1 trillion limit was first approved by the House. The Senate approved the measure by a vote of 64 to 34 even after one senator, William Proxmire, pleaded against the bill for over sixteen hours.

29. **(d)** The Japanese government acted to voluntarily limit its automobile exports for a period of three years. In the first fiscal year (April 1, 1981, to March 31, 1982) the reduction was 7.7 percent. This action was taken to head off import quotas that were being prepared by the U.S. Congress in the face of the increasing U.S. trade deficit with Japan. The deficit for 1981 was estimated at $15 billion, more than $4 billion above the 1978 level. The deficit was partly a result of U.S. imports of Japanese automobiles and other goods.

30. **(a)** In May 1981 the World Health Organization (WHO) voted virtually unanimously (118 to 1) to discourage the use of baby formula and encourage breast-feeding in Third World countries. Formula use in those countries was blamed for contributing to almost 1 million infant deaths a year, largely because impoverished mothers were diluting the formula to make it go further, preparing it with contaminated water, or serving it in unsterilized bottles. The sole dissenting vote was cast by the United States (two senior U.S. officials subsequently resigned in protest). Swiss-based Nestlé Alimentana, S.A., a major formula manufacturer, was later accused of failing to comply with WHO policy and continuing to distribute formula

in Third World countries. Nestlé set up a commission, headed by former U.S. senator and secretary of state Edmund S. Muskie, to investigate the charges, but the Infant Formula Action Coalition, a consumer alliance, called the commission a mere public relations gimmick.

**31. (a)** Budget Director David Stockman was outspoken in many other areas besides the budget. He said the Pentagon was filled with "blatant inefficiency, poor deployment of manpower, contracting idiocy." Stockman, a Michigan Republican who had served two terms in the House, was not trained as an economist. He studied at Harvard University's Institute of Politics and was appointed Reagan's budget director at the age of thirty-four. After an angry Reagan reprimanded him for his remarks in a meeting on November 12, 1981 (which Stockman likened to "a visit to the woodshed after supper"), he offered to resign, but Reagan refused it. In a series of interviews published in the December 1981 issue of *Atlantic Monthly*, Stockman said—among other things—that the budget would not be balanced by 1984 and that the Pentagon was inefficient.

**32. (d)** Spain and Portugal became the eleventh and twelfth members of the European Economic Community (EEC), which represents 320 million consumers and was formed in 1957. They joined Great Britain, France, West Germany, Italy, the Netherlands, Belgium, Greece, Ireland, Denmark, and Luxembourg. As members of the Community, the twelve West European nations have pledged to complete by 1992 what was once considered impossible: the creation of a single unified European marketplace and an end to frontier restrictions. The EEC is the world's largest consumer market, with trading volume more than twice Japan's.

**33. (d)** All of the answers are correct. In 1980 Carter embargoed 17 million metric tons of grain that were to be shipped to the Soviet Union. This was the first time that food had been used as a weapon in the superpower diplomatic struggle. The other embargo items were of much less importance to the Soviets.

**34. (b)** Tough-talking Lee Iacocca brought Chrysler back from the brink of disaster. In 1984 and 1985 his autobiography *Iacocca* was a number-one best-seller, with 2.56 million copies sold. Iacocca was perceived by the public as a man who gets things done. In early 1988, in a *Washington Post* straw poll, he ran a strong third for the Democratic presidential nomination (after New York governor Mario Cuomo and Senator Gary Hart).

**35. (d)** The prime rate, the interest rate banks charge their highest-quality borrowers, reached a record high of 21.5 percent. The inflation rate was 12.8 percent, and mortgage rates reached 17 percent.

**36. (a)** The U.S. government provided loan guarantees of $1.2 billion to Chrysler Corporation when Chairman Lee Iacocca sought help from President Carter. Slumping sales were causing Chrysler to lose $6 million a day. Iacocca turned the company around, repaying the government loans seven years early. His secret? Giving unionized workers a choice between no jobs and less money, persuading suppliers to wait for their money, and emphasizing smaller cars.

**37. (a)** In 1984 the government stepped in to rescue the Continental Illinois Bank, lending it $1 billion, assuming $4.5 billion in bad loans, and guaranteeing all deposits. This came amid a wave of bank failures, including that of Oklahoma City's Penn Square Bank, to which Continental Illinois had made many bad loans. The government estimated that bank failures due to fraud or embezzlement involved losses that rose from $196 million in 1981 to $1.1 billion in 1986.

**38. (d)** Michael Milken of Drexel Burnham Lambert effected something of a financial revolution by popularizing and legitimizing high-risk issues of "junk bonds." Besides producing earnings for the sellers, proponents argue, junk bonds also enable worthy entrepreneurs without blue-ribbon credit ratings to raise money for expansion or acquisition. Critics counter that the bonds have primarily benefited takeover artists and corporate raiders interested only in short-term profit. In any case, junk bonds are here to stay: in 1989 an estimated one quarter of all outstanding corporate stocks were junk bonds, with a value of $180 billion.

**39. (d)** More than 500 of 3150 federally insured thrifts had become insolvent by the beginning of 1988. The year 1989 witnessed federal legislation to bail out distressed savings and loans—at an estimated cost of $300 billion over the next thirty years.

The law also brought about reorganization of U.S. thrift industry regulators. Particularly in the Sun Belt, banks went under partly because they had overextended themselves in the 1970s oil boom, then faced disaster in the oil crash of the 1980s. Part of the problem was insider "back-scratching loans" between savings and loan institutions to finance high-risk schemes. It is possible that one of every four bank failures can be attributed to fraud. In the late 1980s the U.S. government established the Resolution Trust Corporation, a new agency to clean up three hundred failing thrifts and sell or close them within five years; the Department of Justice was given funds to prosecute fraudulent thrift managers. Under the plan endorsed by President George Bush, savings and loan owners were required to follow stricter accounting rules and raise reserve capital from 3 percent to 6 percent of assets.

**40.** **(d)** With a home equity loan the homeowner is given a revolving line of credit. During the first five or ten years the homeowner can withdraw funds up to the line of credit; during the second phase of the loan (which can last another ten years or so) the homeowner cannot withdraw money. The lenders of home equity loans do not care how the borrower spends the money. The loans are risky because interest rates, which are tied to the prime rate, can fluctuate widely.

AP/Wide World Photos

## TEST 5

# *Popular Culture*

*There is a trend towards watching trends.*

—FAITH POPCORN

1.  What was the 1980s event at which more than 140,000 people joined mental forces at select locations across the world?

    a.  the "harmonic convergence"
    b.  "We Are the World"
    c.  "Live Aid"
    d.  the "Age of Aquarius"

2.  Which rock-and-roll band, according to former Secretary of the Interior James Watt, attracted the "wrong element"?

    a.  the Grateful Dead
    b.  Bon Jovi
    c.  Bruce Springsteen and the E Street Band
    d.  the Beach Boys

3.  Which of the following celebrities did *not* promote a perfume product in the 1980s?

    a.  Linda Evans
    b.  Eva Gabor
    c.  Julio Iglesias
    d.  Cher

4.  Which author was granted permission to perpetuate the fictional character of James Bond originally created by Ian Fleming, who died in 1964?

    a.  John le Carré
    b.  Robert Ludlum
    c.  Jeffrey Archer
    d.  John Gardner

5.  What network television program developed from specialized coverage of the Iran hostage crisis?

    a.  "Nightline"
    b.  "20/20"
    c.  "60 Minutes"
    d.  "The Today Show"

**6.** When Queen Elizabeth II visited President Reagan's Santa Barbara, California, ranch in March 1983, what was she served for lunch?

   **a.** burgers and fries

   **b.** chili dogs

   **c.** cold cuts

   **d.** Mexican food

**7.** What is zapping?

   **a.** avoiding commercials by using a VCR and a remote control device

   **b.** developing a tan from quick exposure to ultraviolet rays

   **c.** flying nonstop from coast to coast

   **d.** cooking with microwaves

**8.** Proceeds raised by the "We Are the World" record went to benefit

   **a.** famine-stricken people in Africa

   **b.** homeless people in America

   **c.** Armenian earthquake victims

   **d.** Afghanistan villagers uprooted by war

**9.** In 1989 a product called Premier was introduced but quickly removed from the market. What was it?

   **a.** a car equipped with air bags

   **b.** a home pregnancy test

   **c.** a smokeless cigarette

   **d.** a sugar-free soft drink

**10.** Who was the only human that kids could watch on Saturday morning children's network television in 1987?

   **a.** Captain Kangaroo

   **b.** Bozo the Clown

   **c.** Peewee Herman

   **d.** Mr. Rogers

**11.** What slang term described the 1980s eating ritual of food-loving yuppies?

   **a.** "strafing"

   **b.** "scarfing"

   **c.** "strapping on the feedbag"

   **d.** "grazing"

**12.** Which of the following is *not* an example of Val-Speak?

   **a.** "grody to the max" (nauseating)

   **b.** "tubular" (spectacular)

   **c.** "groovy" (in tune)

   **d.** "gag me with a spoon" (nauseating)

**13.** With what 1980s product were Debbie Reynolds, Jane Fonda, Jane Powell, and Raquel Welch associated?

   **a.** exercise videos

   **b.** salad dressing

   **c.** perfume

   **d.** deodorant

**14.** How did *USA Today*, introduced in 1982, revolutionize the newspaper business?

   **a.** by using color extensively in its editorial pages

   **b.** by providing shorter stories

   **c.** neither of the above

   **d.** both of the above

**15.** How was Batman's long-time partner Robin killed?

   **a.** He fell from a building when he lost his grip on his Bat-rope.

   **b.** He died in the Bat-copter crash.

   **c.** He was ambushed during a drive-by shooting.

   **d.** He was a bombing victim.

**16.** On the "Magnum, P.I." television show, what was Robin Masters's source of income?

   **a.** He wrote adventure novels.

   **b.** It was never disclosed.

**c.** He had been a drug dealer during the 1960s.

**d.** He was a junk bond dealer.

**17.** Why did the U.S. Department of Agriculture object to Wolfgang Puck's line of frozen pizza?

    **a.** It contained no tomato sauce.

    **b.** It was too expensive.

    **c.** It proved addictive in laboratory tests.

    **d.** It violated shape regulations.

**18.** What television series showed that tough guys could wear pastels?

    **a.** "Hill Street Blues"

    **b.** "Jake and the Fat Man"

    **c.** "Miami Vice"

    **d.** "The A-Team"

**19.** Who became popular in 1986 by dancing to the Marvin Gaye hit "I Heard It Through the Grapevine"?

    **a.** Fred Astaire

    **b.** the Joffrey Ballet

    **c.** Disney parade characters

    **d.** clay raisins

**20.** What was the new name of the old soft drink that returned to the marketplace after "New Coke" fizzled?

    **a.** Quality Coke

    **b.** Antique Coke

    **c.** Quintessential Coke

    **d.** Classic Coke

**21.** What is liposuction?

    **a.** a method to vacuum fat away

    **b.** a new kind of kissing

    **c.** the procedure used to create airtight seals in space-craft hatches

    **d.** a patented turbo-speed attachment for household vacuum cleaners

**22.** What is a frequent flyer?

    **a.** a drug addict

    **b.** a person who flies often on airplanes

    **c.** a new kind of sled

    **d.** a toy mechanical bird

**23.** Who hosted "Lifestyles of the Rich and Famous"?

    **a.** Johnny Carson

    **b.** Robin Williams

    **c.** Robin Leach

    **d.** Barbara Walters

**24.** Which of the following words or phrases described the unmarried person with whom you lived during the 1980s?

    **a.** "posslq"

    **b.** "significant other"

    **c.** "domestic partner"

    **d.** all of the above

**25.** In 1980 the familiar red-and-yellow McDonald's sign read "Over 30 billion sold." What number was on the sign in November 1988?

    **a.** 40 billion

    **b.** 60 billion

    **c.** 70 billion

    **d.** 1 trillion

**26.** What are "Super Mario 2," "The Legend of Zelda," and "Punch-out!"?

    **a.** Saturday morning cartoons

    **b.** 1980s hit records

    **c.** Nintendo games

    **d.** instruction videos on boxing

**27.** What are these Italian imports: penne, capelli d'angelo, fusilli, and lumache?

   **a.** ices

   **b.** vegetables

   **c.** herbs

   **d.** pasta

**28.** The television show "Falcon Crest" contributed to the influx of tourists in

   **a.** Aspen, Colorado

   **b.** Martha's Vineyard, Massachusetts

   **c.** San Diego, California

   **d.** Napa Valley, California

**29.** On what part of the body were Deely Bobbers worn?

   **a.** legs

   **b.** head

   **c.** feet

   **d.** wrist

**30.** What was the object in solving the puzzle of the original Rubik's Cube?

   **a.** to dismantle the smaller cubes and reassemble the whole

   **b.** to maneuver three different-colored cubes into each row of the larger cube

   **c.** to change the cube shape into a swan, a saxophone, or a steamroller

   **d.** to align the smaller cubes so that each side of the whole cube has only one color

**31.** What type of cuisine was affected when the U.S. government imposed a temporary ban on the harvesting of redfish in 1986?

   **a.** sushi

   **b.** Cajun

    **c.** Thai

    **d.** Tex-Mex

**32.** What is the Home Shopping Club?

    **a.** a chain of discount stores that sell home furnishings

    **b.** a computer network for real estate transactions

    **c.** a cooperative of individuals who sell merchandise to each other

    **d.** a television program that sells merchandise over toll-free telephone lines

**33.** Which of the following items was *not* a popular toy in the 1980s?

    **a.** Barbie

    **b.** Transformer

    **c.** Teddy Ruxpin

    **d.** Ziggy Marley

**34.** How are the Judds, the popular country-music duo, related?

    **a.** They are sisters.

    **b.** They are mother and daughter.

    **c.** They are cousins.

    **d.** They are father and daughter.

**35.** In a market where yearly revenues may top $1 billion, what do TCBY, Heidi's, and Penguin's sell?

    **a.** women's lingerie

    **b.** pizza

    **c.** hair care products

    **d.** frozen yogurt

**36.** With the last episode of "A Prairie Home Companion" on June 13, 1987, which imaginary American town went off the air?

    **a.** Lake Wobegon, New York

    **b.** Lake Wobegon, Minnesota

   c. Lake Wobegon, South Carolina

   d. Lake Wobegon, Wyoming

**37.** Which of the following activities would a New Age adherent of the 1980s be likely to pursue?

   a. channeling

   b. rebirthing

   c. crystal healing

   d. all of the above

**38.** Which of the following is the name of a dance that was very popular in 1983 and 1984?

   a. slam dance

   b. breakdance

   c. moondance

   d. flashdance

**39.** What activity of the baby boom generation was described by the slang term "cocooning"?

   a. skin rejuvenation through special treatments

   b. couples-only weekend camping trips

   c. staying at home at night instead of going to clubs and restaurants

   d. holistic therapy for dealing with midlife crisis

**40.** Which of the following foods would be found in a trendy 1980s restaurant?

   a. radicchio

   b. tapas

   c. goat cheese pizza

   d. all of the above

# TEST 5: Explanatory Answers

1. **(a)** José Arguelles, an art history teacher from Boulder, Colorado, and the author of *The Mayan Factor: Path Beyond Technology*, thought that during a two-day period beginning on August 16, 1987—when Mars, Venus, and Mercury lined up with the new moon—Earth would move, perilously, from one epic age to another. The gathering of 144,000 people on August 16 in "sacred sites" (Mt. Shasta in California, Central Park in New York City, Ayers Rock in Australia, the pyramids of Egypt) was supposed to bring about a new age of peace and harmony and prevent the end of the world. To harness their spiritual energies, believers in the harmonic convergence meditated and resonated by humming.

2. **(d)** On April 6, 1983, Watt informed the National Park Service that the Beach Boys, a "soft" rock group, had attracted the "wrong element" (which he later explained to mean "drug abuse and alcoholism") when they played at the Washington Mall on July 4, 1982, and they would not be permitted to play there on Independence Day, 1983. He dropped his Beach Boy ban the next day after being summoned to the White House to hear the president, Mrs. Reagan, and Vice President Bush sing the band's praises. Watt left the White House with a present from the president—a life-size replica of a human foot with a hole in it, symbolizing where he had shot himself. Watt's choices to replace the Beach Boys were popular singer Wayne Newton and military bands.

3. **(b)** The craze for celebrity perfumes was in the air in the 1980s. Cosmetic conglomerates used endorsements from the stars to market new scents: Linda Evans had Krystal, named after her character in the television show "Dynasty"; Julio Iglesias marketed Only; Cher endorsed a fragrance called Uninhibited. The trumpeter and band leader Herb Alpert took a more entrepreneurial approach. He spent five years mixing and sniffing in a lab at home before he concocted Listen, a floral fragrance for women that he marketed successfully in California boutiques.

4. **(d)** James Bond, agent 007 on Her Majesty's Secret Service, lived on in Gardner's books: *License Renewed* in 1981, *For*

*Special Services* in 1982, *Ice Breaker* in 1983, *Role of Honor* in 1984, and *Nobody Lives Forever* in 1986.

**5. (a)** Originally created as a special network report on the status of the American hostages held in Iran in the early 1980s, "Nightline" found a regular spot on ABC's schedule in March 1980. In the years after the hostages returned to America "Nightline" became one of television's most respected news/interview shows primarily because of host Ted Koppel's superior interviewing skills.

**6. (d)** After a tough drive through unusually stormy weather to Reagan's Rancho Cielo, the queen was served *caldo tlalpeno*, a chicken soup seasoned with chipotle chiles; enchiladas filled with ground beef, cheese, and olives; chiles rellenos; tacos; rice; refried beans; and guacamole. For dessert there were orange slices with kirsch and butter cookies.

**7. (a)** One definition of the verb *zap* is to move with sudden speed or swift action. With the advent of prerecorded broadcast programming played back on home VCRs at the viewer's convenience, advertisers worried about the zapping trend. Their concerns were justified. Remote control devices allow viewers to fast-forward through commercials or other uninteresting portions of prerecorded video programming.

**8. (a)** On January 28, 1985, some of the country's top recording artists gathered in Los Angeles to record "We Are the World," written by Lionel Ritchie and Michael Jackson, to benefit those suffering from famine in Africa. The record was released on March 7, 1985. Among the forty-six singers collectively known as USA (United Support of Artists) for Africa were Tina Turner, Bruce Springsteen, Ray Charles, Diana Ross, Bob Dylan, Billy Joel, Paul Simon, Stevie Wonder, and Steve Perry. The song begat a video and an album and raised $50 million.

**9. (c)** In March 1989, RJR Nabisco, Inc., withdrew Premier, its smokeless cigarette, from the market. Premier was supposed to be the answer to the increasing discontent with smoking in public places. The company reportedly spent more than $300 million on what the *Wall Street Journal* called "one of the most stunning new-product disasters in recent history." To "smoke" the complicated cigarette, one sucked in air through its carbon-heated tobacco jacket and flavor capsule to produce a smoke cooled by filtering. Each pack of Premiers came with a four-page instruction booklet. In addition to its complexity and the "hernia effect" of trying to draw in air, the cigarette failed because it tasted awful unless it was lighted with a special butane lighter.

10. **(c)** "Peewee's Playhouse" was the show featuring humans and their interaction. The deliciously silly Peewee Herman and his coterie of friends (Miss Yvonne, Captain Carl, Reba the mail lady, a Latino lifeguard), furniture (Chairy the chair, Magic Screen, a talking window who announced visitors), and play-mates encouraged young, impressionable viewers to use their imaginations for entertainment. Peewee was always showing ways to have fun with stuff kids would normally have available. Some stations decided to run "Peewee's Playhouse" in a late-night time slot to lure hip adults into the fun.

11. **(d)** The "grazing" phenomenon—eating snacks all day long or eating small portions of different foods—originated in England in the early 1980s and quickly caught on in America. By grazing, food lovers were able to sample exotic cusines, new vegetables, new methods of presentation, and new ethnic tastes that were proliferating. The grazing concept also coin-cided with the trend of eating small portions of healthful foods.

12. **(c)** Val-Speak, a 1980s form of teenager slang, originated in the San Fernando Valley, California, with female high schoolers ("Vals") who hung out at malls. It became famous when, in 1982, Moon Unit Zappa, a San Fernando Valley girl then 14, imitated the speech of her schoolmates at the dinner table. The result was the song "Valley Girl," recorded by Moon Unit and her musician father, Frank, former leader of the Mothers of Invention rock group. In the song Moon—as Andrea, the stereotypical Valley Girl—takes listeners on an aural tour of her life, with descriptions of her gross, saliva-covered retainer and someone else's grody dried food that she encounters when her mother makes her do the dishes.

13. **(a)** During the 1980s each star produced an exercise or workout videotape for the home market. Jane Fonda is the best known for her series of workout tapes, including "Jane Fonda's Prime Time Workout" (1984) and "Jane Fonda's Complete Workout" (1989). Raquel Welch taught women how to "Lose 10 Pounds in 3 Weeks" (1988). Jane Powell suggested

her audience "Fight Back with Fitness" (1986). Debbie Reynolds followed her first workout video, "Do It Debbie's Way," with "Couples Do It Debbie's Way" (1988).

14. **(d)** The Gannett Corporation introduced *USA Today* on September 15, 1982. The paper was controversial and revolutionary from its first issue for three main reasons: (1) *USA Today* was the first newspaper to demonstrate the power of extensive use of color in its editorial pages. Newspapers all over the country followed suit as soon as finances allowed. (2) *USA Today* carried shorter stories than other newspapers. It was edited for travelers, business people, and readers with limited time. Critics unkindly referred to this aspect of the paper as fast-food journalism. (3) It was the first general-interest newspaper to cover the nation as a whole. Each issue carried news briefs from all fifty states.

15. **(d)** Batman's foe, the Joker, did it in 1988. In a grisly series of panels, readers saw the Joker beat Robin with a crowbar. He was still alive, however, when the Joker left a bomb in the warehouse where the beating had occurred. It was the bomb blast that finally killed Robin. The Robin who died, however, was Jason Todd, not Dick Grayson, the original Robin. Apparently, Todd was not popular with Batman's publisher, DC Comics, or with readers. The company sponsored a reader poll to determine Robin/Todd's fate. Of 10,614 reader responses, 5343 voted to let him die and 5271 voted for his survival.

16. **(a)** Adventure and thriller novelist Robin Masters, though never seen on the show, played a big role. He owned Robin's Nest, the estate where Magnum occupied the guest house and majordomo Jonathan Quail Higgins brought traditional English correctness to the tropics. Masters often called or recommended clients to Magnum or hosted, in absentia, a bevy of interesting guests who used his estate during their Hawaiian visits. But he was always away researching or writing his adventure novels and rarely spent a night in his own house. One running subtheme of the show led viewers to believe that Robin was, in fact, Higgins. Magnum believed it. Higgins denied it.

17. **(a)** The USDA's regulations define a pizza as a dough-based product containing cheese and tomato sauce. Puck, the owner of Spago, the Los Angeles restaurant as famous for its exotic

pizza as for its show-biz glitterati clientele, thought tomato sauce had a cheap image and opted for other ingredients. After negotiating, Puck agreed to add chunks of tomato to his pesto sauce on the pizzas. Agriculture authorities were satisfied, and the pizzas were allowed to be sold.

**18. (c)** The fast-cut, hip "Miami Vice," with its rock-video-like cinematography, also was noted for its men's clothes—in keeping with a show known as much for its style as its content. Italian designers supplied the cast with unstructured jackets over lavender and neon-pink T-shirts worn with beltless, pleated pants—a style that spread to the general public as the Vice Look.

**19. (d)** The California Raisins—cool in their sunglasses and tennis shoes—first appeared in a television commercial in September 1986 doing a conga line to "I Heard It Through the Grapevine." The raisins were so popular that by the end of 1988 they had sold an estimated $500 million worth of T-shirts, bed sheets, lunch boxes, toys, and almost three hundred other products, not to mention raisins. Will Vinton's studio in Portland, Oregon, brought the clay raisins alive through Claymation, a type of stop-action animation. Vinton was also responsible for the "Noid," the obnoxious pizza destroyer featured in Domino's Pizza commercials.

**20. (d)** On April 23, 1985, after five years of experimentation, Coca-Cola announced it was changing the formula of the world-famous soft drink to a sweeter, less-carbonated version. The change, partly a reaction to the increasing popularity of Pepsi-Cola, was not the first in the nearly one-hundred-year-old recipe, but it was given enormous publicity. The company returned the old formula to an Atlanta, Georgia, bank vault and then awaited rave reviews and big sales for its New Coke. However, these expectations were dashed. Most dedicated Coke drinkers hated the new version of their favorite. On July 10, 1985, Coca-Cola decided to reintroduce the original-formula soft drink, henceforth known as Classic Coke. Resurrecting the older formula was considered one of the most dramatic turnarounds in marketing history.

**21. (a)** *Lipo-* (from the Greek word *lipos,* meaning "fat") denotes a relationship to fats or lipids. Therefore, liposuction literally means sucking or vacuuming the fat away. The technique, performed properly under the correct conditions, successfully removed unwanted fat cells from midsections and thighs all over the country during the 1980s.

22. **(b)** One of the phenomena of the 1980s was frequent flyer programs, in which airlines kept track of miles flown by individual passengers, allowing them to accumulate "free miles" for every mile flown. For their free miles customers were rewarded with free tickets or upgrades in service classes. The first such program was offered in 1980 to business travelers by Western Airlines, but the idea became widespread after American introduced its Advantage program a year later. Originally developed as a method to build customer loyalty after airline deregulation in the late 1970s, frequent flyer programs were eventually offered by nearly every airline.

23. **(c)** Television viewers with a penchant for peeking into the lives of the rich could hardly refuse Leach's invitation to join him as he toured and partied with the wealthy and well known. On every broadcast he wished his viewers the same "champagne wishes and caviar dreams" he was having. Only Robin— with his disarming Cockney accent—could get us into those bathrooms, staterooms, closets, and offices of people with whom we were unlikely ever to cross paths. Who else would know about places like the Villa d'Oro, a Hong Kong house made largely of gold, down to an 18-karat-gold fence?

24. **(d)** Throughout the decade marketing firms, demographics researchers, advice columnists, manners mavens, and the U.S. Census Bureau struggled to create an acceptable label for a sometimes delicate domestic arrangement. "Posslq" was the sociological code word for "person of opposite sex sharing living quarters." In polite society live-ins were referred to as "significant others." In census-speak "domestic partner" was the euphemism for roommate, significant or not.

25. **(c)** In eight years the fast-food king of the Golden Arches more than doubled the number of hamburgers it had sold since its beginnings in 1955, when Ray Kroc opened his own Golden Arches store on a ten-year contract with Maurice and Richard McDonald, who operated the prototype stand in San Bernardino, California.

26. **(c)** "Super Mario 2," "The Legend of Zelda," and "Punch-out!" are game cartridges for the Nintendo entertainment system.

Nintendo, Ltd., one of the major manufacturers of electronic toys in Japan, revitalized the home market for video games in the late 1980s by offering more computer power and sophisticated graphics in its system. The small Nintendo computer console plugs into the television; the software is the game cartridges. Players, mostly adolescent boys, use two hand-held controllers, a light gun, or a joystick to maneuver characters through an electronic universe of adventures and hazards. Nintendo games were in nearly 20 million homes by the end of the decade, and more than fifty thousand calls a day from obsessive players poured into Nintendo's game-counseling hot line.

**27. (d)** Americans consumed a lot of Italian pasta during the 1980s—yearly consumption went up tenfold from 1975 to 1986, from 10 million pounds to 100 million pounds. Although spaghetti remained the most popular pasta, cooks and restaurant chefs also served the thin angel's hair capelli d'angelo, the corkscrew-shaped fusilli, the quill-shaped penne, the snail-shaped lumache, and other kinds of the approximately four hundred pastas produced in Italy. Pasta was a prized food in the 1980s because of its versatility in cuisine and its low-fat complex carbohydrates.

**28. (d)** "Falcon Crest" portrayed the seamy side of wine moguls in the Napa Valley and helped fuel business for one of California's hottest tourist attractions. In 1987 alone about 2.5 million visitors journeyed to Napa County to visit the wineries, including Spring Mountain vineyard, the location where some of the scenes from "Falcon Crest" are filmed, and Chateau Boswell with its "magic castle." In addition to Cabernet, Chardonnay, and Sauvignon Blanc, the wineries sell tram rides, picnic lunches, T-shirts, corkscrews, and cookbooks to the tourists. Some wine connoisseurs and local grape growers think things in Napa County have gone too far and the wineries should get back to the business of making wine.

**29. (b)** Deely Bobbers caught on in 1982 as frivolous headgear with no purpose except silliness. Deely Bobbers are headbands that sprout springy, antenna-like stalks with plastic balls, stars, hearts, or pinwheels at the end. The novelty was created by thirty-eight-year-old John Mincove of Bellevue, Washington, who had them manufactured in Hong Kong and Taiwan. John

Belushi wore Deely Bobbers on "Saturday Night Live" when he appeared as a killer bee. They were popular at the Knoxville World's Fair and sold well at toy stores and other retail shops.

**30. (d)** Rubik's Cube has six sides, each with a different bright color. The sides are divided top to bottom and side to side into three rows that each have three smaller cubes that can be turned 360 degrees to reveal other colors. The puzzle solver must scramble the smaller cubes and align them again into one solid color on each of the six sides. There are 43,252,003,274,489,856,000 potential color patterns in the cube. It was created in 1974 by Ernö Rubik, a Hungarian architect and professor, who used the cube as a teaching tool in the study of three-dimensional objects. Rubik's Cube—also called the Hungarian Horror—became the "world's most-asked-for plaything" in 1980. Ideal Toy Corp., the licensed distributor, sold about 5 million cubes a year at the height of the craze. There were sanctioned spinoffs (like the Magic Cube, which could be twisted into the shape of a swan, saxophone, or steamroller), counterfeit versions from Taiwan and Hong Kong, and copycat puzzles, including a British cube commemorating the royal wedding that featured likenesses of Prince Charles and Princess Diana on two sides and the Union Jack on the other four.

**31. (b)** The craze for Cajun cooking contributed to a shortage of redfish, which are harvested in the Gulf of Mexico. Blackened redfish is a popular Cajun menu item prepared by dipping the fish in butter, then in a peppery herb mix, and searing it until blackened (burned) in a special heavy iron skillet. Cajun cuisine comes from Louisiana, where the descendants of French-Canadians from Nova Scotia serve up spicy dishes, like gumbo and jambalaya, that include red and black peppers, chicken, sausage, crab, and shrimp.

**32. (d)** The Home Shopping Club was the first of many successful cable television programs that sell products to home viewers. A 24-hour program, Home Shopping Club started in 1982 in Clearwater, Florida, and became popular for offering reliable products from closeouts and liquidations at an average price of $33. A national phenomenon in the 1980s, television shopping clubs sell jewelry, appliances, and knickknacks touted by jovial, chatty hosts to home viewers who place their credit-card orders over toll-free 800 numbers. The market for shopping at home from the television screen reached $17 million in the fiscal year 1986–1987.

**33.** **(d)** Ziggy Marley, son of the late reggae star Bob Marley, performs in a band called the Melody Makers with his brother and two sisters. Barbie, Transformer, and Teddy Ruxpin are all part of America's 1980s toy world. Mattel's Barbie—the teenage doll—continued to attract a young following in the 1980s with her new evening wardrobe, a personal computer, an attache case, and an exercise room. Transformers by Hasbro are malleable plastic models, such as insects and dinosaurs, that a child can transform into something else; a robot Transformer, for example, turns into a powerful microscope. Teddy Ruxpin combines two toy trends of the 1980s—teddy bears and high tech. The animated bear, made by Worlds of Wonder, talks and tells stories from illustrated storybooks with the help of an internal cassette.

**34.** **(b)** Naomi Judd and her daughter, Wynonna Judd, revitalized the country-music scene in the first part of the decade with albums such as *Rockin' in Rhythm.* A native of Ashland, Kentucky, Naomi gave birth to Wynonna when she was eighteen years old. After living in California, where she worked as a secretary and a salesclerk in a health food store, Naomi moved back home with her two daughters. (She had never cottoned to California—when asked her sign, she would say, "Baptist.") Naomi sang around the house while Wynonna taught herself to sing and play guitar and studied to become a registered nurse. Mother and daughter eventually bought a $30 cassette recorder at K-Mart, and Wynonna, during a nursing assignment, got a top country-music producer to listen to their homemade tape. They were signed by RCA in Nashville, made the Country Top 20 with their debut single, and went on to win a Grammy in 1985.

**35.** **(d)** TCBY (The Country's Best Yogurt), Heidi's, and Penguin's are just some of the frozen-yogurt chains that caught on in the 1980s. Health-conscious Americans lined up to buy the frozen dessert, which typically has less fat and fewer calories than ice cream: premium ice cream has 175 calories per half-cup serving, whereas frozen yogurt averages about 105. The advertisers of Penguin's Place put it this way: "Eat like a pig.

Look like a fox." Not all frozen yogurt is healthful, however. Many brands have additives, and some have enough sugar to bring their calorie count up to ice cream's. Also, toppings like jelly beans, crumbled cookies, and granola aren't kind to the waistline.

**36.** **(b)** Lake Wobegon, Minnesota, was the quintessential rural Midwest town created by humorist Garrison Keillor, the host of the popular "Prairie Home Companion" radio show. The show ended in 1987, after thirteen years, when Keillor quit to pursue a writing career and took with him Lake Wobegon, its peculiar and charming citizenry, and its notable establishments (the Chatterbox Cafe, the Sidetrack Tap, and Bertha's Kitty Boutique).

**37.** **(d)** An eclectic mix of spiritual beliefs and practices taken from astrology and primitive religions, with a dash of Eastern mysticism and modern therapeutic techniques, New Age culture (which owes a debt to the counterculture of the 1960s) has claimed a lot of media attention, partly because of famous adherents like actress Shirley MacLaine. (It was MacLaine who popularized channeling with her 1985 book, *Dancing in the Light.*) Channeling refers to a person's ability to act as a medium for an "ancient" or "alien" being with a message for those on earth. Rebirthing is a therapeutic process of simulating one's own birth. Crystal healing involves the use of mineral crystals to effect changes in health and vitality.

**38.** **(b)** An acrobatic dance style known as "breaking" developed in the streets of the Bronx, New York, in the early 1980s. Highly athletic and full of stylized spins, rolls, and dives, breaking evolved into a competitive performance among street gangs, who used dancing instead of fighting to challenge each other. Films such as *Flashdance* (1983), *Footloose* (1984), and *Breakin'* (1984), along with a burgeoning dance club scene, helped promote breakdancing to tremendous popularity.

**39.** **(c)** Staying home was not a new idea, but when the baby boom generation did it, the trend had to be labeled with its own buzzword. Cocooning provided yet another market to be tapped, and television commercials featured young, attractive stay-at-homes having much more fun around the house—with

their VCRs, down comforters, and Cuisinarts—than they
would have if out painting the town.

**40.** **(d)** Radicchio, an outrageously expensive lettuce, found its
way into salads in restaurants patronized by hip yuppies.
Tapas, or little grilled and marinated appetizer dishes from
Spain, provided 1987's new food trend. And by the end of the
decade goat cheese pizza, a California cuisine novelty in the
early 1980s, was almost a new American classic.

AP/Wide World Photos

# TEST 6

# Science and Technology

*Technology increases what we can do, but it cannot teach us the right thing to do.*

*—POPE JOHN PAUL II*

1. In 1983 a new form of sound recordings known as CDs appeared on the market. What does "CD" stand for?

   a. coded disc

   b. cassette disc

   c. compact disc

   d. cellular disc

2. What is the primary cause of the "greenhouse effect"?

   a. water vapor condensation

   b. carbon dioxide

   c. chlorofluorocarbons (CFCs)

   d. nuclear waste

3. In 1985 a British scientific expedition found a huge hole in the earth's ozone layer over the Antarctic. What caused this hole?

   a. ultraviolet radiation

   b. chlorofluorocarbons (CFCs)

   c. acid rain

   d. the greenhouse effect

4. In 1988 it was announced that ordinary aspirin could help prevent heart attacks. Why?

   a. Aspirin reduces stress.

   b. Aspirin dilates blood vessels.

   c. Aspirin reduces cholesterol levels.

   d. Aspirin reduces blood clotting.

5. A computer program secretly entered into a computer to sabotage or destroy its contents is called a(n)

   a. clone

   b. virus

   c. zapper

   d. intruder

6. How does the B-2 Stealth bomber avoid detection?

   a. The plane's "flying wing" design travels faster than radar waves.

b. The plane's surface is coated with radar-dampening materials that soak up radar waves.

c. The plane carries a mobile Midgetman missile to preemptively attack enemy detectors.

d. The plane flies at altitudes below the threshold of radar detection.

7. Superconductor technology is being developed to

   a. provide a means of transmitting electrical current without energy loss from electrical resistance

   b. reach absolute zero ($-273.15$ C)

   c. produce lightweight metallic alloys for space vehicles

   d. produce ceramic compounds that can be efficiently burned as fuel

8. Which of the following nations/agencies did not launch a spacecraft to observe the return of Halley's Comet in 1986?

   a. the United States

   b. the Soviet Union

   c. the European Space Agency

   d. Japan

9. In October 1988 the Shroud of Turin, venerated for centuries as Jesus Christ's burial cloth, was proved by carbon-14 tests to be

   a. authentic

   b. a medieval forgery

   c. the burial cloth of St. Peter

   d. still a complete mystery

10. Who was the first recipient of a permanent artificial heart?

   a. Murray P. Haydon

   b. Baby Fae

   c. Dr. Barney Clark

   d. William J. Schroeder

**11.** Americans became very cholesterol-conscious in the 1980s. What is cholesterol?

    **a.** a waxy substance that is the main cause of coronary artery disease in the United States

    **b.** a substance produced in the body and essential to good health

    **c.** a dietary substance found in dairy products and animal fats

    **d.** all of the above

**12.** What does "nuclear winter" mean?

    **a.** a nuclear freeze

    **b.** the behavior of atomic particles at absolute zero

    **c.** the aftermath of large-scale nuclear war

    **d.** a nuclear power plant shutdown

**13.** The U.S. space probe *Voyager 2* is known for its photographs of

    **a.** Neptune

    **b.** Uranus

    **c.** Saturn

    **d.** all of the above

**14.** Gene-splicing technology is being developed to

    **a.** produce more effective drugs and vaccines

    **b.** "design" plant and animal life forms for use in medical research and industry

    **c.** mine copper by breaking down its naturally occurring compound into pure metal

    **d.** all of the above

**15.** In 1988 the U.S. Patent Office issued a patent for the first genetically altered mammal. What was that mammal?

    **a.** a mouse

    **b.** a rat

    **c.** a guinea pig

    **d.** a cat

**16.** The new generation of video technology that has produced a dramatic improvement in television picture quality is called

    **a.** cable TV

    **b.** MTV

    **c.** HDTV

    **d.** videodisc

**17.** Radon is a naturally occurring gas that

    **a.** depletes the ozone layer

    **b.** causes cancer

    **c.** is an economical fuel

    **d.** is a coolant in superconductor technology

**18.** The new telecommunications technology that transmits text and images over telephone lines is called

    **a.** computer electronic mail

    **b.** fax

    **c.** fiberoptical telex

    **d.** magnetic resonance imaging

**19.** In 1984 Dr. Robert Gallo announced that he had isolated the cause of AIDS. What is it?

    **a.** a parasite

    **b.** a virus

    **c.** a bacterium

    **d.** a fungus

**20.** In 1987, for the first time in almost four centuries, a certain astronomical event occurred close enough to Earth to be visible to the naked eye. What was it?

    **a.** a meteor shower

    **b.** a comet

c. a supernova or exploding star

d. a black hole

**21.** In 1987 a major medical study reported that osteoporosis in postmenopausal women can be effectively treated with

a. niacin supplements

b. AZT

c. cyclosporin A

d. estrogen supplements

**22.** In 1984 Boston doctors surgically repaired a damaged organ, using the first successful implant of laboratory-cultured replacement tissue. What organ did they repair?

a. the liver

b. the skin

c. a kidney

d. the intestine

**23.** On January 28, 1986, the U.S. space shuttle *Challenger* exploded. What was the cause of the explosion?

a. a computer malfunction

b. bad launch weather

c. leaky O-ring seals

d. an electrical short circuit

**24.** What is thought to be the primary cause of acid rain?

a. sulfur dioxide from air pollution

b. atmospheric testing of nuclear weapons

c. ozone depletion

d. plastic

**25.** In 1986 the Soviet Union launched a space vehicle named *Mir*, which means "peace." It is the world's first

    **a.** permanently manned space station

    **b.** international communications satellite

    **c.** telescope in space

    **d.** probe landing on Venus

**26.** In October 1984 an infant known to the public only as "Baby Fae" underwent a headline-making surgical procedure. What was it?

    **a.** She was separated from a Siamese twin joined to her at the head.

    **b.** She received a heart transplant from a baboon.

    **c.** She received transplants of laboratory-cultured skin over 95 percent of her body.

    **d.** She was "born" from an artificial womb after her mother died in the eighth month of pregnancy.

**27.** "Biometric" security is rapidly replacing locks, keys, and guards at research labs, computer centers, and other high-security buildings. This new technology employs sensors that scan the user's

    **a.** fingerprints

    **b.** blood vessel patterns in the retina of the eye

    **c.** voice

    **d.** all of the above

**28.** On March 23, 1989, what event of scientific interest occurred that narrowly missed becoming a global disaster?

    **a.** Electrical interference from an aurora borealis triggered a computerized nuclear missile launch program that aborted one minute before firing.

    **b.** A large asteroid came within 450,000 miles of hitting earth.

    **c.** A nuclear power plant in Brazil was vandalized, nearly releasing its radioactive core material into the atmosphere.

    **d.** A deadly bacteria strain was accidentally released during a laboratory experiment but was contained at the last moment.

**29.** In 1986 paleontologists announced the discovery of the oldest known bird fossils, which supported the evolutionary theory that birds developed from dinosaurs. This fossil was named

    **a.** Archaeopteryx

    **b.** Protoavis

    **c.** Archaeosaurus

    **d.** Protosaurus

**30.** Scientist Stephen Hawking became internationally recognized in the 1980s as the

    **a.** director of the historic Human Genome Project

    **b.** discoverer of a possible cure for cancer

    **c.** creator of the "superstring" theory of the universe

    **d.** most brilliant theoretical physicist since Einstein

**31.** The new field of micromachinery uses

    **a.** microwaves

    **b.** microscopic silicon-chip motors

    **c.** microorganisms

    **d.** nuclear-power by-products

**32.** In the late 1980s the computer graphics field developed sophisticated 3-D image processing. What is this new technique used for?

    **a.** design and engineering of consumer products

    **b.** visualizing surgical procedures and scientific research

    **c.** architectural design and model-building

    **d.** all of the above

**33.** Air bags and/or automatic seat belts will be mandatory equipment in all new U.S. cars by 1990. Which of the following groups has supported this ruling throughout the 1980s?

   **a.** U.S. automobile manufacturers

   **b.** the Reagan administration

   **c.** automobile insurance companies

   **d.** the U.S. Department of Transportation

**34.** "String theory," a new field of theoretical physics, postulates that

   **a.** the universe has ten dimensions

   **b.** gravity can be mathematically accounted for, which is a major failing of quantum theory

   **c.** the universe is composed of elementary particles shaped like loops, or "strings," vibrating with energy

   **d.** all of the above

**35.** The slang term for the new technology that computerizes, monitors, and automates all of the electrical and energy systems of a building is

   **a.** "smart"

   **b.** "solar"

   **c.** "digital"

   **d.** "robotic"

**36.** In 1989 the U.S. Congress funded the historic Human Genome Project. What will the project do?

   **a.** study, map, and interpret the entire set of coded genetic information contained in human DNA

   **b.** research and develop a cure for genetically caused diseases

   **c.** construct a sophisticated computer model of the human body's systems

   **d.** collect blood samples from every American for genetic testing

**37.** In 1988 the most spectacular archaeological find in the Western Hemisphere was announced. It was the gold-laden tomb of a priest of the Moche people in

   a. Venezuela

   b. Peru

   c. Brazil

   d. Honduras

**38.** The key device that facilitated the 1985 discovery of treasure on the sunken Spanish galleon *Nuestra Señora de Atocha* was

   a. side-scanning sonar

   b. a high-speed magnetometer

   c. jets of water

   d. a 17th-century report

**39.** Radial keratotomy, the trendy new eye surgery, is designed to correct

   a. astigmatism

   b. crossed eyes

   c. nearsightedness

   d. farsightedness

**40.** A new crime-fighting technique known as "genetic fingerprinting" may link a suspect to a crime by testing DNA patterns in

   a. tissue samples

   b. a drop of blood

   c. semen

   d. all of the above

# TEST 6: Explanatory Answers

1. **(c)** CDs were developed in Japan by means of digital sound reproduction technology. Music is "translated" into a binary code of zeros and ones at the rate of 44,100 digits per second and imprinted onto a 4.7-inch-diameter aluminum and plastic disc. The disc surface is scanned by a laser beam and the coded information is then translated back into a sound signal.

2. **(b)** A measurable global warming trend known as the "greenhouse effect" is primarily traced to increased levels of carbon dioxide ($CO_2$) in the atmosphere. $CO_2$ is formed by the burning of fossil fuels such as oil and coal. Many scientists fear that unless the greenhouse effect is brought under control, the climate changes will precipitate environmental crises. Adding to the problem is the fact that humans are systematically destroying rainforests, which are natural absorbers of $CO_2$. Carbon dioxide in the atmosphere traps infrared radiation (heat), thus warming up the earth's surface.

3. **(b)** CFCs, commonly found in air conditioners and refrigerators, Styrofoam, and aerosol cans, have been around for fifty years. Released into the air, CFCs react chemically with the earth's delicate ozone layer 15 miles above the ground. The chemical reaction destroys ozone, and because ozone absorbs the sun's ultraviolet (UV) radiation, the result is that more UV radiation reaches earth. UV is known to cause many kinds of biological damage, including genetic mutation, sunburn, skin cancer, and even the weakening of the human immune system.

4. **(d)** Blood clots are formed in part by "platelet" cells. Aspirin inhibits the clumping together of platelets by reducing the body's ability to produce prostaglandin, a chemical that helps make the platelets stick together.

5. **(b)** In 1988 there was an epidemic of computer virus attacks on an estimated quarter of a million U.S. computers. The phenomenon disrupted or shut down personal computers, electronic bulletin boards, university offices, businesses, and even the U.S. Department of Defense. Like biological viruses, computer viruses can multiply, "infecting" thousands of machines as the disruptive program spreads to other programs.

6. **(b)** Among the radar-deflecting features of the B-2 Stealth bomber are special windows treated to shield the plane's interior from radar waves and a honeycombed material on the plane's leading edge. The honeycomb "baffles" (absorbs) the radar waves, preventing them from bouncing off the plane's surface. Unveiled in 1988 by the Northrop Corporation after ten years of development, the B-2 is estimated to cost about $530 million per plane.

7. **(a)** Superconductivity, or the complete absence of electrical resistance, has been observed and produced in certain metallic substances since 1911 but only at extremely cold temperatures. The expense of producing these cold temperatures made the technology cost-prohibitive. But in 1986 and 1987 scientists discovered that certain ceramic compounds developed superconductivity at temperatures that were not nearly so cold. This discovery made the widespread practical application of superconductors at least theoretically possible.

8. **(a)** The January 1986 space shuttle *Challenger* disaster aborted the U.S. launch of a comet-watching vehicle, but an American probe called *Pioneer 12*, launched in 1978, observed the comet from its orbit near Venus. The Japanese probes *Sakigake* and *Suisei* and the Soviet Union's *Vega 1* and *Vega 2* sent images and data back to earth, and the European Space Agency's *Giotto* took photos of the comet's nucleus from a distance of only 335 miles.

9. **(b)** Three independent laboratories performed carbon-14 analysis on tiny swatches cut from the shroud. All three found that the shroud had been woven between 1260 and 1390—over 1200 years after the crucifixion. Still a mystery is how the ghostly image of a crucified man got on the shroud.

10. **(c)** Retired dentist Barney Clark at age sixty-one became the first recipient of a permanent artificial heart on December 2, 1982. The heart, designed by Dr. Robert Jarvik, was implanted in a $7\frac{1}{2}$-hour operation by Dr. William DeVries in Salt Lake City, Utah. Clark died on March 23, 1983, from circulatory collapse and multiorgan failure. The mechanical heart remained functional to the end.

11. **(d)** Found primarily in the blood, cholesterol is manufactured by the body's cells and is also ingested from food sources. It

is necessary for building cell membranes and sex hormones, as well as for aiding digestion. Too much blood cholesterol, however, can cause fat deposits on artery walls and lead to heart attacks. A diet rich in animal proteins and saturated fats can increase blood cholesterol to a dangerous level.

12. **(c)** "Nuclear winter" was coined in a scientific paper published in 1983. It described the global effects of a major thermonuclear war. Detonation of nuclear weapons would, according to computer-modeled weather studies, cause firestorms big enough to send dense clouds of soot and dust into the atmosphere, blocking the sun's heat and light for weeks or months. The resulting global cooling and darkening could kill all plant and animal life on the planet.

13. **(d)** In 1989 *Voyager 2* sent back photos of Neptune, including a spectacular look at what appeared to be active ice volcanoes on Neptune's moon, Triton. The spacecraft had already photographed Uranus in 1986 and Saturn in 1981. Launched in 1977, *Voyager 2* first flew by Jupiter in 1979. After the encounter with Neptune, the spacecraft headed into interstellar space.

14. **(d)** Gene-splicing, or recombinant DNA technology, is a fast-growing field that "engineers" specific changes in the genetic codes of living organisms. Genetic traits can be enhanced, suppressed, added, or deleted by using special chemical enzymes, and the resulting changes are permanent and inheritable. "Designing" new plants, animals, and microorganisms is a controversial biotechnology because it involves living things and eventually will be able to genetically mutate human beings. Certain drugs, such as insulin and the human growth hormone called interferon, have been produced through gene-splicing, and animals have been "designed" for research and increased food production. The bacterium *Thiobacillus ferrooxidans* is already used in about 10 percent of U.S. copper production.

15. **(a)** In 1987 the U.S. Supreme Court ruled that living animals that had been "human made," or genetically altered, were patentable. In 1988 Harvard University received the first patent issued for a form of animal life, a laboratory mouse genetically altered to make it more susceptible to cancer. According to

Harvard researchers, the mouse—called "C-Myc"—will hasten the development of new cancer drugs and therapies.

16. **(c)** HDTV stands for high-definition television, and it utilizes a new standard of broadcast-signal quality. American television broadcasts transmit a 525-line image, whereas the new HDTV (developed in Japan) transmits a picture formed by 1000 to 1250 lines on a wider-format screen. The picture quality is similar to a 35-mm motion picture image. However, TV sets currently in use will not be able to receive HDTV signals adequately; and the new HDTV sets, as well as HDTV broadcast equipment, will be expensive. Over-the-air HDTV broadcasts in the United States are expected in the mid- to late 1990s.

17. **(b)** Radon is a radioactive gas produced by the decay of uranium in the earth. It can enter houses and tap water from underground pipes and cracks. The U.S. government's Environmental Protection Agency estimates that 10 percent of American homes have dangerously high levels of radon. Second only to cigarette smoking, radon is a leading cause of death from lung cancer in the United States.

18. **(b)** "Fax" means "facsimile transmission," and fax technology utilizes existing telephone lines to transmit visual information. The image is electronically scanned by the fax machine, which translates the information into electrical patterns that travel over phone lines and are then translated back into graphic form by the receiving fax machine.

19. **(b)** AIDS, or acquired immune deficiency syndrome, first appeared in the United States in 1981. Invariably fatal, it works to destroy the body's immune system, leaving the way open for other diseases, infections, and forms of cancer that normally could be warded off. Caused by the HTLV-III virus (human T-cell lymphotropic virus, type III) living within bodily fluids, the infection is passed through the exchange of such fluids, primarily blood and semen. The disease can lie dormant in a person's body for years, producing no symptoms, but that person can still infect others with the virus at any time.

20. **(c)** In the first several months of 1987 astronomers observed a supernova, or death of a star, in the Greater Magellanic Cloud. It was the brightest such event observed on earth since 1604, estimated at approximately 1 billion times the brightness

of our sun. When its nuclear fusion power was spent, the star collapsed inward, producing a shock wave that exploded the outer shell of the star as gravitational energy was liberated. Called SN 1987A, the supernova actually exploded fifty thousand years ago, but the light it generated didn't reach the earth until 1987.

21. **(d)** Osteoporosis, a bone-weakening condition prevalent among older women, can be treated with estrogen (female hormone) supplements to reduce the risk of bone fracture and poor healing. Estrogen, which the body no longer produces after menopause, contributes to bone growth and strength.

22. **(b)** Doctors at Boston's Shriners Burn Institute took small patches of intact skin from a burn victim and cultured it to grow new skin. The new growth was then grafted into the patient's burned area, where it was not rejected. The "test-tube" skin produced about half a square yard within three months.

23. **(c)** The O-ring problem was pinpointed just weeks after the accident; a suspicion had already existed before launch that the rubber O-rings might not function adequately in cold weather. January 28 was an especially cold day, and the O-rings' failure to seal properly allowed hot exhaust gases to escape, ignite, burn through a support strut, and cause a fuel tank to collapse and explode. When the official Rogers Commission report came out four months later, it also acknowledged that NASA's entire shuttle program had been pushed too fast and too hard. As a result of the *Challenger* accident, the U.S. space shuttle program, which had begun with the flight of the *Columbia* in 1981, was halted until 1989.

24. **(a)** Automobiles and power plants burn fossil fuels such as oil and coal, producing a sooty residue containing sulfur dioxide. Released into the air, the sulfur forms sulfuric acid. Such acidified rain has killed or damaged trees all over Europe, the United States, and Canada; in 1986 it was reported that 50 percent of the conifers in Switzerland were dead or dying because of acid rain damage.

25. **(a)** The Soviet space station *Mir* was placed in orbit on February 19, 1986. Three weeks later the Soviet cosmonauts Vladimir Solovyou and Leanid Kizim, launched into space

aboard *Soyuz T-15*, activated *Mir*. The space station, which weighs 46,300 pounds, contains laboratories for experiments, living space for cosmonauts, work and exercise areas, and six docking ports so that it can be docked simultaneously with six spacecraft, including cargo, passenger, and research ships. On December 29, 1987, Colonel Yuri Romanenko returned to earth after spending 326 days aboard *Mir*—a single-mission space endurance record. A comparable U.S. space station should be operational by 1996.

26. **(b)** Born with a defective heart, "Baby Fae" received the healthy heart of a young baboon who had been killed specifically for the transplant operation. Performed at Loma Linda University Medical Center in California, it was the first animal-to-human transplant. Because the baboon's blood type did not match the infant's, she died twenty days after the operation.

27. **(d)** Biometric security systems operate by means of computerized sensors. A finger, eye, or voiced phrase is presented to the machine, which encodes the visual or sound information into digital form and compares it to finger, eye, or voice prints already stored in the computer's memory. The measurement of a person's physical traits (biometrics) offers an advantage as a "key" to opening a locked door because each key is unique. No one can steal the user's unique characteristics, and the user has no key to lose or password to forget.

28. **(b)** "Earth grazers," asteroids that travel close to earth, are not common. However, 1989FC, the asteroid that passed by the earth on March 23, was the closest since 1937 and was estimated to be between 100 yards and half a mile across. Although the asteroid was 450,000 miles away from earth, in cosmic terms the distance was short. Made of solid rock, 1989FC would have had an impact equaling the power of thousands of H-bombs. 1989FC orbits the sun and will pass close to earth again in 1990 and 2015. Asteroids of that size are common in the universe and run into earth about once every 100,000 years.

29. **(b)** The 225-million-year-old fossil remains of Protoavis, or "first bird," were found in western Texas in 1984. About the size of a crow, Protoavis is more "birdlike" than the 150-million-year-old Archaeopteryx, which scientists had presumed for over a hundred years to be the first bird. Protoavis

had no back teeth (resulting in a lightweight jawbone); it had well-developed wings, a wishbone, and a breastbone that indicated a physiology well suited for flight. The fossil's age supports the theory that birds constitute a branch of the dinosaurs' evolutionary tree.

**30. (d)** A professor at Cambridge University in England, Hawking is most widely known for his study of black holes. His theories have advanced theoretical physics along the path toward a "Grand Unification" theory that could explain the nature of all forces and events in the physical universe. Afflicted with amyotrophic lateral sclerosis (Lou Gehrig's disease), Hawking cannot walk or speak. He uses a computerized communications system that he operates with one hand. Hawking is the author of the best-selling *A Brief History of Time* (1988).

**31. (b)** Engineers around the world are shrinking gears, turbines, and motors to microscopic dimensions by etching patterns on tiny silicon chips. The techniques used in this revolutionary technology have produced turbines and working gears that are 125 microns in diameter, with gear teeth that are 15 microns wide (less than one-fifth the thickness of a human hair). The silicon micrometers will be so small that sixty thousand of them will fit into 1 square inch of space. The potential uses of micromachinery are vast—from surgical techniques and communications equipment to industrial and military applications.

**32. (d)** Realistic three-dimensional images on a two-dimensional computer screen have been made possible by new, more powerful computer chips. The chips enable the computer to encode, store, and manipulate the literally billions of mathematical calculations that produce a detailed, natural-looking, moving, three-dimensional image on a flat screen. Products from sneakers to automobiles are currently designed and engineered on 3-D computer graphics systems. Doctors can model the entire human body as well as plan or rehearse surgical procedures. Scientists can conduct experiments without needing a laboratory, and architects can draw, change, and even visually "enter" a 3-D model of a building.

**33. (c)** Auto insurance companies and safety activists estimate that highway deaths could be reduced by up to 40 percent by the use of air bags and/or automatic seat belts. At one time the U.S. Department of Transportation did endorse air bags, inflatable cushions that shield passengers from the impact of a crash. But the department backed down under auto industry pressure against installing the expensive equipment in new cars. In 1981 the Reagan administration canceled previous rulings that air bags or seat belts be required in all U.S. cars by 1984. It took a Supreme Court ruling to persuade the administration to reconsider its decision.

**34. (d)** The "string" model of the universe is not new but had been abandoned as unworkable until about 1980, when it was revived primarily by Edward Witten, a theoretical physicist at the Princeton, New Jersey, Institute for Advanced Studies. Called the next step after quantum theory, string theory is able to account for gravity within a "unified" theory of universal forces and matter—if a ten-dimensional idea is accepted. But six of the ten dimensions remain hidden from us because they are tightly rolled up into microscopic dimensions. Why? No one is certain, but perhaps they failed to expand after the Big Bang.

**35. (a)** "Smart" technology features computerized wiring that links together a number of systems in the building—heating, cooling, television, telephone, gas and electric appliances, and security systems. Programmed to function at top energy efficiency, microprocessors issue commands to water lawns, turn off lights, and adjust heating levels. Industrial applications are vast, and the smart factory is not only managed by similar controls but also includes computer-aided design, engineering, and manufacturing.

**36. (a)** The genome is an individual's complete genetic code, the sum total of information needed to produce a human being. The nucleus of each human cell contains the genome in the form of DNA. The estimated number of genes in the genome is about 100,000; only about 4500 of them have been identified. Nobel Prize winner James Watson, director of the Human Genome Project, said that the project will be "the ultimate tool for understanding ourselves at the molecular level." It is estimated that the project will take fifteen years and cost $3 billion, and the information gathered will fill a million-page book.

**37. (b)** The 1500-year-old burial site, 420 miles from Lima, was the tomb of a warrior priest of the Moche people, a civilization that preceded the Incas. Although the Moche never developed a written language, they were a highly sophisticated people, and scientists claim that the cache of artifacts uncovered rivals those found in the tomb of King Tutankhamen in Egypt. The centerpiece of the find was the body of the warrior priest, splendidly attired in exquisite gold, silver, and jeweled ornaments.

**38.** **(d)** Although Mel Fisher and his crew used the most advanced underwater detection machinery available—including side-scanning sonar to provide a detailed chart of the ocean floor, a high-speed magnetometer to identify the metal in ship fittings, and jets of water to uncover objects buried under ocean silt—it was a 17th-century salvors' report found by doctoral student Eugene Lyon which led Fisher to the underwater reef near the Marquesas Keys off Key West, where the *Atocha* was eventually discovered. The treasure, estimated to be worth $400 million, included silver ingots and gold coins.

**39.** **(c)** By 1988 more than 200,000 nearsighted Americans had undergone radial keratotomy, an eye operation developed in the Soviet Union in 1974. The surgery, which takes about a half hour, involves changing the shape of the cornea, the rounded transparent tissue that covers the iris and pupil. Incisions are made on the cornea; and as the cornea heals, it flattens out in the center, changing the angle of light rays that enter the eye. Despite the growing popularity of the procedure, a study by the National Eye Institute indicated that 26 percent of patients emerge with undercorrected eyes and 16 percent with overcorrected eyes.

**40.** **(d)** Genetic fingerprinting techniques are based on the fact that everyone has a unique DNA pattern, except for identical twins. DNA contains all of an individual's genetic information in chemical codes. Tommy Lee Andrews became the first person convicted in a criminal case in the United States when DNA in his blood matched the DNA in semen found on a rape victim. To date DNA fingerprints have been introduced in at least eighty murder and rape trials.

AP/Wide World Photos

## TEST 7

# *Scandals*

*Greed is not a bad thing. Everybody should be a little greedy. . . . You shouldn't feel guilty.*

—*IVAN BOESKY*

1. Which former Miss America was involved in a 1988 bribery conspiracy trial in New York?
   a. Bess Myerson
   b. Vanessa Williams
   c. Tawney Godin (Little)
   d. Phyllis Ann George

2. Two successive presidents of what U.S. labor union were indicted while in office in the 1980s?
   a. the American Federation of Musicians
   b. the Longshoremen's Association
   c. the Teamsters
   d. the United Mineworkers of America

3. Which of the following Reagan staff members got into trouble for illegal lobbying?
   a. Richard V. Allen and Raymond J. Donovan
   b. Michael K. Deaver and Lyn Nofziger
   c. James Watt and David Stockman
   d. all of the above

4. Which of the following religious leaders was jailed in 1984 for income tax evasion?
   a. Jimmy Swaggart
   b. Baba Ram Dass
   c. Sun Myung Moon
   d. Bhagwan Shree Rajneesh

5. Socialite Claus von Bulow was accused of trying to kill his wife by what means?
   a. arsenic
   b. staging an accidental shooting
   c. staging an auto accident
   d. insulin injection

**6.** What TV evangelist claimed God would "call him home" if he didn't raise $8 million fast?

   **a.** Jim Bakker

   **b.** Jimmy Swaggart

   **c.** Jerry Falwell

   **d.** Oral Roberts

**7.** In 1983 a West German magazine announced the discovery of a sixty-two-volume diary supposedly written by which of the following World War II leaders?

   **a.** Benito Mussolini

   **b.** Joseph Stalin

   **c.** Adolf Hitler

   **d.** Winston Churchill

**8.** In which of the following undercover operations did FBI agents pose as Arab sheiks?

   **a.** Abscam

   **b.** the DeLorean case

   **c.** Irangate

   **d.** Wedtech

**9.** Prep school headmistress Jean Harris shot her lover, Scarsdale diet doctor Herman Tarnower, because

   **a.** he refused to marry her

   **b.** he took a new mistress

   **c.** she was hooked on amphetamines that he gave her

   **d.** all of the above

**10.** The Greenpeace scandal in France in 1985 arose out of that organization's protest against

   **a.** nuclear testing

   **b.** killing of seals

   **c.** whaling operations

   **d.** colonialism

**11.** In 1989 the House Ethics Committee accused Jim Wright, Speaker of the U.S. House of Representatives, of violations stemming from

    **a.** improper gifts

    **b.** book sales

    **c.** his wife's job

    **d.** all of the above

**12.** After charges of Nazi war crimes were raised against the former UN secretary general in the mid-1980s, Kurt Waldheim was

    **a.** tried and convicted in his native Austria

    **b.** extradited to Israel for trial

    **c.** elected president of Austria

    **d.** totally exonerated of all charges

**13.** The head of which of the following agencies resigned in 1983 after being cited for contempt of Congress?

    **a.** the Office of Management and Budget

    **b.** the Central Intelligence Agency

    **c.** the Environmental Protection Agency

    **d.** the Housing and Urban Development Agency

**14.** Maverick automaker John DeLorean was accused of what crime?

    **a.** cocaine trafficking

    **b.** embezzlement

    **c.** tax evasion

    **d.** all of the above

**15.** Jim Bakker, founder and head of the PTL religious empire until brought down by a sex scandal in 1987, was ordained in what denomination?

    **a.** the Assemblies of God

    **b.** the Methodist Church

    **c.** the Baptist Church

    **d.** the Congregationalist Church

**16.** Vanessa Williams, the first black Miss America (1983), gave up her title for what reason?

   **a.** She was secretly married.

   **b.** There were rumors of a lesbian affair.

   **c.** She had posed for nude photographs.

   **d.** She wanted to pursue a movie career.

**17.** U.S. attorney general Edwin Meese was accused of which of the following ethical lapses?

   **a.** taking bribes

   **b.** violating conflict-of-interest laws

   **c.** filing a false tax return

   **d.** all of the above

**18.** The governor of which state was impeached in 1988?

   **a.** Tennessee

   **b.** Alabama

   **c.** Maryland

   **d.** Arizona

**19.** The Helmsley hotel chain became embroiled in what scandal in 1988?

   **a.** tax evasion

   **b.** prostitution

   **c.** bankruptcy

   **d.** trafficking in stolen goods

**20.** Adman Khashoggi, a middleman in the Iran-*contra* affair, was also implicated in which other 1980s scandal?

   **a.** the DeLorean affair

   **b.** improper payments to House Speaker Jim Wright

   **c.** the financial improprieties of Ferdinand and Imelda Marcos

   **d.** illegal junk bond transactions

**21.** What entertainment industry figure won a lawsuit against the *National Enquirer?*

    **a.** Paul Newman

    **b.** Frank Sinatra

    **c.** Jane Fonda

    **d.** Carol Burnett

**22.** Which of the following companies was involved in defense procurement scandals in the 1980s?

    **a.** Rockwell International

    **b.** Hughes Aircraft

    **c.** Northrop

    **d.** all of the above

**23.** Who was the investment banker who received suitcases stuffed with money in exchange for insider trading tips?

    **a.** Martin Siegel

    **b.** Dennis Levine

    **c.** Boyd Jeffries

    **d.** Charles Atkins

**24.** Aldo Gucci, manufacturer of luxury leather goods, served a year in prison for

    **a.** writing bad checks

    **b.** trafficking in stolen goods

    **c.** tax evasion

    **d.** securities fraud

**25.** In 1986 stock manipulator Ivan Boesky agreed to cooperate with the U.S. government in its investigations of insider trading. In exchange for that,

    **a.** all charges were dropped against Boesky

    **b.** he was banned for a year from trading in securities

    **c.** he was fined $100,000

    **d.** he was fined $100 million and sentenced to jail

**26.** New York City's "Mayflower Madam" was so called because

    **a.** her ancestors came over on the Mayflower

    **b.** she worked out of the Mayflower Hotel

    **c.** she catered to social-register customers

    **d.** of all of the above

**27.** Gary Hart withdrew his candidacy for president in May 1987 when it was alleged he had an affair with

    **a.** Jessica Hahn

    **b.** Donna Rice

    **c.** Fawn Hall

    **d.** Rita Jenrette

**28.** In 1989 whiz kid and entrepreneur Barry Minkow was convicted of fraud and conspiracy relating to his business, which was

    **a.** an auto repair company

    **b.** a rug cleaning company

    **c.** a chain of grocery stores

    **d.** a toy manufacturer

**29.** Who set up a gun-running operation in the Iran-*contra* affair, ran his own private treasury, lied to Congress, destroyed government documents, yet emerged as a national hero?

    **a.** Robert McFarlane

    **b.** William Casey

    **c.** Robert Poindexter

    **d.** Oliver North

**30.** Michael Milken, the junk bond king of Drexel Burnham Lambert, was charged with

    **a.** stock manipulations

    **b.** insider trading

    **c.** racketeering

    **d.** all of the above

**31.** Joe Hunt's "Billionaire Boys Club" was founded to
   a. help underprivileged boys
   b. enrich Joe Hunt
   c. promote sports among youth
   d. all of the above

**32.** When former Philippine first lady Imelda Marcos was arraigned on racketeering charges in New York City in 1988, who posted her bail?
   a. tobacco heiress Doris Duke
   b. financier Adnan Khashoggi
   c. the John Birch Society
   d. a group of wealthy Marcos loyalists

**33.** John Tower, President George Bush's nominee for secretary of defense, was rejected for
   a. alcoholism
   b. womanizing
   c. accepting payments from defense contractors
   d. all of the above

**34.** A 1981 Pulitzer Prize–winning newspaper article, later revealed to be a fake story, was about
   a. Jimmy, an eight-year-old heroin addict
   b. Lulu, a teenage unwed mother
   c. José, a thirteen-year-old crack seller
   d. Pat, a hemophiliac AIDS victim

**35.** In 1984 the CIA caused a scandal with its manual on
   a. the home manufacture of bombs
   b. computer hacking
   c. deep-cover operations
   d. guerrilla operations in Nicaragua

**36.** At the 1988 Seoul Olympics what event did Canadian Ben Johnson win, only to be stripped of his medal?
   a. the 400-meter hurdles
   b. the javelin throw

    **c.** the decathlon

    **d.** the 100-meter dash

**37.** In 1989 Cincinnati Reds manager Pete Rose was banned from baseball because

    **a.** he used drugs

    **b.** he punched an umpire

    **c.** he fixed a baseball game

    **d.** he gambled on baseball games

**38.** What eminent American publishing family was in the news in 1982 due to a scandalous divorce?

    **a.** the Hearsts

    **b.** the Coxes

    **c.** the Pulitzers

    **d.** the Chandlers

**39.** On August 21, 1987, Clayton Lonetree was sentenced to thirty years in prison on charges of spying for the Soviet Union. Lonetree was

    **a.** a defense contractor

    **b.** a career diplomat

    **c.** an office clerk at the Pentagon

    **d.** a sergeant in the U.S. Marine Corps

**40.** The Walker family gained notoriety for

    **a.** check fraud

    **b.** welfare fraud

    **c.** insider trading

    **d.** espionage

# TEST 7: Explanatory Answers

1. **(a)** Myerson, Miss America of 1945, was acquitted after a highly publicized trial in 1988 for conspiracy to bribe a New York State judge. The ambitious former beauty queen—an unsuccessful candidate for the U.S. Senate in 1980, then a TV consumer affairs reporter—was appointed Cultural Affairs Commissioner for New York City in 1982 after helping Mayor Ed Koch get elected. Twice married and divorced, Myerson fell in love with a New York contractor, Andy Capasso, who was married. In Capasso's 1983 divorce trial Myerson was accused of trying to bribe the judge for a favorable settlement by giving the judge's daughter a job.

2. **(c)** In 1981 interim Teamsters president Roy L. Williams was indicted and convicted of plotting to bribe a U.S. senator to delay a trucking deregulation bill. Williams was released after three years in prison and died shortly thereafter. In 1986 his successor, Jackie Presser, was indicted in a payroll-padding scheme but nonetheless was reelected to a five-year term as union president. Presser died in July 1988. (While Presser was awaiting trial in 1988, the U.S. Department of Justice filed suit to remove the union's leaders and "take back the Teamsters from the Mafia.")

3. **(b)** Former White House deputy chief of staff Deaver and former presidential advisor Nofziger both ran afoul of new laws regulating the lobbying activities of government officials once they have left office. Nofziger was found guilty in 1988 of violating the prohibition on lobbying one's former agency within a year of leaving government. His conviction, however, was reversed by a federal appeals court in June 1989. Deaver was convicted of perjury, also in 1988, for lying about his lobbying activities. According to *Time* magazine, "Deaver began peddling his government connection with an avidity that was shocking even by jaded Washington standards."

4. **(c)** Sun Myung Moon, South Korean evangelist and founder of the Unification Church, was convicted of tax evasion in the state of New York. His followers, called "Moonies," regard him as a manifestation of God. When Moon was charged with not reporting interest on a $1.6 million bank account, he claimed that the money belonged to the church. After his conviction,

he mounted a huge media campaign that influenced his release in 1985, after serving thirteen months of an eighteen-month sentence. Moon's overall U.S. empire is extensive and includes political groups, media organizations, and businesses as well as religious organizations.

**5. (d)** The Danish-born von Bulow earned a law degree from Cambridge (England) and worked for J. Paul Getty before his 1966 marriage to American heiress Martha ("Sunny") Crawford. For most of their fourteen-year marriage the couple lived in uppercrust affluence in Newport, Rhode Island, raising Sunny's two children by a previous marriage and their one daughter. In 1980, when Sunny lapsed into a coma from which she will never awaken, the two older children and a maid cast suspicion on von Bulow, accusing him of inducing the coma with an insulin injection. Von Bulow was convicted of attempting to murder his wife in 1982; the conviction was overturned in 1984; a new trial in 1985 resulted in his acquittal.

**6. (d)** A pioneering TV evangelist who took to the medium in the 1950s, Roberts also founded a $500 million complex, including Oral Roberts University and the City of Faith medical complex, near Tulsa, Oklahoma. On March 22, 1987, Roberts announced that he would remain in the university's 200-foot prayer tower until he had raised $8 million for medical scholarships. His deadline was the end of the month, and if the money was not forthcoming, he warned, God might "call Oral Roberts home." On April 1, Roberts announced that the money had been raised. A Florida dog-track owner had put up $1.3 million of the donations, which was accepted despite the fact that Methodists like Roberts abhor gambling.

**7. (c)** The diaries, supposedly written by Hitler between 1932 and 1945, turned out to be forgeries, and the perpetrators of the hoax proved to be veteran investigative reporter Gerd Heidemann and document dealer Konrad Kujau, both West Germans. Heidemann persuaded his magazine, *Stern*, to pay $3.8 million for the diaries, which Kujau scribbled furiously to complete, improvising ("must not forget to get tickets for the Olympic games for Eva") when he ran out of historical inspiration. Experts soon picked up on the mundane asides as well as the historical errors. Both Heidemann and Kujau were brought to trial and convicted.

8. **(a)** During the two-year sting operation that became known as Abscam (for "Arab scam"), FBI agents pretended to be wealthy Arabs seeking to buy political favors. Results of the investigation, announced in early 1980, implicated thirty-one public officials, including one U.S. senator and seven members of the House of Representatives; some were captured on videotape accepting $25,000 and $50,000 bribes. Seven of the eight legislators were convicted on Abscam charges, including Senator Harrison A. Williams, Jr. (D, N.J.), who resigned from the Senate in 1982 after his trial.

9. **(d)** Shortly after they met in 1966, Tarnower, then fifty-seven, asked Harris, then forty-three, to marry him. But he never followed through on his offer. Instead, the haughty, overbearing cardiologist from Scarsdale used Harris to help edit his best-selling diet book, then kept her on a string for fourteen years, eventually finding himself a younger mistress. Also, for years Tarnower had been giving Harris a powerful amphetamine, which may have helped to alter her moods and to precipitate the tragedy. On May 10, 1980, Harris shot and killed her lover. At her trial she refused to plead mitigating circumstances, was convicted of murder, and was sentenced to fifteen years to life.

10. **(a)** The Greenpeace ship *Rainbow Warrior* intended to sail into a French bomb-test area in the South Pacific Ocean to protest French nuclear testing. On July 10, 1985, while the ship was anchored in Auckland, New Zealand, a bomb went off on board, sinking the ship and killing one passenger. In the ensuing scandal (called "underwatergate" because the bomb was planted under water) two French agents were convicted of manslaughter, the French minister of defense resigned, and the head of French intelligence was dismissed. The real crime, it was said in France (where the atomic bomb is a matter of national pride), was in bungling the operation and getting caught.

11. **(d)** Wright (D, Tex.), who succeeded Tip O'Neill as Speaker of the House in 1986, was charged in April 1989 by the House Ethics Committee with accepting improper gifts, including the use of a car and an apartment offered by a Fort Worth businessman. Also questionable was a salary paid to Wright's wife by the same Fort Worth businessman for an allegedly

"phantom" job. Another charge involved Wright's book, *Reflections of a Public Man*, which he sold in bulk to lecture groups, thus collecting royalties in lieu of honoraria, which are subject to income limits. On May 31, 1989, Wright, tired of intense media coverage but still protesting his innocence, gave an impassioned speech before the House in which he announced his intention to resign to "bring this period of mindless cannibalism to an end." Wright was the first Speaker ever to quit in midterm for any reason.

**12.** **(c)** Despite allegations of involvement in Nazi war crimes in the Balkans during World War II, Waldheim was elected president of Austria in 1986. He has consistently maintained that he was "only a clerk" in the German army, but an international group of historians concluded in 1988 that Wehrmacht lieutenant Waldheim was "excellently informed" of war crimes, knowledge that he subsequently tried to conceal. In 1987 the U.S. Department of Justice barred him from entering the United States, saying that its investigation found a "prima facie case" that Waldheim had taken part in Nazi war crimes.

**13.** **(c)** Anne McGill Burford resigned as head of the Environmental Protection Agency in 1983 after she received a contempt citation from the House of Representatives for failure to provide subpoenaed documents on hazardous waste treatment. Her refusal came amid allegations that preferential treatment had been given to industrial polluters who contributed to Republican election campaigns. Rita Lavelle, head of the EPA's toxic-waste-cleanup program, was also cited for contempt and was later convicted of perjury for lying about her involvement in decisions concerning the cleanup liability against her former employer; she served three months in prison.

**14.** **(d)** A gifted engineer and genius at self-promotion, DeLorean left General Motors in 1973 to design and manufacture his own New Age sports car—safe and economical as well as beautiful. As the first cars rolled off production lines in 1981, DeLorean found himself in serious financial difficulty. In 1982 he was charged with planning to sell $24 million worth of cocaine in a desperate effort to shore up his failing auto company. At his 1984 trial in Los Angeles, DeLorean was shown on government tapes discussing the cocaine deal, but jurors decided he had been a victim of entrapment and acquitted him. DeLorean was subsequently charged and also acquitted of tax evasion, mail fraud, and embezzling millions from his auto company, which went bankrupt in 1984.

**15.** **(a)** Bakker, who was driven from his ministry after admitting to an extramarital tryst with a church secretary, was ordained in 1964 by the Assemblies of God, a Pentecostal group with 2 million members. He preached an eclectic gospel of prosperity through prayer—sort of a "cheerful materialism"—and shared Pentecostal beliefs in faith healing and speaking in tongues. More than just gospel, he offered viewers of his television show a kind of religious soap opera featuring the trials and tribulations of his own family. In September 1989 Bakker went on trial in Charlotte, North Carolina, facing charges of fraud and other financial misdealings.

**16.** **(c)** Williams, a native of Millwood, New York, gave up her Miss America title in 1984 after it was revealed that she had posed for nude photographs. While a student at Syracuse University in 1982, she had tried her luck at modeling, posing nude with another woman (out of curiosity, she explained). Although the photographer promised Williams complete confidentiality, he sold the pictures to *Penthouse* magazine, which published them in September 1984. In the ensuing public furor, 67 percent of the respondents to a *Glamour* magazine poll said Williams deserved to lose her crown.

**17.** **(d)** When White House counselor Edwin Meese was appointed attorney general in 1985 by President Reagan, confirmation proceedings took more than a year as various charges of ethical misconduct were investigated, then dropped. Two years later, Meese was embroiled anew in charges of taking bribes or gratuities from Wedtech, a government contractor, and of issuing rulings on two telephone companies in which he held stock. Meese was also accused of tax evasion. In 1988 a special prosecutor's report concluded that Meese "probably" violated conflict-of-interest laws, but there was insufficient evidence to prove financial gain or corrupt intent. After months of controversy Meese finally resigned, claiming the investigation had vindicated him. However, a 1989 report issued by the Department of Justice said that if Meese were still in office, "disciplinary action" should be taken against him for "conduct which should not be tolerated of any government employee, especially not the Attorney General."

18. **(d)** A perennial candidate for public office, Phoenix car dealer Evan Mecham was the surprise winner in a three-way race for governor of Arizona in 1986. He promptly offended nearly everyone with his racist and sexist remarks. He also canceled the paid state holiday for Martin Luther King Jr.'s birthday and cut $50 million from the state education budget. In April 1988 the Arizona state senate convicted Mecham of misconduct (obstructing an investigation and illegally lending state funds) and removed him from office. Undaunted, Mecham said he would run again.

19. **(a)** New York real estate magnate Harry Helmsley and his wife, Leona, widely advertised as the "queen" of the Helmsley hotel empire, were charged with tax evasion in 1988. Harry Helmsley, whose first big real estate deal was the purchase of the Empire State Building in 1961, began building his hotel chain in the 1970s. By the end of the 1980s it was estimated that he had amassed a fortune in excess of $1.4 billion. The couple was charged with allegedly evading more than $1.2 million in taxes. The indictment stated that numerous personal items— including a $130,000 indoor-outdoor stereo system, $500,000 in jade objects, and a $45,000 silver clock—were listed as business expenses on the couple's tax forms. In August 1989 Leona was convicted on 33 counts of tax evasion (husband Harry, 88, was found incompetent to stand trial).

20. **(c)** Khashoggi, an international wheeler-dealer who at one time earned exclusive commissions on 80 percent of U.S. military sales to his native Saudi Arabia, is accused of helping Ferdinand and Imelda Marcos hide money and property stolen from the Philippine government. In 1989 the U.S. government charged him with racketeering, conspiracy, obstruction of justice, and mail fraud for his dealings with the former Philippine leader and his wife. At the height of his wealth in the late 1970s this consummate middleman was worth an estimated $4 billion. Khashoggi later claimed to have suffered financial reverses, including a $10–$15 million payment ("bridging money") he supposedly lent the secret U.S. Iran-*contra* operation and never got back.

21. **(d)** Many stars have threatened to sue the Florida-based scandal sheet, and there are frequent rumors of out-of-court settlements between celebrities and the tabloid; but Burnett,

TV's "clown princess," sued the *Enquirer* and won a $1.6 million libel action in 1981. At issue was an article that described her as publicly drunk in a Washington, D.C., restaurant. The award was subsequently cut in half, and Burnett promptly donated the money to journalism scholarships.

**22.** **(d)** In the 1980s, despite record-high defense budgets, contracts were fewer and larger, leading to a "get-rich-quick" mentality among contractors. Norththrop was alleged to have falsified test reports, Rockwell was indicted for double billing, and it was alleged that Hughes paid for confidential information regarding the bidding of contracts. In 1988 fifty-five of the top one hundred contractors were being investigated in 274 cases of alleged procurement fraud.

**23.** **(a)** Martin Siegel was the top investment banker at Kidder Peabody, earning $2 million a year at age thirty-seven in 1986. For a two-year period beginning in 1982 he leaked confidential inside information about upcoming corporate takeovers to arbitrageur Ivan Boesky. Siegel's payoffs for the information were delivered in an amazingly simple—some say stupid—manner: on three occasions, he met Boesky's agents at a prearranged site, uttered a secret password, and received a suitcase full of cash (payoffs totaled $700,000). Arrested in February 1987, Siegel pleaded guilty to two felony counts.

**24.** **(c)** Aldo Gucci, former head of his family's international chain of boutiques that sell leather goods and other luxury accessories, was fingered by his son Paolo. Angered because his father, brother, and cousins once beat him up at a board meeting, Paolo was eager to reveal his father's financial indiscretions. In 1986 Aldo pleaded guilty, paid the back taxes he owed, and got a one-year sentence. Because of the family's continual squabbles the Gucci boutiques have lost ground to competitors such as Valentino and Ferragamo.

**25.** **(d)** Boesky, the former "wizard of arb" (arbitrage), made a fortune betting on the outcome of corporate takeovers. His success, it turned out, rested on insider information as well as luck and skill. In November 1986 he pleaded guilty to conspiracy and agreed to pay $100 million in fines and penalties. Also, Boesky agreed to cooperate with the U.S. government in its investigations of insider trading. In December 1987 he was sentenced to three years in a minimum-security prison in Lompoc, California.

26. **(a)** Sidney Biddle Barrows's ancestors did arrive on the *Mayflower*, a fact the former debutante capitalized on in her 1986 memoir, *Mayflower Madam*, which described her life as the operator of an upscale "escort" service. The vice squad shut her business down in 1984, and Barrows pleaded guilty to promoting prostitution, for which she was fined $5000. The blueblood madam's bevy of high-class prostitutes worked only at Manhattan's best addresses and often carried credit-card machines in their attaché cases. However, Barrows probably earned more money from her book (rumored to have fetched a $250,000 advance) than she did as a madam.

27. **(b)** Hart bowed out of the 1988 race for president after the press reported that he had spent the night with a young woman in his Washington, D.C., town house. Reporters had staked out the town house after Hart, annoyed for years by reports of his "womanizing," challenged the press to "put a tail" on him, saying that reporters would only be bored with the results. However, the town house incident was immediately followed by revelations that the houseguest, Miami model Donna Rice, had also spent a night with Hart aboard the yacht *Monkey Business* on a sailing jaunt from Florida to Bimini Island in the Bahamas. Within days of the disclosure Hart dropped out of the race, saying that he did not want to subject his family and friends to further rumors and gossip. At that time he was ahead in public opinion polls for the Democratic nomination. Six months after withdrawing, Hart tried unsuccessfully to revive his candidacy.

28. **(b)** At the age of fifteen Barry Minkow started ZZZZ Best Carpet Cleaning out of his parents' garage and built it into a $100 million operation—on paper. The energetic entrepreneur was able to convince wealthy investors and sophisticated bankers that he had lucrative contracts to restore fire- and flood-damaged buildings. His staff, meanwhile, was cooking the books showing money from those contracts—most of them total fabrications—in order to keep current and potential investors satisfied that ZZZZ Best was spiraling upward. Tried and convicted on fifty-seven counts of fraud and conspiracy, Minkow, age twenty-three, was sentenced to twenty-five years

in prison. The judge in the case said to Minkow, "You're dangerous because you have this charisma, this gift of gab, this ability to communicate, but you have no conscience."

**29. (d)** Marine lieutenant colonel Oliver North, the central figure in the Iran-*contra* scandal, has continually claimed that his secret and controversial actions were taken with the full knowledge of his White House superiors. The scandal was disclosed in 1986 when it was discovered that money from the sale of U.S. arms to Iran was being diverted to aid Nicaraguan rebels in defiance of congressional bans. North stood trial in 1989 and was convicted on three felony charges: altering and destroying top-secret documents, aiding and abetting in an obstruction of Congress, and receiving an illegal gratuity. However, he was acquitted on nine other felony charges. He was later sentenced to a three-year suspended prison term and a $150,000 fine. His trial raised more questions than it answered. The key issue still to be resolved is to what extent former president Ronald Reagan and President George Bush were involved in the covert scheme and its cover-up. Public opinion polls have consistently shown sympathy toward North, supporting his portrait of himself as a patriotic pawn in "a chess game played by giants."

**30. (d)** In 1989 a federal grand jury in Manhattan indicted Michael Milken on charges of federal racketeering, insider trading, stock manipulation, defrauding his clients, and a host of other crimes—a total of ninety-eight felony counts. Milken, who almost single-handedly created the lucrative junk-bond market, faces a maximum jail sentence of 520 years in what is the largest securities fraud case in U.S. history. The government's indictment calculated that Milken's salary and bonuses amounted to $554 million in 1984–86 and $550 million in 1987. The former head of the junk-bond department of the investment firm of Drexel Burnham Lambert, Milken was first implicated by the testimony of convicted arbitrageur Ivan Boesky, who told prosecutors of alleged stock-fraud deals with Milken and Drexel.

**31. (b)** The Billionaire Boys Club ("BBC") was a group of overprivileged California men, most in their early twenties, who wore Italian suits and drove expensive cars. Articulate and a wizard with numbers, Joe Hunt founded the group in 1983 to engage in various financial enterprises, originally financed by the members' parents and rich friends. But when the money ran out and huge debts needed to be paid, Hunt resorted to high-risk business schemes in a last-ditch effort to recoup his loses. Hunt's grand plans backfired, especially a business deal with Ron Levin, whose mastery of the con game rivaled the scam talents of Hunt. After learning that Levin had conned him in a multimillion-dollar hoax, Hunt killed his former business partner. The twenty-seven-year-old Hunt was convicted of murder in 1987.

32. **(a)** Imelda Marcos and her entourage flew to New York from Hawaii in her friend Doris Duke's private jet for arraignment on charges of embezzling more than $100 million from the Philippine government. The money, according to a federal grand jury, was funneled through secret bank accounts and ultimately used to purchase artworks and real estate in Manhattan. Because Ferdinand Marcos was too ill to travel, he was temporarily excused from the arraignment. Claiming that the Marcoses did not have the required $5.3 million in bail money, Imelda turned to her longtime friend Doris Duke, who immediately pledged the money. The reclusive and eccentric Duke, the only child of tobacco magnate James Duke, is worth an estimated $800 million.

33. **(d)** John Tower's rejection for the post of secretary of defense marked the first time in thirty years that the full Senate, by a vote of 53 to 47, had refused a president's cabinet choice. An extensive investigation into Tower's past repeatedly pointed up allegations of drinking and womanizing. In addition, the former Republican senator and chairman of the Armed Services Committee had received $750,000, during $2\frac{1}{2}$ years in which he was out of office, from major defense contractors. In the end, all of the factors contributed to his downfall—although the Democrats, led by Senator Sam Nunn, focused on Tower's excessive drinking, which Tower said existed in the 1970s but was no longer a problem.

34. **(a)** After receiving a Pulitzer Prize for local reporting, Janet Cooke (then twenty-six) of the *Washington Post* admitted that she had made up the story of an eight-year-old addict whose mother allowed her lover to inject the boy with heroin. The Pulitzer Prize was returned and Cooke resigned.

**35.** **(d)** The CIA's anti-Sandinista primer on insurgency, called *Psychological Operations in Guerrilla Warfare,* caused an uproar because it revealed that the U.S. government was encouraging the rebel forces in Nicaragua to commit political assassinations. The eighty-nine-page booklet, written in Spanish, recommended use of "selective violence" to "neutralize" Sandinista public officials "such as court judges, police, and state security officials." Disclosure of the existence of the manual evoked a moral outcry as well as a charge that the document was in direct violation of a 1981 executive order, signed by President Reagan, that prohibited even indirect participation in assassinations. CIA director William Casey said that the passages regarding murders and shootings had been taken out of context; President Reagan said that the whole thing was a big misunderstanding caused by the fact that the word "remove" was incorrectly translated to "neutralize" in the Spanish version of the manual.

**36.** **(d)** At the 1988 Seoul Olympics, Canadian sprinter Ben Johnson exploded off the blocks in the 100-meter dash finals and won the gold medal with a 9.79-second world-record time. However, he tested positive for anabolic steroids, a banned substance, in a post-race urinalysis. The International Olympic Committee stripped Johnson of his medal the following day, awarding it to the second-place finisher, Carl Lewis of the United States.

**37.** **(d)** On August 24, 1989, Bart Giamatti, then commissioner of major league baseball, announced that superstar Pete Rose was banned from baseball for life for gambling on baseball games, including bets on his own team. Although he is technically ineligible for baseball employment, Rose can apply for reinstatement in August 1990. Before becoming manager of the Cincinnati Reds, Rose dazzled fans in his twenty-four seasons as a player. He set the record for hits (4,256), games played (3,562), and 200-plus-hit seasons (10). Throughout the proceedings leading up to the lifetime ban, Rose continuously denied that he bet on baseball.

**38.** **(c)** The 1982 divorce of Roxanne Pulitzer and publishing heir Herbert "Peter" Pulitzer, Jr., filled the headlines with stories of drugs, sex, and the good life in Palm Beach, Florida. Among the most titillating revelations in the highly publicized divorce trial were the stories of threesome frolics in the Pulitzer bed and the fact that Roxanne sometimes took a trumpet to bed with her (to talk to the dead, she explained). When the nineteen-day trial ended, Roxanne was awarded $2000 a month for only two years, a car, and some jewelry. The insult was compounded by the judge's decision to award custody of the Pulitzers' twin sons to their father. Roxanne subsequently posed nude for *Playboy* magazine and wrote a tell-all memoir, *The Prize Pulitzer.*

**39.** **(d)** A jury of eight Marine Corps officers found Sergeant Clayton Lonetree guilty of thirteen counts of espionage committed during the time he served as a guard at U.S. embassies in Moscow and Vienna. His crimes included conspiring with the enemy, disclosing the identity of U.S. intelligence agents, and handing over the blueprints of American embassies to the Soviets. Although other marines were implicated in the security breaches, only Lonetree was convicted, sentenced to prison, and dishonorably discharged. While embarrassed U.S. government agencies tried to minimize the damage, Secretary of Defense Caspar Weinberger characterized the Soviet penetration of American security as "massive."

**40.** **(d)** John A. Walker, Jr., a retired navy officer, was arrested in 1985 and charged with selling classified documents to the Soviets. His son Michael, a navy seaman, and his brother Arthur, also a retired naval officer, were arrested as well. John Walker had apparently been a spy for fifteen years. He and his brother Arthur were sentenced to life terms in prison. In exchange for his cooperation, Walker won a reduced sentence, twenty-five years, for his son Michael.

AP/Wide World Photos

# Words and Language

*Language developed out of our deep
inner need to complain.*

—LILY TOMLIN

**1.** In 1986 a new drug abuse epidemic began, involving a form of cocaine called

  **a.** blow

  **b.** freebase

  **c.** crack

  **d.** classic coke

**2.** In 1984 the media focused on a group of Americans described as young, devoted to career success, preoccupied with health and physical fitness, and avid consumers of fashionable goods and services. Who are they?

  **a.** preppies

  **b.** yuppies

  **c.** trendies

  **d.** boomers

**3.** Using computers to produce, assemble, and duplicate pages of text and graphics is called

  **a.** number crunching

  **b.** desktop publishing

  **c.** cloning

  **d.** downloading

**4.** Who first described Ronald Reagan's fiscal policies as "voodoo economics"?

  **a.** Paul Volcker

  **b.** George Bush

  **c.** Alan Greenspan

  **d.** David Stockman

**5.** During the 1988 presidential election campaign, candidates often relied on advice given by consultants popularly known as

  **a.** wisdom makers

  **b.** spin doctors

c. caucus watchers

d. media wizards

**6.** In 1983 the Reverend Jesse Jackson coined a phrase describing the part of the electorate he claimed was ignored by Ronald Reagan. What was the name of that group?

a. Moral Majority

b. Rainbow Coalition

c. Rainbow Warriors

d. People for the American Way

**7.** Secretary of the Interior James G. Watt resigned from office in October 1983 after referring to his Coal Advisory Commission as

a. "a black, a woman, two Jews, and a cripple"

b. "low-level munchkins"

c. "an effete corps of impudent snobs"

d. "the Seven Dwarfs"

**8.** President Ronald Reagan's popularity was somewhat dimmed by the "gender gap," which was his

a. lower approval rating from women than from men

b. constant reference to women as "girls"

c. lack of women appointees to high public office

d. none of the above

**9.** What country did President Reagan characterize in 1983 as an "evil empire"?

a. Iran

b. Libya

c. the Soviet Union

d. Nicaragua

**10.** Personal computer technology in the late 1980s developed a "super" PC called a

a. sampler

b. workstation

    c. modem

    d. mainframe

**11.** The Soviet Union's General Secretary Mikhail Gorbachev popularized the Russian word *glasnost*, which means

    a. "restructuring"

    b. "openness"

    c. "Westernization"

    d. "reform"

**12.** What does the acronym MADD stand for?

    a. Mothers Against the Department of Defense

    b. Mutual Assured Destabilization and Destruction

    c. Mothers Against Drunk Drivers

    d. Missile and Arms Development and Deployment

**13.** Which of the following terms best describes a feminist approach to environmental concerns?

    a. dual regionalism

    b. equal ecology

    c. Mother Earth politics

    d. ecofeminism

**14.** During the 1980s many U.S. states passed or considered resolutions to declare which language(s) to be "official"?

    a. English

    b. English and Spanish

    c. English and Native American Indian languages

    d. English, Spanish, and Native American Indian languages

**15.** A popular term that describes the abundance of illegal and unethical activities that took place in the Reagan administration is

    a. Beltway banditry

    b. credibility gap

    **c.** sleaze factor

    **d.** off-the-shelf operation

**16.** Television news and commentary in the 1980s has increasingly come to rely on "sound bites." What are they?

    **a.** sarcastic or ironic comments

    **b.** the practice of cutting off interviews in midsentence

    **c.** quick, captionlike comments or excerpts of speech

    **d.** tiny microphones actually positioned inside the newscaster's mouth

**17.** The official designation of "Star Wars," the proposed U.S. space-based missile defense system, is

    **a.** ABM

    **b.** START

    **c.** INF

    **d.** SDI

**18.** Young computer enthusiasts who break into private, corporate, or governmental computer systems and explore or alter information are called

    **a.** corporate raiders

    **b.** hackers

    **c.** networkers

    **d.** terminators

**19.** A couch potato is a person who

    **a.** likes to nap on the couch

    **b.** has very simple tastes

    **c.** likes to stay home and watch television

    **d.** eats a lot of potato chips

**20.** The controversial South African policy of complete separation of the races under white rule is called

    **a.** sanction

    **b.** apartheid

    c. constructive separation

    d. homeland rule

**21.** "Pro-life" is a term describing advocacy of

    a. a woman's right to seek a legal abortion

    b. the belief that abortion should be illegal

    c. abolition of the death penalty

    d. the right of animals not to be subjected to medical research experiments

**22.** "McPaper" is the nickname for

    a. a high-speed computer printer made by Apple

    b. the newspaper *USA Today*

    c. a newspaper recycling system

    d. a company newsletter for McDonald's employees

**23.** Congresswoman Patricia Schroeder of Colorado was quoted as saying

    a. Defense contractors were "the Welfare Queens of the Reagan administration"

    b. "America is man enough to elect a woman president"

    c. Ronald Reagan's presidency was "Teflon-coated"

    d. all of the above

**24.** It was the diet and health buzzword of the 1980s, with power not only to prevent cancer and lower cholesterol but also to aid in weight loss. What is it?

    a. gelato

    b. salsa

    c. fiber

    d. carbohydrates

**25.** In August 1984 Ronald Reagan said, "My fellow Americans, I am pleased to tell you that I've signed legislation that will outlaw Russia forever. We begin bombing in five minutes." He said this while

    a. making a guest appearance on the TV show "Saturday Night Live"

**b.** testing the microphone before taping a radio speech

**c.** rehearsing a possible declaration-of-war announcement

**d.** joking with a delegation from the American Legion

**26.** In 1984 the question "Where's the beef?" was originally asked in reference to

   **a.** the voter's choice of candidates in the presidential election

   **b.** a hamburger patty at a fast-food restaurant

   **c.** an argument between a talk show host and guest

   **d.** a U.S. trade embargo on Argentine meat

**27.** The California-based youth movement advocating a violent enforcement of white supremacy and neo-Nazi values is called

   **a.** skinheads

   **b.** talking heads

   **c.** eraserheads

   **d.** metalheads

**28.** Which of the following acronyms does *not* refer to a health condition that was focused on in the 1980s?
   **a.** ARC
   **b.** PID
   **c.** PMS
   **d.** PTL

**29.** Which of the following books published in the 1980s contains unflattering memoirs of the Reagan White House?
   **a.** *Behind the Scenes* by Michael Deaver
   **b.** *For the Record* by Donald Regan
   **c.** *Speaking Out* by Larry Speakes
   **d.** all of the above

**30.** In 1980 the United Nations Educational, Scientific, and Cultural Organization (UNESCO) reported that what percent of the world population is illiterate?
   **a.** 29 percent
   **b.** 12 percent

    c. 64 percent

    d. 5 percent

**31.** The phenomenon of "dumping" caused problems for American manufacturing businesses in the 1980s. What was it?

    a. selling products below manufacturing cost, thus creating unfair competition

    b. production line failures caused by program memory loss in computers

    c. a trend in which executives left their companies, with little or no advance notice, for better-paying jobs

    d. none of the above

**32.** "User friendly" describes

    a. a place where illegal drugs can easily be bought

    b. the appeal of secondhand items purchased at flea markets and garage sales

    c. the ease with which a computer can be operated

    d. an insincere display of goodwill

**33.** The Nicaraguan guerrillas who have been fighting the Sandinista government are called "*contras*" because

    a. their weapons have been smuggled in as contraband

    b. the word means "against" in Spanish, and the guerrillas are opposed to the Sandinistas

    c. it means "contrast," and their politics contrast with those of the Sandinistas

    d. it means "freedom fighters" in Spanish

**34.** Who would be most likely to use a "golden parachute"?

    a. a corporate raider

    b. a top executive whose company was bought out in a corporate takeover

    c. a junk bond broker

    d. an insurance salesman

**35.** First Lady Nancy Reagan's "Just Say No" campaign was against

   **a.** satanic rock and roll lyrics

   **b.** drugs

   **c.** alcohol

   **d.** premarital sex

**36.** In the 1980s the phrase "peace through strength" was used to mean

   **a.** a reduction in nuclear weapons

   **b.** a buildup of nuclear weapons

   **c.** an increase in negotiated peace settlements in the Middle East and Central America

   **d.** an enforcement of economic sanctions against South Africa to effect a peaceful change in government

**37.** In 1982 President Reagan encouraged U.S. companies to invest in "enterprise zones," which would be located in

   **a.** Third World countries

   **b.** federal prisons

   **c.** undeveloped rural areas

   **d.** inner-city ghettos

**38.** "The L word" was a familiar phrase used in the 1988 presidential campaign to describe Michael Dukakis. The "L" stood for

   **a.** left-wing

   **b.** libertarian

   **c.** liberal

   **d.** loser

**39.** What novelist Anthony Burgess called "the greatest publishing event of the century" is the unveiling of the second edition of the *Oxford English Dictionary*. It

   **a.** costs $2,500

   **b.** is twenty volumes long

**c.** will be available in software form

**d.** all of the above

**40.** Which female head of government is known as the "Iron Lady"?

**a.** Indira Gandhi

**b.** Margaret Thatcher

**c.** Corazon Aquino

**d.** Benazir Bhutto

# TEST 8: *Explanatory Answers*

1. **(c)** Crack, the most powerfully addicting form of cocaine, is so named because it is "cooked" with baking soda and water into a crystalline form that makes a cracking sound while heating. The effects of the drug are explosively powerful. Crack is cheap and the user can be physiologically addicted in just a few weeks. Within two years of its appearance the use of crack had spread throughout many U.S. cities and suburbs, and it has been pinpointed as a major cause of urban crime.

2. **(b)** In March 1983 columnist Bob Greene first used the term "yuppie" (young urban professional). It quickly became, after the publication of *The Yuppie Handbook* in 1984, the nickname for an emerging American social class arising from the baby-boom generation. Yuppies are generally described as college-educated men and women with professional or managerial jobs who strive for a life-style centered on material rewards, career achievements, and physical fitness. The definition of the term was quickly mutated to "young upwardly mobile professionals," to reflect yuppie dedication to the accumulation of wealth and status.

3. **(b)** Coined by Apple Computer, Inc., in 1985, "desktop publishing" or electronic publishing, describes an expanding world of revolutionary techniques used in the mass production of printed information. Computers can now process not only text but also graphics, thus eliminating the need for costly paste-up and typesetting services. Sometimes even the need for a print shop is eliminated if the computer printer is capable of producing a finished product. Essential to the success of desktop publishing is the increasing affordability of high-quality laser printers, which can turn out ads, brochures, reports, and documents quickly, cheaply, and professionally. Within one year of its introduction, desktop publishing had inspired a magazine and six books devoted to the subject.

4. **(b)** In April 1980, George Bush was running against Ronald Reagan for the Republican presidential nomination. During that campaign Bush dismissed Reagan's plan to balance the budget—with a complex scheme of tax cuts that would stimulate economic activity—as "voodoo economics." In office as Reagan's vice president, Bush was asked about the memorable

phrase, but he denied ever saying it. However, the news department at NBC found the videotape of Bush's comments and aired it in February 1982.

5. **(b)** "Spin doctors" derived their nickname from a comparison of politics to sports—a player can put "spin" on the ball to gain a competitive advantage. Politically speaking, a spin doctor prescribes corrective actions or comments to improve public perception of a candidate's actions or statements. In the 1988 presidential election campaign, intense media coverage of the candidates resulted in a daily analysis of their every word. Thus, the spin doctors were called in to give advice on how each point should be played in the ever-changing game of politics.

6. **(b)** In 1983 and 1984 Jesse Jackson became the first black man to seriously pursue the presidential nomination from a major party. He described his constituency as a "rainbow coalition" of blacks, women, Hispanics, and other minorities— those who had not profited from Reaganomics. Jackson is chairman of the National Rainbow Coalition, Inc., a civic organization based in Chicago. In 1988 Jackson again ran for the Democratic party's presidential nomination and scored impressive victories in the primary elections.

7. **(a)** Appointed secretary of the interior by Ronald Reagan in 1981, James Watt claimed that he meant no harm by the offensive statement. It was, however, the last of a series of abrasive comments made throughout his almost three-year tenure, and it culminated in widespread outrage that forced his resignation. In addition, Watt's environmental policies had consistently alarmed conservationists. When denounced for opening public lands to big oil drillers and miners, Watt often countered by calling his critics Communists.

8. **(a)** Throughout his presidency Reagan had lower approval ratings among women than among men on issues regarding the economy, defense spending, international relations with the Soviets, Central America, the Middle East, the U.S. nuclear arms buildup, and equal rights for women. In a 1983 Gallup poll 65% of women agreed with the statement that Reagan had "an old-fashioned attitude toward women."

9. **(c)** Ronald Reagan first used the term "evil empire" on March 8, 1983, while addressing the National Association of Evan-

gelicals in Orlando, Florida. He encouraged his listeners to oppose any freeze or reduction in the U.S. buildup of nuclear weapons and characterized the Soviet Union as "the focus of evil in the modern world."

**10. (b)** Workstations have been called "second-generation personal computers" and "personal mainframes" because they offer significant advantages over a simple desktop PC. Originally developed for scientific and engineering use, workstations became, by the end of the 1980s, the fastest-growing area in the computer industry. Workstations can produce highly detailed graphics and edit text at up to sixty times the power of a standard PC.

**11. (b)** General Secretary Mikhail Gorbachev came to power in 1985 and instituted a new approach to leadership in the Soviet Union. He captured international headlines by openly criticizing the Soviet system, proposing new election procedures and advocating economic reform. In June 1987 he championed the passage of new laws taking effect in January 1988 to officially "promote a nationwide discussion of important questions of state life." This new concept was called *glasnost,* or "openness," and it aimed to introduce a new climate of democratization, fairness, and participation for all Soviet citizens.

**12. (c)** MADD was organized in May 1980 by Candy Lightner, whose thirteen-year-old daughter was killed by a drunk driver out on bail after his third drunk-driving offense. Seeking to toughen penalties for drunk-driving convictions, MADD has helped to pass new legislation by mobilizing public opinion against permissive attitudes toward drunk drivers. By 1989 MADD had evolved into an international organization with more than 600,000 members in the United States.

**13. (d)** In 1980 a conference took place in the United States entitled "Women and Life on Earth: Ecofeminism in the 1980s." Since then the term has been used to describe the work of activists and scholars who have analyzed the last five thousand years of history as a patriarchal mode of domination and as the exploitation of both women and nature. Ecofeminist thought has explored the matriarchal, nature-oriented "goddess" cultures of ancient times as models of ecological balance. The ecofeminist movement of the 1980s has produced such influential books as Carolyn Merchant's *Death of Nature* (1983) and Riane Eisler's *Chalice and the Blade* (1987).

**14. (a)** There is no "official" language provision in the U.S. Constitution, and there has always been a multitude of tongues spoken in melting-pot America. But in 1983 the organization U.S. English was founded to promote a constitutional amendment making English the only "official" American language. Since 1984 seventeen states have passed resolutions to this effect, and many other states are considering such measures. Advocates claim that large numbers of Hispanic immigrants threaten to make the United States a bilingual nation. Opponents claim that "English only" measures discriminate against Asian and Hispanic immigrants.

**15. (c)** Laurence Barrett is credited with coining "sleaze factor" in his 1983 book *Gambling with History*. Writer Thomas Riehle cataloged no less than twenty-eight Reagan administration scandals from 1981 to 1984. In Reagan's second term the most famous scandals included the Iran-*contra* affair, Attorney General Edwin Meese's embroilments in the Wedtech Corporation conflict-of-interest case, and White House aide Michael Deaver's perjury conviction for lying about illegal lobbying activities.

**16. (c)** The highly edited, quick-jump style of television news coverage in the 1980s was a response not only to an information-saturated modern world but also to the audience-grabbing advertising techniques of Madison Avenue. Rather than airing a public figure's entire newsworthy statement, television news programs lifted out the punchiest one-liners for broadcast. That sort of coverage favors the astute phrase-maker and has led critics to complain that the sound-bite style prevents accurate, complete news reporting.

**17. (d)** SDI stands for Strategic Defense Initiative. A highly controversial plan, SDI would cost billions of dollars and would rely on technology not yet developed. President Ronald Reagan introduced the plan in 1983 as a space-based defense against possible Soviet nuclear missile attack and estimated that the laser- and particle-beam weapons technology could be ready by the turn of the century. Critics have labeled the plan "bizarre" and technologically questionable, and the U.S. Congress has voted to reduce the SDI budget. Reagan consistently defended SDI, calling it "a vital insurance policy." However, the U.S. National Academy of Sciences, in a 1986 poll of its members, received an 8 to 1 vote against SDI.

18. **(b)** In 1983 the popular movie *War Games* featured a young computer hacker who easily gained access to a high-security military computer system and inadvertently instructed it to launch a nuclear attack. The movie highlighted a growing subculture of adolescent computer users who hack, or gain unauthorized entry, into other computer systems. Fascinated with computer technology and tempted by the challenge of roaming undetected through the secret data banks of businesses and government, hackers play by their own rules. According to hackers, if no damage is done, then hacking should not be illegal. Another hacker contention is that information should not be private property. In the summer of 1983 the FBI staged a series of dramatic raids to seize the computers of the 414s, a group of hackers in Milwaukee who had broken into more than sixty computer systems, including the Los Alamos National Laboratory and the Memorial Sloan-Kettering Cancer Center.

19. **(c)** The "World-Famous Couch Potatoes" marched in the Pasadena, California, "Doo Dah Parade" in 1980, but not until 1987 did the term receive national attention. By then the popularity of VCRs had soared, and Americans were staying home in record numbers to watch TV instead of going out for a night on the town. Couch potatoes are so named because the couch is their preferred spot to spend an evening watching television, and potatoes have eyes with which to see many television programs. The credo of the couch potato is "Say it loud—I'm a spud and I'm proud."

20. **(b)** Apartheid is the system of racial segregation and white supremacy that exists in the Republic of South Africa. It excludes blacks (the majority population) from participation in the country's government and places severe restrictions on virtually every aspect of their personal lives. Under apartheid blacks cannot vote or run for public office; they cannot own land, travel, or work without permits. Some liberalization measures were instituted in South Africa in the 1980s partly as a result of the growing international outrage and protest aimed against the oppressive policy. However, racial tensions

in the country continue to escalate, often causing eruptions of widespread violence.

**21. (b)** "Pro-life" and "pro-choice" issues received much media attention in the 1980s as battle lines were drawn between groups opposed to abortion on religious grounds and those who upheld the Supreme Court's 1973 decision that established a woman's right to abortion. Pro-life advocates generally believe that abortion is the taking of a human life and is wrong under any circumstance. Some pro-life advocates have promoted their beliefs by bombing abortion clinics, staging demonstrations across the country, and harassing doctors who perform abortions.

**22. (b)** In 1982 the newspaper *USA Today* made its debut. It featured a multitude of graphics, full-color photos, and short, celebrity-news-oriented articles, all in an exceptionally easy-to-read format. Called "McPaper" for its journalistic resemblance to junk food, *USA Today* became a profitable enterprise in 1987 after five years in the red. The "Mc" designation has also been used to disparage other products of mass culture; the singer Madonna was termed "McDonna" by one critic.

**23. (d)** Congresswoman Patricia Schroeder of Colorado withdrew from the race for the Democratic party presidential nomination in 1988, but she left behind a colorful legacy of political observations, including remarks about defense contractors, women, and politics. The "Teflon-coated presidency" referred to Ronald Reagan's uncanny ability to remain unsullied by the numerous scandals surrounding his administration; his public image remained untouched even by his own frequent gaffes.

**24. (c)** Dietary fiber made news in 1987, largely as a result of studies showing that blood cholesterol levels could be lowered with a diet low in fat and high in fiber, primarily oat bran. Other grains, as well as fruits, vegetables, and legumes, also contain dietary fiber. The National Cancer Institute and the American Dietetic Association both recommend a daily intake of about 30 grams of fiber, not only for good nutrition but also because the risk of colon cancer, the second leading cause of cancer deaths in the United States, can be reduced by a high-fiber diet. In addition, fiber-rich foods help dieters feel full without overloading on calories.

**25. (b)** Reagan's supporters passed off the bombing statement as a joke, but the incident underscored fears that not only was the president trigger-happy but he also had poor judgment. Tass, the Soviet news agency, remarked that the statement was "unprecedentedly hostile." Although the remark was highly publicized and criticized, Reagan won a historic landslide reelection just over two months later.

**26. (b)** Clara Peller was the elderly lady who asked the famous question in a Wendy's hamburger television commercial in January 1984. The commercial ridiculed competing fast-food restaurants for having tiny hamburger patties on oversize buns. The catch-phrase caught on with the public, and it soon appeared on a deluge of merchandise, including "Where's the beef?" T-shirts, dolls, coffee mugs, greeting cards, and wastebaskets. Clara Peller became an instant, if brief, celebrity, and Wendy's saw a 15 percent increase in sales in the first month the commercial was aired.

**27. (a)** With a preference for military-style close-cut hair, soldiers' fatigues, and leather jackets, the skinheads are thought to be an extremist offshoot of the early 1980s punk movement. They live primarily in California, although small groups are found in many large U.S. cities. Skinheads advance their white supremacist beliefs by physically attacking members of racial minorities, tattooing themselves with swastikas, and painting racist graffiti.

**28. (d)** PTL refers to "Praise the Lord," a televangelist ministry run by Jim and Tammy Bakker until a sex scandal in 1987 forced their resignations. ARC, or aids-related complex, is a medical condition afflicting those infected with the AIDS virus. Its symptoms are not as severe as those of a fully developed case of AIDS. PID, or pelvic inflammatory disease, refers to an advanced state of pelvic infection as a result of untreated diseases such as chlamydia or gonorrhea. PMS, premenstrual syndrome, received increased attention in the 1980s as women learned that the emotional volatility, bloating, depression, and pains associated with their monthly menstrual cycles comprised an actual medical condition.

**29. (d)** At the end of the Reagan presidency a number of "tell-all" books began to appear, written by former White House staffers who had daily contact with the president. None of the books was particularly flattering. Former White House aide Michael Deaver penned *Behind the Scenes* (1988), which included stories about the presidential habit of falling asleep at cabinet meetings. White House chief of staff Donald Regan revealed in *For the Record* (1988) that First Lady Nancy Reagan used an astrologer's services to help schedule her husband's presidential agenda. White House press secretary Larry Speakes admitted in *Speaking Out* (1988) that many of the statements attributed to the president by the press were in fact concocted by White House staffers.

**30.** **(a)** Almost one third of the world's population—814 million people—cannot read or write, according to a 1980 UNESCO report. The ten nations with the highest illiteracy rates were India, Indonesia, Bangladesh, Pakistan, Nigeria, Brazil, Ethiopia, Egypt, Iran, and Afghanistan. The UNESCO study projected 884 million illiterates by 1990.

**31.** **(a)** Dumping became a problem when mass production techniques made vast product overruns possible and when rapidly changing technologies made overnight obsolescence a reality. In 1985 and 1986 dumping emerged as a major problem between the United States and Japan. The Japanese microelectronics industry sold computer memory chips at such low prices that three U.S. semiconductor firms asked the International Trade Commission to levy a dumping tax on the Japanese manufacturers. The Japanese promised to stop dumping the computer chips, but in 1987 the U.S. Department of Commerce assessed worldwide sales of the chips and concluded that the Japanese were still selling them at up to 60 percent below cost.

**32.** **(c)** Many PC users are not technological wizards and do not want to learn elaborate codes, processes, and computer languages in order to use their computers. "User friendly" was coined to describe hardware or software that is easy to use, not complicated or intimidating, and efficient.

**33.** **(b)** In 1979 Nicaraguan president Anastasio Somoza was overthrown by the Marxist, Soviet-backed Sandinistas. In 1981 the U.S. government began sending millions in financial support to the rebel *contras* fighting against the Sandinistas in what was to become a decade-long guerrilla war. In 1984, as a result of the widespread perception that the *contras* were perhaps more of a terrorist organization than "freedom fighters," Congress cut off any further money "for the purpose of overthrowing the government of Nicaragua." In 1985, President Reagan, who remained committed to aiding the *contras*, called them "the moral equivalent of our Founding Fathers," and the next year Congress voted to reinstate both military and humanitarian aid to the rebels.

**34. (b)** In the 1980s traditional job security for top executives was shaken by corporate takeovers. The phenomenon spawned the "golden parachute," which is business jargon for a lucrative termination agreement with an executive who is fired or demoted following a corporate takeover. The agreements, which are now standard in many top-level employment contracts, can be worth as much as $10 million for the chairman of a large corporation.

**35. (b)** Nancy Reagan's crusade against drug abuse gained momentum each year of her husband's tenure as president, and by 1986 "Just Say No," which began as a catch-phrase encouraging young people to resist peer pressure to try drugs, had become a foundation with Mrs. Reagan as its honorary chairman. With a resonance beyond the subject of drug use, "Just say no" became a popular comment applicable to many situations, from alcohol to sex. In the later 1980s statistics showed that many middle-class youths were losing interest in drugs but that drug abuse—especially use of crack—was still on the rise in the inner city.

**36. (b)** The political rhetoric of military preparedness changed somewhat in the 1980s. In the earlier years "peace through strength" was endorsed by President Reagan and his supporters as the most effective policy toward the "evil empire" of the Soviet Union. The phrase was also used to characterize the "Star Wars" plan, introduced in 1983. After Mikhail Gorbachev's rise to power in 1985, the United States and the Soviet Union made significant efforts to reduce the nuclear arms buildup, and by November 1987, President Reagan had altered his viewpoint on the subject. He said, "I had a plan . . . to deal from strength . . . I think today we see and are trying to make some changes."

**37. (d)** U.S. companies were offered attractive incentives, such as reduced government regulations and tax credits, if the companies would establish businesses in designated "enterprise zones," defined as zones that meet the criteria of "pervasive poverty, unemployment, and general distress." Although there are now thirty-seven states with enterprise zones, it is uncertain whether or not the program has made any lasting impact on the communities in which they are located. Secretary of Housing and Urban Development Jack Kemp has made enterprise zones a top priority and plans to create seventy new zones by 1993.

**38. (c)** During the 1988 presidential campaign, Democratic candidate Michael S. Dukakis was reluctant to call himself a liberal. The word itself became a cause célèbre and was called "the L word." Republicans used the phrase often to chide Dukakis for not owning up to his legacy and policies. In October 1988, a month before the election, Dukakis finally admitted to being a liberal "in the tradition of John F. Kennedy, Franklin D. Roosevelt, and Harry S Truman."

**39. (d)** The second edition of the *Oxford English Dictionary*, known as OED2, contains 21,728 pages and defines 616,500 words and terms, using nearly 60 million words. Called "the leading repository for the English language," the twenty-volume OED2 carries a stiff price—$2500. The electronic version will be available in 1991.

**40. (b)** Thatcher, Great Britain's Conservative party leader, was elected prime minister in 1979, reelected in 1983, and reelected to an unprecedented third term in 1987. She earned her reputation as the "Iron Lady" for her fierce determination and her combative personality.

AP/Wide World Photos

# TEST 9

# Arts and Entertainment

*To me, the most perfect play ever written will be one word.*

**—SYLVESTER STALLONE**

1. A work by which of the following artists commanded the highest price ever paid for a painting at auction during the 1980s?
   a. Pablo Picasso
   b. Vincent van Gogh
   c. Paul Gauguin
   d. Claude Monet

2. What theme do the following movies have in common: *Rocky, Flashdance,* and *Working Girl?*
   a. boy-meets-girl love story
   b. the search for lost treasure
   c. from rags to riches
   d. murder and mayhem at teen summer camps

3. Which pioneering composer of the rock musical wrote the music for the Broadway hits *Cats* (1982) and *Phantom of the Opera* (1987)?
   a. Leonard Bernstein
   b. Stephen Sondheim
   c. Andrew Lloyd Webber
   d. Quincy Jones

4. Which of the following black American opera stars gave her farewell performance at New York's Metropolitan Opera in 1985?
   a. Marian Anderson
   b. Leontyne Price
   c. Jessye Norman
   d. Kathleen Battle

5. The Academy Award-winning film *Out of Africa* (1985) is based on the adventures of
   a. Ernest Hemingway
   b. Isak Dinesen
   c. Albert Schweitzer
   d. Beryl Markham

**6.** Leonardo da Vinci's notes on the properties of water were purchased by and renamed for which wealthy collector in 1980?

   **a.** Armand Hammer

   **b.** Nelson Rockefeller

   **c.** Norton Simon

   **d.** Bunker Hunt

**7.** Which actor-comedian plays an obstetrician on a popular sitcom and is a best-selling author?

   **a.** Bill Cosby

   **b.** Richard Pryor

   **c.** Eddie Murphy

   **d.** Red Foxx

**8.** Which European artist working in Southern California became rich and famous in the 1980s for his paintings of swimming pool suburbia?

   **a.** Claes Oldenberg

   **b.** David Hockney

   **c.** Henry Moore

   **d.** Piet Mondrian

**9.** Who is Helga?

   **a.** a Swedish rock star

   **b.** Hollywood's new Greta Garbo

   **c.** a Pennsylvania housewife and artist's model

   **d.** creator of a new health and fitness fad

**10.** What best describes the writing style of author Gabriel Garcia Marquez, Nobel Prize winner for literature in 1982?

   **a.** magic realism

   **b.** surrealism

   **c.** neo-geo

   **d.** minimalism

**11.** Which former child singing star recorded *Thriller*, one of the best-selling record albums of all time, in 1983?

   **a.** Little Richard

   **b.** Stevie Wonder

   **c.** Prince

   **d.** Michael Jackson

**12.** *Satyagraha* (1980), *Akhenaten* (1984) and *1000 Airplanes on the Roof* (1989) are the titles of

   **a.** short stories by Woody Allen

   **b.** poems by Allen Ginsberg

   **c.** sitar compositions by Ravi Shankar

   **d.** operas by Philip Glass

**13.** The shooting of which of the following films resulted in a fatal accident for which charges were brought against the director and crew?

   **a.** *The Twilight Zone*

   **b.** *Platoon*

   **c.** *The Stunt Man*

   **d.** *Top Gun*

**14.** *M. Butterfly*, the 1988 Tony Award-winning Broadway play, draws on which of the following sources?

   **a.** the opera *Madame Butterfly*

   **b.** an actual diplomatic scandal

   **c.** a sexual identity crisis

   **d.** all of the above

**15.** What is MTV?

   **a.** a cable channel featuring music videos

   **b.** a TV capable of stereophonic sound

   **c.** "simulcasting," or simultaneous radio and TV broadcasting

   **d.** a talk show about music

**16.** Which actor, known for his he-man roles, also co-wrote the screenplay that rocketed him to stardom?

   **a.** Charles Bronson

   **b.** Charlton Heston

   **c.** Chuck Norris

   **d.** Paul Hogan

**17.** Which artist was best known for multiple silkscreens of Marilyn Monroe, Mao, and Campbell's soup cans?

   **a.** Andy Warhol

   **b.** Jasper Johns

   **c.** Jackson Pollock

   **d.** Mark Rothko

**18.** The richest woman in the entertainment industry in 1988, according to *Forbes* magazine, was

   **a.** Jane Fonda

   **b.** Madonna

   **c.** Oprah Winfrey

   **d.** Whitney Houston

**19.** Which captain of industry wrote a best-selling autobiography in 1984?

   **a.** Donald Trump

   **b.** Ted Turner

   **c.** H. Ross Perot

   **d.** Lee Iacocca

**20.** Robin Williams did *not* star in which of the following films?

   **a.** *Moscow on the Hudson* (1984)

   **b.** *The World According to Garp* (1982)

   **c.** *Popeye* (1980)

   **d.** *The Blues Brothers* (1980)

**21.** Which Russian-born pianist returned to Moscow in 1986, after 60 years, to give a triumphant concert?

    **a.** Vladimir Horowitz

    **b.** Artur Rubinstein

    **c.** Vladimir Feltsman

    **d.** Vladimir Ashkenazy

**22.** Which former singer became mayor of Palm Springs, California, in 1988?

    **a.** Rudy Vallee

    **b.** Clint Eastwood

    **c.** Sonny Bono

    **d.** Andy Williams

**23.** Which artist specializes in "wrapping" nature and man-made structures in special packages?

    **a.** Louise Nevelson

    **b.** Christo

    **c.** Jasper Johns

    **d.** Robert Rauschenberg

**24.** Which of the following movies had the most sequels?

    **a.** *Rocky*

    **b.** *Crocodile Dundee*

    **c.** *Halloween*

    **d.** *Friday the Thirteenth*

**25.** John Williams, appointed conductor of the Boston Pops Orchestra in 1980, is also a celebrated

    **a.** society bandleader

    **b.** country-western singer

    **c.** Hollywood film composer

    **d.** pop song writer

**26.** Which defecting Russian dancer appeared in a 1985 movie about being trapped back in the Soviet Union?

    **a.** Gudonov

    **b.** Nureyev

c. Baryshnikov

d. Makarova

**27.** Which "investigative" TV journalist made screaming headlines when he opened Al Capone's vault, and when he delved into satanism?

a. Morton Downey, Jr.

b. Maury Povich

c. Dan Rather

d. Geraldo Rivera

**28.** The works of which nineteenth-century author, creator of Scrooge and Fagin, were adapted to stage and screen in the 1980s?

a. Mark Twain

b. Charles Dickens

c. Victor Hugo

d. Gustave Flaubert

**29.** Which of the following artists specialized in paintings of desert flowers and skulls?

a. Georgia O'Keeffe

b. Helen Frankenthaler

c. Louise Nevelson

d. Lee Krasner

**30.** Which actor played a member of the opposite sex in the 1983 film *Tootsie*?

a. Linda Hunt

b. Dustin Hoffman

c. Dan Ackroyd

d. John Belushi

**31.** Tom Wolfe, author of *The Electric Kool-Aid Acid Test* (1968) and *The Right Stuff* (1975), ventured into fiction with

a. *Bonfire of the Vanities*

b. *The Color Purple*

    **c.** *Red Storm Rising*

    **d.** *The Bourne Supremacy*

**32.** Who is Max Headroom?

    **a.** a talk show host

    **b.** a computer-generated humanoid

    **c.** a British comedian

    **d.** an animated cartoon character

**33.** Folk-rock singer Paul Simon captured the music of Africa on his smash 1987 album called

    **a.** *Graceland*

    **b.** *The Joshua Tree*

    **c.** *Higher Love*

    **d.** *Born to Run*

**34.** What is colorization?

    **a.** computerized matching of makeup and wardrobe colors

    **b.** the casting of blacks in ethnic-neutral roles

    **c.** the rekeying of old black-and-white movies in color

    **d.** none of the above

**35.** The exterior of the Louvre Museum in Paris was altered in the late 1980s by the nearby construction of a glass pyramid designed by architect

    **a.** Philip Johnson

    **b.** I. M. Pei

    **c.** Buckminster Fuller

    **d.** Minoru Yamasaki

**36.** "Born in the U.S.A." is the signature song of what popular singer?

    **a.** Barry Manilow

    **b.** Peter Gabriel

    **c.** Billy Joel

    **d.** Bruce Springsteen

**37.** A Tony Award-winning Broadway play and subsequent film titled *Amadeus* featured which major composer?

   **a.** Wolfgang Mozart

   **b.** Ludwig van Beethoven

   **c.** George Gershwin

   **d.** Johann Sebastian Bach

**38.** Which of these Academy Award-winning films had no female stars?

   **a.** *Platoon* (1986)

   **b.** *The Last Emperor* (1987)

   **c.** *Chariots of Fire* (1981)

   **d.** *Gandhi* (1982)

**39.** What country-western singer founded Farm Aid in 1985?

   **a.** Roy Orbison

   **b.** Glenn Campbell

   **c.** Willie Nelson

   **d.** Patsy Cline

**40.** What is performance art?

   **a.** dance

   **b.** filmed versions of pop music

   **c.** multimedia events

   **d.** rock music

# TEST 9: Explanatory Answers

1. **(b)** Two works by Dutch painter van Gogh (1853–1890) pulled in record-high bids at auction in 1987. A Japanese insurance company bid $39.9 million in March 1987 for one of a *Sunflowers* series. *Irises* (1889) went for a record $53.9 million in November 1987.

2. **(c)** These three movies all feature working-class types—a jock, a factory worker, and a secretary—who dream of making it big in all-American Horatio Alger style. In the *Rocky* movies (I through IV, 1976–85), a two-bit boxer and underdog wins long shots at various championships. In *Flashdance* (1983) a girl welder undergoes a metamorphosis from barroom dancer to prima ballerina. And in *Working Girl* (1988) a secretary successfully plots in her boss's absence to make it big on Wall Street.

3. **(c)** At a time when the conventional musical was declining and serious opera was at a standstill, British composer Lloyd Webber merged both forms into big, flashy box office bonanzas. Following on the success of *Jesus Christ Superstar* (1971) and *Evita* (1978), he drew on a collection of poems by T. S. Eliot to create *Cats*. In *Phantom of the Opera* he updates another old story, about a masked figure living in the bowels of the Paris Opera, masterminding the career of a soprano for whom his love is unrequited. Lloyd Webber has also composed a *Requiem*, which climbed to the top of pop charts in 1985.

4. **(b)** Born in Mississippi in 1927, Price won a scholarship to the Juilliard School of Music in New York. She toured the United States and Europe with *Porgy and Bess* (1952–55), then made concert and TV appearances until receiving her first invitations to sing with major opera companies. In 1959 she became the first black woman to sing at La Scala in Milan, and in 1961 she made her debut at New York's Metropolitan Opera. Price's greatest roles were the lead in *Aida* and Leonora in *Il Trovatore*, both by Verdi.

5. **(b)** Writer Karen Blixen, who took the pen name Isak Dinesen, was born in Denmark and married a Danish baron, with whom she moved to Africa in 1914 to run a coffee plantation. Farming was not a success, nor was her marriage, but during

her seventeen years in Africa, Blixen fell in love with a British big-game hunter and became a first-class storyteller. Her stories and her life were superbly adapted for the screen in this 1985 film.

6. **(a)** A doctor and multimillionaire industrialist (Occidental Petroleum, which he bought as a tax shelter for retirement, became the seventh largest U.S. oil company), Hammer paid a record $5,126,000 for Leonardo's thirty-six-page notebook, which he promptly rechristened the Codex Hammer. Protracted negotiations with Southern California museums to house Hammer's treasures failed in the late 1980s, and the nonagenarian collector was last rumored to be considering building his own $30 million art center.

7. **(a)** "The Cosby Show," which ran consistently at the top of the Nielsen ratings in the mid-1980s, features Cosby and a family of five children and is based on everyday problems from Cosby's own family life. Cosby's TV children have been described as role models for his theories of education and family, the subject of several books he has written.

8. **(b)** Hockney (born 1937), an Englishman, first came to California in 1963, drawn by the climate of hedonism as well as the sunshine. Working in a figurative, representational style, he began to paint the pictures of swimming pools, boys in showers, and palm trees and sunshine for which he now earns $500,000 to $2 million each. In the 1980s Hockney branched out to design opera sets and costumes and also experimented with cubist perspectives and photo collages. A major 1988 retrospective of Hockney's work traveled from Los Angeles to New York and London.

9. **(c)** Andrew Wyeth (born 1917), one of the most highly respected of contemporary American artists, startled the art world in 1985 with the revelation that he had secretly withheld some 240 works he had painted during the previous fifteen years, all featuring a Pennsylvania neighbor named Helga Testorf. Many of the portraits were highly erotic nudes, suggesting an intimate artist-model relationship. Publisher Leonard E. B. Andrews bought the whole group of Helga portraits, which were published in a 1987 book.

10. **(a)** Critics describe the style popularized by Colombian-born Garcia Marquez as "magic realism"—a mixture of reality and

fantasy, history and myth. "The problem is," the author explains, that in Latin America "reality resembles the wildest imagination." Garcia Marquez's novels feature dolls that grow, people who communicate regularly with the dead, men with five thousand children, and in his latest, *Love in the Time of Cholera* (1988), lovers whose union is frustrated by reality for fifty-one years.

11. **(d)** Michael Jackson, the most famous member of the musical Jackson family, made his singing debut at age five in 1963. Breaking away from his siblings in the 1980s, he recorded a fabulously successful album *Thriller* (1982), followed by another runaway hit, *Bad* (1987). He also acquired a reputation for personal eccentricity: wearing jeweled gloves, appearing everywhere with his pet chimp, and undergoing extensive cosmetic surgery. An astute businessman, Jackson bought the rights to the Beatles' songs, collected $15 million from Pepsi for commercials, and went on an extremely lucrative world tour in 1987. *Forbes* magazine listed him at the top of its top-forty money earners in the entertainment industry in 1988, with $60 million in revenue.

12. **(d)** Working in a style called minimalism, composer Glass specializes in extensive and hypnotic repetition of melodic fragments or chord sequences, frequently set to texts of incomprehensible phrases. His themes, however, are on an epic scale, dealing with such topics as Gandhi (*Satyagraha*) and ancient Egypt (*Akhenaten*). In 1988 Glass won a $325,000 commission from the Metropolitan Opera, the highest ever paid for a serious opera, to create a work commemorating the five hundredth anniversary of Columbus's discovery of America, titled "The Voyager."

13. **(a)** During shooting for a feature film adaptation of Rod Serling's *Twilight Zone* (1983), a huge special-effects explosion caused a helicopter to crash, killing veteran actor Vic Morrow and two child extras. As a result, director John Landis (*The Blues Brothers*, 1980; *Trading Places*, 1983) and other crew members were tried for involuntary manslaughter, the first such trial arising from an accident on a movie set. They were acquitted in 1987, and Landis went on to greater success as director of *Coming to America* (1988). Witnesses who testified that production safety was lax, however, have found themselves blackballed in Hollywood as troublemakers.

**14. (d)** Posted to China in 1964, French diplomat Bernard Boursicot fell in love with Peking opera star Shi Peipu, who presented him with a son in 1966. Blackmailed by the Chinese, Boursicot agreed to pass secret documents in order to protect his lover and child. He was finally able to get them out of China in 1982, only to be charged with espionage back in France. During their trial and imprisonment Peipu was revealed to be a man, having learned as an actor to impersonate women. Reversing the story of the opera *Madame Butterfly*, in which a woman is the victim, playwright David Henry Hwang explores elements of the sexual identity crisis of our age—role reversals and sexual ambiguity.

**15. (a)** MTV, a 24-hour cable channel that began in the early 1980s, features music videos, or dramatized film versions of pop songs. These short films, which trace their origin to the Beatles films of the 1960s, were originally intended as promotional gimmicks to sell records, then took on a life of their own. Local stations have begun to pick up the innovative music videos, characterized by high-voltage imagery and slick editing, and in 1984 the first annual MTV Video Music Awards were presented.

**16. (d)** Paul Hogan, first known in the United States for his TV commercials for his native Australia, co-wrote his first two starring vehicles, *Crocodile Dundee* and *Crocodile Dundee II*.

**17. (a)** With his pale hair and big glasses, Warhol was almost as instantly recognizable as Marilyn and Mao. A leading guru of pop culture, he made films, wrote books and published a magazine, and acted in films, on TV, and in commercials. He was everywhere, usually with the beautiful people. Warhol died suddenly in 1987, at age fifty-six, after routine surgery. One of his Marilyn paintings recently fetched $4 million.

**18. (b)** All four are listed among the *Forbes* top forty, with pop singer Madonna (real name: Louise Ciccone), who earned gross income of $46 million in 1987–88, ranking first among women and ninth overall. (Her *True Blue* album alone sold 5 million copies in 1987–88.) Talk show hostess Oprah Winfrey came in second among women, fourteenth overall, with $37 million gross in the same two-year period; and pop singer Whitney Houston was third (seventeenth overall) with $30 million.

Actress and exercise maven Jane Fonda ranked thirtieth overall, with $23 million gross income.

**19.** **(d)** In *Iacocca: An Autobiography*, Iacocca explains his homespun philosophy of business success, describing how he was fired as president of Ford Motor Company and three days later took over the equivalent position at ailing Chrysler Corporation, where he got a government loan and introduced the K car to turn Chrysler around.

**20.** **(d)** The rapid-fire comedian graduated from TV's "Mork and Mindy" (1978–82) to go his own individual way in films, tailoring each role to his particular genius. For *Moscow on the Hudson*, for example, Williams learned both Russian and saxophone. In *Good Morning, Vietnam* (1987), Williams used his brilliant improvisations as a DJ in war-torn Vietnam.

**21.** **(a)** Horowitz (born 1904), who fled Russia at age twenty-one, made a triumphal return in 1986, his first trip home in sixty years. Known throughout his long career for his dazzling technique and daredevil recklessness at the keyboard, Horowitz has been called the most charismatic pianist since Liszt, playing in that grand romantic tradition. His two concerts in the Soviet Union in 1986, both mobbed, were recorded and televised in the United States.

**22.** **(c)** Bono, best known as the other half of the "Sonny and Cher Comedy Hour" (1971–1975), found his career slumping after his divorce. Reduced to guest spots on TV's "The Love Boat" and "Fantasy Island," he went into the restaurant business in Los Angeles and Palm Springs, then into local politics.

**23.** **(b)** Environmental artist Christo (Javacheff), born in Bulgaria in 1935, moved to New York in 1964. He soon began "packaging" or wrapping public buildings and spaces in plastic or canvas, temporarily altering the relationship between people and their environment. In the 1970s Christo erected huge curtains across a Colorado canyon and a running fence in the northern California hills, both events commemorated on film. In the 1980s, Christo again made headlines by wrapping eleven small islands off Miami in flamingo pink plastic (1983) and covering the venerable Pont Neuf in Paris with beige sheeting (1985), for two weeks each.

**24.** **(d)** Stallone's rags-to-riches *Rocky* has been through four incarnations and is due for a fifth. *Crocodile Dundee*, starring Australia spokesman Paul Hogan, has had only one sequel as of 1989, and the thriller *Halloween* has had two. There have been seven gory installments of *Friday the Thirteenth*.

**25.** **(c)** Before succeeding Arthur Fiedler as conductor of the Boston Pops, Williams (born 1932) was a highly successful film composer and winner of three Academy Awards (for *Fiddler on the Roof*, *Jaws*, and *Star Wars*). His subsequent film credits include *Raiders of the Lost Ark* (1981), *E.T., the Extraterrestrial* (1982), and most recently, *Indiana Jones and the Temple of Doom* (1989). Williams has been very popular in Boston for his performances and recordings of excerpts from his film scores.

**26.** **(c)** Baryshnikov (born 1948), formerly of Leningrad's Kirov Ballet, defected in 1974 and became head of the American Ballet Theater in 1980. Between dancing assignments he found time to make his movie debut in *The Turning Point* (1977). In the 1985 film *White Nights* he played a defector who got trapped behind the Iron Curtain when his plane was forced to land there in an emergency. The dancer also made headlines for his affairs with ballerina Gelsey Kirkland, who wrote a tell-all book, and with actress Jessica Lange, who bore him a daughter in 1981.

**27.** **(d)** Is it news or entertainment, critics asked, when Rivera opened Capone's vault in 1986 and found nothing but a few gin bottles. "Tabloid TV" and "teleporn," they said, when Rivera did a two-hour documentary on devil worship. Whatever you call it, the fans love Geraldo's aggressive and highly personal style of show business, which may even include a fistfight to get a story.

**28.** **(b)** The 1980s saw Broadway productions of Dickens's *Mystery of Edwin Drood* (1985) and *The Life and Adventures of Nicholas Nickleby* (1981, New York), the latter an 8½ hour marathon. Among many films adapted from Dickens in the 1980s were Bill Murray's *Scrooged* (1988) and an animated Disney version of Oliver Twist called *Oliver and Company* (1988).

**29.** **(a)** The preeminent American woman artist of the twentieth century, O'Keeffe (1887–1986) specialized in bold flower forms and the harsh landscapes of New Mexico, where she lived for the last forty years of her life. Originally a schoolteacher, she was first exhibited in 1916 by photographer Alfred Stieglitz, whom she later married, at his New York gallery. A major retrospective of O'Keeffe's work was presented in 1988.

**30. (b)** Dustin Hoffman pulled off a tour de force as the aspiring actor who takes a feminine role in a soap opera. Hunt won an Academy Award for her portrayal of a man in *The Year of Living Dangerously* in 1983.

**31. (a)** Wolfe's first novel, the best-selling *Bonfire of the Vanities* (1988) describes the downfall of a plutocrat. Wolfe, who coined the term "plutography" to mean "depicting the acts of the rich," describes the 1980s as a decade of affluence, status, and greed. *The Color Purple* is Alice Walker's Pulitzer Prize-winning novel, and *Red Storm Rising* and *The Bourne Supremacy* were written, respectively, by Tom Clancy and Robert Ludlum.

**32. (b)** Max Headroom (the name is taken from "maximum headroom," or clearance) has been described as a computerized version of Johnny Carson. He was created in England in 1985 and brought to U.S. cable TV the same year to provide a bridge between music videos. Headroom is actually played by actor Matt Frewer wearing a prosthetic chin and slicked-down hair, and the image is then altered with special effects, animation, computer graphics, and a synthesized voice.

**33. (a)** "Graceland," the album's title song, referring to Elvis Presley's home, is actually about lost love, but in a larger sense refers to our rock-and-roll roots, the real subject of this album. Paul Simon (born 1942), formerly of Simon and Garfunkel, traveled to Africa to find happy, funky rhythms for *Graceland*, which he then combined with his own quirky lyrics. Simon toured the United States with South African musicians such as the group Ladysmith Black Mombaza, Miriam Makeba, and Hugh Masekela. The other albums listed are by U2, Steve Winwood, and Bruce Springsteen.

**34. (c)** The biggest current proponent of colorization is media mogul Ted Turner, founder of his own successful Cable News Network and the new TNT (Turner Network Television), which shows primarily old movies. Because he believes many viewers are bored by black and white, Turner, who also owns MGM's film library, plans extensive colorization, over the protests of movie purists. Turner explains: "I think the movies look better in color, pal, and they're my movies."

**35. (b)** Purists were strictly opposed to construction of a modern glass pyramid and reflecting pool, completed in 1989, in the courtyard of the Louvre. Architect Pei argued that the pyramid's geometry and glass are neutral and do not clash with the classically designed former palace. The public seems to agree with a French newspaper, which declared in headlines that "The pyramid is very beautiful after all."

**36. (d)** Springsteen (born 1949) burst into the popular consciousness (and conscience) in 1975, when he simultaneously made the covers of *Time* and *Newsweek*. Hailed as the "new Bob Dylan," he seemed to be chasing the elusive American dream rather than criticizing it, as Dylan did. A serious, committed artist who identifies strongly with his working class background, Springsteen gives concerts in aid of Vietnam veterans and Amnesty International. A musical retrospective of his work was released in 1987.

**37. (a)** *Amadeus* is the story of Mozart as told by one of his archrivals in eighteenth-century Vienna, the Italian composer Antonio Salieri, a musical mediocrity who was acutely jealous of the uncouth young genius. Despite its rather highbrow theme, the story (by Peter Shaffer) had a great critical and popular success on both stage (1984) and screen (1985).

**38. (a)** All four of these films are strongly masculine in orientation and casting, but only *Platoon*, a grim drama about the Vietnam War, had no featured actresses.

**39. (c)** Singer/songwriter Nelson (born 1933) has recorded twenty-five albums in the last ten years, mostly sad honky-tonk songs about love, God, and family. He is probably best known for his number-one hit "On the Road Again" (1980). A farm boy from Texas, he also founded Farm Aid in 1985, giving concerts to benefit the nation's farm poor.

**40.** **(c)** Performance art, loosely defined as any multimedia art form, actually may include any of the above. Performance artists have been known to juxtapose elements of music, dance, recitation, newsreel footage, computer graphics, and video, and the results may be grotesque, surreal, hi-tech, or funny.

AP/Wide World Photos

# TEST 10

# *Sports*

Any man who watches more than three consecutive football games on TV in one day can be declared legally dead.

—DR. JOYCE BROTHERS

**1.** Which NBA player retired in 1989 as the league's all-time top scorer?

   **a.** Bill Walton

   **b.** Kareem Abdul-Jabbar

   **c.** Larry Bird

   **d.** Julius (Dr. J.) Erving

**2.** In 1988 Susan Butcher won one of the world's most grueling races for the third year in a row. Name the race.

   **a.** the Indianapolis 500

   **b.** the Tour de France

   **c.** the Boston Marathon

   **d.** the Iditarod Sled Dog Race

**3.** Who was the last major-league baseball player to hit forty home runs and have forty stolen bases in the same season?

   **a.** Orel Hershiser

   **b.** Darryl Strawberry

   **c.** Jose Canseco

   **d.** Don Mattingly

**4.** Who became the first player in eighteen years to win the pro tennis Grand Slam in 1988?

   **a.** Martina Navratilova

   **b.** Steffi Graf

   **c.** Gabriela Sabatini

   **d.** Mats Wilander

**5.** What event caused the United States, Japan, Canada, China, and other countries to boycott the 1980 Moscow Olympics?

   **a.** the downing of KAL flight 007

   **b.** the use of steroids by Soviet athletes

   **c.** the inclusion of South African athletes in the games

   **d.** the Soviet invasion of Afghanistan

**6.** Which NFL team dominated the league in the 1980s, winning three Super Bowls in a seven-year span?

   **a.** the San Francisco 49ers

   **b.** the Washington Redskins

   **c.** the Los Angeles Raiders

   **d.** the Denver Broncos

**7.** What team did the U.S. hockey team defeat to win the gold medal in the 1980 Winter Olympics at Lake Placid?

   **a.** Canada

   **b.** the Soviet Union

   **c.** Sweden

   **d.** Finland

**8.** In 1980, Genuine Risk became the first

   **a.** filly to win the Kentucky Derby in sixty-five years

   **b.** horse in ten years to win the Triple Crown

   **c.** horse ridden by a woman jockey to win the Preakness

   **d.** filly to break the track record at Churchill Downs

**9.** In 1985 who became the youngest player ever to win the men's singles title at the Wimbledon tennis tournament?

   **a.** Jimmy Connors

   **b.** Boris Becker

   **c.** John McEnroe

   **d.** Pat Cash

**10.** How much money was the United States Football League awarded in its 1986 antitrust lawsuit against the NFL?

   **a.** $1

   **b.** $1,000

   **c.** $100,000

   **d.** $10,000,000

**11.** Who won the men's and women's gold medals in singles tennis the first year tennis returned as an official Olympic sport?

    **a.** Miloslav Mecir and Steffi Graf

    **b.** John McEnroe and Chris Evert

    **c.** Ivan Lendl and Martina Navratilova

    **d.** Boris Becker and Gabriela Sabatini

**12.** Who replaced Peter Ueberroth as commissioner of major league baseball?

    **a.** Bill White

    **b.** Bowie Kuhn

    **c.** George Steinbrenner

    **d.** Bart Giamatti

**13.** Name the only NBA team to win back-to-back championships in the 1980s.

    **a.** the Boston Celtics

    **b.** the Los Angeles Lakers

    **c.** the Houston Rockets

    **d.** the Detroit Pistons

**14.** Greg LeMond became the first American to win what famed international sports event in 1986?

    **a.** the Le Mans auto race

    **b.** the New York Marathon

    **c.** the Tour de France bicycle race

    **d.** the British Open golf tournament

**15.** Play was almost halted in the 1988 NFL divisional playoff game between the Chicago Bears and the Philadelphia Eagles because of what climatic condition?

    **a.** snow

    **b.** fog

    **c.** rain

    **d.** lightning

**16.** Who was the first athlete to win five gold medals in individual events at one Olympics, Winter or Summer?

   **a.** Mark Spitz

   **b.** Florence Griffith-Joyner

   **c.** Eric Heiden

   **d.** Carl Lewis

**17.** Who dominated international men's diving in the 1980s?

   **a.** Mark Spitz

   **b.** Bruce Kimball

   **c.** Matt Biondi

   **d.** Greg Louganis

**18.** Whose career record for base hits did Pete Rose break in 1985?

   **a.** Hank Greenberg's

   **b.** Ty Cobb's

   **c.** Honus Wagner's

   **d.** Babe Ruth's

**19.** In the autumn of 1988, Stacy Allison and Peggy Luce became the first American women to

   **a.** climb Mt. Everest

   **b.** cross the Atlantic in a balloon

   **c.** fly nonstop around the world

   **d.** kayak the length of the Amazon River

**20.** Name the player who broke Jim Brown's NFL all-time rushing record.

   **a.** Eric Dickerson

   **b.** Franco Harris

   **c.** Tony Dorsett

   **d.** Walter Payton

**21.** Which athlete at the 1984 Los Angeles Olympics duplicated Jesse Owens's feat of winning the 100-meter race, the 200-meter race, the 4 × 100 relay, and the long jump?

    **a.** Carl Lewis

    **b.** Edwin Moses

    **c.** Evelyn Ashford

    **d.** Daley Thompson

**22.** Name the women's tennis player who dominated Wimbledon in the 1980s, winning six consecutive singles titles to break Suzanne Lenglen's record.

    **a.** Chris Evert

    **b.** Billie Jean King

    **c.** Martina Navratilova

    **d.** Evonne Goolagong Cawley

**23.** Nolan Ryan broke what major league baseball record in 1983?

    **a.** home runs

    **b.** stolen bases

    **c.** consecutive games played

    **d.** strikeouts

**24.** How many consecutive games did the Columbia University football team lose before winning one in 1988?

    **a.** forty

    **b.** forty-four

    **c.** fifty

    **d.** fifty-five

**25.** In the biggest trade in NHL history the Edmonton Oilers sent Wayne Gretzky to which team?

    **a.** the Chicago Blackhawks

    **b.** the Calgary Flames

    **c.** the Buffalo Sabres

    **d.** the Los Angeles Kings

**26.** American track stars Florence Griffith Joyner and Jackie Joyner-Kersee

    **a.** are sisters-in-law

    **b.** each set a world record at the 1988 Olympics

    **c.** share the same coach

    **d.** all of the above

**27.** Name the winningest coach in college football history, who surpassed Bear Bryant's career record in 1985.

    **a.** Bo Schembechler

    **b.** Joe Paterno

    **c.** Lou Holtz

    **d.** Eddie Robinson

**28.** Where was the design secret that helped *Australia II* successfully challenge for the America's Cup in 1983?

    **a.** in the stern

    **b.** in the sails

    **c.** in the mast

    **d.** in the keel

**29.** Over whom did Mary Decker trip in the 3000-meter final at the 1984 Olympics at Los Angeles?

    **a.** Evelyn Ashford

    **b.** Zola Bud

    **c.** Maricica Puica

    **d.** Wendy Sly

**30.** What team did Notre Dame beat in the Fiesta Bowl in January 1989 to remain undefeated and win a record eighth national championship in college football?

    **a.** Nebraska

    **b.** West Virginia

    **c.** Miami

    **d.** Penn State

**31.** Who was the fifty-seven-year-old jockey who got his thousandth stakes victory on a horse named "Peace" on April 30, 1989?

   **a.** Eddie Arcaro

   **b.** Pat Valenzuela

   **c.** Bill Shoemaker

   **d.** Laffit Pincay, Jr.

**32.** Name the golfer who, in 1986 at the age of forty-six, won his sixth Masters Tournament.

   **a.** Tom Watson

   **b.** Jack Nicklaus

   **c.** Arnold Palmer

   **d.** Lee Trevino

**33.** At the Seoul Olympics in 1988, Carl Lewis

   **a.** became the first long jumper ever to win a gold medal in consecutive Olympic Games

   **b.** had the highest gold medal total of any athlete

   **c.** tested positive for steroids

   **d.** won every event he entered

**34.** Which NHL team won four consecutive Stanley Cups in the 1980s?

   **a.** the Montreal Canadiens

   **b.** the Philadelphia Flyers

   **c.** the New York Islanders

   **d.** the Edmonton Oilers

**35.** What team went "wire-to-wire" in the 1984 season to win the World Series?

   **a.** the Detroit Tigers

   **b.** the Los Angeles Dodgers

   **c.** the St. Louis Cardinals

   **d.** the San Diego Padres

**36.** What did the Louisville and Indiana college basketball teams have in common in the 1980s?

   **a.** two NCAA tournament victories

   **b.** head coach Bobby Knight

   **c.** NCAA probation

   **d.** drug-related player deaths

**37.** Which boxer did Sugar Ray Leonard beat in 1987, coming out of retirement to regain the middleweight title?

   **a.** Roberto Duran

   **b.** Hector (Macho) Camacho

   **c.** Leon Spinks

   **d.** Marvelous Marvin Hagler

**38.** Over what issue did major-league baseball players strike in 1981?

   **a.** the lengthened season

   **b.** free agency

   **c.** World Series compensation

   **d.** the designated hitter rule

**39.** Edwin Moses' gold-medal performance in the 1984 Los Angeles Olympics marked his ninetieth consecutive victory in the finals of what event?

   **a.** the 100-meter dash

   **b.** the pole vault

   **c.** the 400-meter hurdles

   **d.** the high jump

**40.** How many times did New York Yankees owner George Steinbrenner fire manager Billy Martin in the 1980s?

   **a.** three

   **b.** four

   **c.** five

   **d.** six

# TEST 10: *Explanatory Answers*

1. **(b)** Kareem Abdul-Jabbar played his last regular-season game for the Los Angeles Lakers on April 23, 1989. The 7-foot, 2-inch center retired at age forty-two, after twenty professional seasons, with an NBA career-record total of 38,387 points. Abdul-Jabbar, who had changed his name from Lew Alcindor, played on three NCAA title teams at UCLA. He helped win six NBA Championships, five with the Lakers and one with the Milwaukee Bucks, for whom he played from 1970 to 1975.

2. **(d)** The Iditarod Sled Dog Race, which bills itself as "The Last Great Race on Earth," runs 1200 miles between Anchorage and Nome. Susan Butcher became the first musher ever to win it three straight years (1986–88). Libby Riddles was the first woman to win the Iditarod, in 1985.

3. **(c)** Oakland Athletics right fielder Jose Canseco hit forty-two home runs, had forty stolen bases, and was named the American League MVP in the 1988 season. His power hitting helped the A's to the American League pennant. The A's defeated the Boston Red Sox in the playoffs in four straight games, aided by Canseco's three home runs. However, they lost in the World Series to the Los Angeles Dodgers in five games.

4. **(b)** Steffi Graf of West Germany became only the sixth tennis player in history to win the Grand Slam, dominating the singles championships at the Australian Open, French Open, Wimbledon, and the U.S. Open tournaments in one calendar year. In those four major competitions, Graf won 54 of 56 sets and 335 of 434 games in 27 matches.

5. **(d)** On January 4, 1980, President Jimmy Carter warned that the Soviet Union's "continued aggressive actions" in Afghanistan would force the United States to pull out of the 1980 Summer Olympics in Moscow. The subsequent withdrawal was a heartbreaking experience for American athletes. More than fifty nations joined the American-led boycott.

6. **(a)** The San Francisco 49ers, under head coach Bill Walsh, won Super Bowls XVI, XIX, and XXIII, spanning the 1981 through 1988 seasons. Quarterback Joe Montana was named most valuable player of the first two of those Super Bowls;

wide receiver Jerry Rice was MVP of the third. Walsh retired as head coach following the Super Bowl XXIII victory in January 1989 but remained with the team in an executive capacity.

7. **(d)** Forty-eight hours after upsetting the powerful Soviet team 4–3, the U.S. hockey team defeated Finland 4–2 to win the gold medal in the 1980 Winter Olympics at Lake Placid, New York. In the exciting and emotional game against the Soviet Union, the youngest-ever American hockey team rallied three times for the victory amid chants of "U.S.A.! U.S.A.!"

8. **(a)** Genuine Risk, ridden by jockey Jacinto Vasquez, won the Kentucky Derby in 1980, becoming the first filly to win the race in sixty-five years and only the second ever to do it. She ran the race in 2:02, the ninth-fastest Derby time ever recorded at Churchill Downs.

9. **(b)** Boris Becker of West Germany was seventeen years old when he defeated South African Kevin Curren to win the men's singles title at the 1985 Wimbledon tennis tournament. Becker was the youngest player ever to win at Wimbledon; Bjorn Borg was twenty; Jimmy Connors twenty-one; and John McEnroe, twenty-two when they won. Becker came back to win at Wimbledon again in 1986 and 1989.

10. **(a)** The USFL was awarded $1 by a U.S. district court jury in its $1.7 billion antitrust suit against the NFL. The USFL claimed that the NFL had used monopoly power to prevent the younger league from obtaining television contracts. A federal jury found that the NFL had violated antitrust laws but nonetheless fined the NFL only $1. The verdict came on July 29, 1986, after an eleven-week trial. The USFL folded soon afterward, many of its top players going to NFL teams.

11. **(a)** Czech Miloslav Mecir defeated American Tim Mayotte to win the men's gold medal in singles tennis, and West German Steffi Graf defeated Gabriela Sabatini of Argentina to win the women's gold medal at the 1988 Seoul Olympics. It marked the return of tennis to full-medal Olympic status after an absence of sixty-four years. Tennis had been a demonstration sport at the 1968 and 1984 Olympics.

12. **(d)** Bart Giamatti, a former president of Yale and of major-league baseball's National League, replaced outgoing commis-

sioner Peter Ueberroth on April 1, 1989, but died of a heart attack only five months later. Bill White, a black with impeccable baseball credentials (including thirteen years as a Giants first baseman), was named to replace Giamatti as National League president in February 1989.

**13. (b)** When they defeated the Detroit Pistons to win the 1988 NBA crown, the defending champion Los Angeles Lakers became not only the only team in the 1980s to win back-to-back titles but also the first team to repeat in nineteen years. The last NBA team to repeat as champion was the 1968–69 Boston Celtics. In the 1980s the Lakers won five NBA championships (1980, 1982, 1985, 1987, and 1988); they lost three times in the finals (1983, 1984, and 1989).

**14. (c)** After placing second to teammate and French cycling legend Bernard Hinault in the 1985 Tour de France, twenty-five-year-old American Greg LeMond won the prestigious 23-day bicycle race in 1986. LeMond could have won the 1985 event but was ordered by his team, La Vie Claire, to let Hinault win. LeMond had finished third in 1984. In 1989 LeMond was again victorious in the closest race to the finish line in Tour de France history.

**15. (b)** The Bears and Eagles began play at Chicago's Soldier Field in brilliant sunshine, but late in the second quarter fog blew in from Lake Michigan and blanketed the field. Officials allowed the game to continue because they could see both goalposts from the center of the field. But broadcasters, fans in the stands, television viewers, and even players on the sidelines had little or no view of the second half of the game, won by Chicago 20–12.

**16. (c)** American speed skater Eric Heiden won five gold medals in individual events—the 500-, 1000-, 1500-, 5000-, and 10,000-meter races—at the 1980 Winter Olympics at Lake Placid, New York. In becoming the first athlete ever to win five individual golds, Heiden bested such stellar Olympic performers as Mark Spitz, Paavo Nurmi, and Jesse Owens, all of whom won medals in team as well as individual events. Heiden set a world record in his 10,000-meter victory.

**17. (d)** Greg Louganis is considered by many to be the greatest diver of all time. Since winning the silver medal for the United

States in platform diving as a sixteen-year-old at the 1976 Montreal Olympics, Louganis has won five Olympic medals overall, five world titles, and forty-seven national titles. In Los Angeles in 1984 he became only the third diver in Olympic history to win the springboard and platform events at the same Olympics. He repeated the feat at the 1988 Seoul Olympics, then announced his retirement from competition.

18. **(b)** Cincinnati Reds first baseman Pete Rose, forty-four, and in his twenty-third major league season, got his 4192nd hit on September 11, 1985. The hit, a single to left field against San Diego Padres pitcher Eric Show, broke the fifty-seven-year-old record held by Detroit Tigers legend Ty Cobb. That date also was the fifty-seventh anniversary of Cobb's last at-bat.

19. **(a)** Though 220 climbers had scaled Mt. Everest, no American woman ever had reached the 29,108-foot summit until Stacy Allison did it on September 29, 1988. (She had failed in an attempt the previous year, spending five days trapped by a storm in a snow cave at 26,000 feet.) Three days later, Peggy Luce, a support climber on the same Northwest American Everest Expedition team, also scaled the peak.

20. **(d)** Chicago Bears running back Walter Payton finished the 1984 season with a career total of 13,309 rushing yards, eclipsing Jim Brown's twenty-year-old record of 12,312. Brown played for the Cleveland Browns from 1957 to 1965. Payton retired following the 1987 season with a thirteen-year career total of 16,726 yards.

21. **(a)** American Carl Lewis won four events at the 1984 Los Angeles Olympics. By winning gold medals in the 100- and 200-meter races, the 4 × 100 relay, and the long jump, he duplicated the amazing performance of American Jesse Owens in the 1936 Berlin Olympics.

22. **(c)** Martina Navratilova won the women's singles title at Wimbledon six years in a row, 1982–87, breaking the record of five set by Suzanne Lenglen in 1919–23. Overall, Navratilova has won eight singles titles and is tied with record holder Helen Wills Moody. Lenglen won six titles overall, adding a victory in 1925. Billie Jean King also won six Wimbledon singles titles (1966–68, 1972–73, and 1975).

23. **(d)** Houston Astros pitcher Nolan Ryan broke Walter Johnson's long-standing major-league strikeout record of 3508 on April 27, 1983. On August 22, 1989, Ryan, who had been signed by the Texas Rangers in 1988, struck out thirteen Oakland Athletics batters to become the first major league pitcher with more than 5000 career strikeouts.

24. **(b)** Columbia finally won a football game on Saturday, October 8, 1988, defeating Princeton 16–13. The victory came almost five years to the day from their last victory, 21–18 over Yale on October 15, 1983. The Lions' streak of forty-four consecutive losses is an NCAA major college record.

25. **(d)** On August 9, 1988, the NHL and the entire nation of Canada were rocked by the news that Wayne Gretzky of the Edmonton Oilers, the league MVP for six straight years, had been traded to the Los Angeles Kings. In the trade the Oilers got $15 million in cash, two players, negotiating rights to another player, and first-round draft picks in 1989, 1991, and 1993. The Kings got Gretzky and two players, plus the negotiating rights to another player.

26. **(d)** Florence Griffith Joyner is married to Jackie Joyner-Kersee's brother Al. Both women are coached by Jackie's husband, Bob Kersee. At the 1988 Seoul Olympics, Griffith Joyner (nicknamed Flo Jo) won four medals: gold in the 4 × 100 relay and 100- and 200-meter races and a silver in the 4 × 400 relay. She set a world record with a 21.34-second time in the 200. Joyner-Kersee won two gold medals: in the long jump and heptathalon, which she won with a world-record score of 7291 points.

27. **(d)** Grambling head coach Eddie Robinson got victory number 324 in October 1985 to pass Alabama's Paul (Bear) Bryant as college football's winningest coach. The victory came against Prairie View A&M, 27–7. Going into the 1989 season, Robinson still was the Tigers head coach.

28. **(d)** Thanks to a revolutionary keel design, challenger *Australia II* in September 1983 broke the 132-year reign of the United States in the America's Cup yacht race (the longest winning streak in sports). The Australian yacht and skipper John Bertrand fought back from a 3–1 deficit to tie the best-of-seven series off Perth, Australia, then came from behind to

win the final race against America's *Liberty* and her skipper, Dennis Conner. The America's Cup was returned to the United States in 1987 when Conner and *Stars and Stripes* successfully challenged, beating *Kookaburra III* in Freemantle, Australia.

**29. (b)** Mary Decker led the 1984 Olympic women's 3000-meter final from the gun. But coming out of a turn after 1600 meters, barefoot young South African Zola Budd (racing for Great Britain) passed Decker. As Budd cut inside, their legs tangled and Decker fell. Decker pulled a hip muscle and was unable to get up; Budd finished the race in tears. Maricica Puica of Rumania was the winner.

**30. (b)** Notre Dame, coached by Lou Holtz and quarterbacked by Tony Rice, defeated the Mountaineers of West Virginia 34–21 in the Fiesta Bowl. The victory gave the Fighting Irish a 12–0 record for the 1988 season and their eighth national championship, the most for any school in history. West Virginia was 11–0 going into the game.

**31. (c)** Bill Shoemaker won his thousandth career stakes victory on "Peace" in the Premiere Handicap race on April 30, 1989. The fifty-seven-year-old Shoemaker (4 feet, 11 inches; 98 pounds) has more career stakes victories than any jockey in racing history. He also is the winningest jockey ever in overall career victories, with 8810 by August 1989.

**32. (b)** When forty-six-year-old golf great Jack Nicklaus won the Masters Tournament at Augusta, Georgia, in April 1986, it marked his sixth victory in the event. Nicklaus previously had won the Masters in 1963, 1965, 1966, 1972, and 1975. He won in 1986 with a dramatic final round score of 65.

**33. (a)** Carl Lewis came home from the 1988 Olympics in Seoul with two gold medals and a silver. His first gold was won in the long jump, making him the only athlete ever to win that event in consecutive Olympic Games. He was awarded his second gold in the 100-meter dash when the winner, Canadian Ben Johnson, was disqualified. Lewis won his silver in the 200-meter race.

**34. (c)** The New York Islanders began the decade with four consecutive NHL championships, winning the Stanley Cup in the 1980–83 seasons. The Edmonton Oilers then took over, winning the Stanley Cup four of the next five seasons (1984–85 and 1987–88).

**35.** **(a)** The Detroit Tigers defeated the San Diego Padres 4 games to 1 to win the 1984 World Series. The Tigers, who won 111 games in the regular season, became the first team since the 1927 Yankees to lead the pennant race from opening day and then win the World Series.

**36.** **(a)** The Louisville Cardinals and Indiana Hoosiers each won the NCAA Final Four basketball tournament twice in the 1980s. The Cardinals won in 1980 and 1986. The Hoosiers followed them each time, winning in 1981 and 1987. The 1987 victory marked Indiana's fifth NCAA title and head coach Bobby Knight's third in twelve years.

**37.** **(d)** After being in retirement for almost three years (and fighting only once in five), boxer Sugar Ray Leonard made a spectacular comeback. He defeated Marvelous Marvin Hagler for the WBC middleweight title at Las Vegas in April 1987. Leonard won the exciting twelve-round fight on a split decision. It was Hagler's first loss in eleven years; he previously had defended his title twelve times.

**38.** **(b)** On June 12, 1981, major-league baseball players went on strike after hitting an impasse with owners over a number of issues involving free agency and free agent compensation. It was the first strike within a season in progress in major-league American sports. Play resumed on August 10, making it the longest stoppage in baseball history. Over the seven-week period, 713 games were canceled.

**39.** **(c)** Edwin Moses, the gold-medal winner in the 400-meter hurdles at the 1976 Montreal Olympics, repeated his performance at the Los Angeles Olympics in 1984, extending his streak of consecutive victories in finals of that event (dating back to 1977) to ninety. Moses' remarkable streak was ended after more than a decade, at 107 in 1987.

**40.** **(a)** Billy Martin was fired as New York Yankees manager three times (as of May 1989) in the 1980s and five times overall. Yankees owner George Steinbrenner had fired Martin in 1978, 1979, 1983, 1985, and 1988. When Bucky Dent took over the Yankees late in 1989, it was New York's nineteenth managerial change in eighteen years.

AP/Wide World Photos

## TEST 11

# Celebrations and Milestones

*I want everyone to have a wonderful time.*

—SARAH FERGUSON
*(on the eve of her marriage to Prince Andrew)*

1. On July 23, 1986, some 300 million people viewed the wedding of Prince Andrew, second son of Queen Elizabeth II. What was his place in line to the throne?
   a. first
   b. second
   c. third
   d. fourth

2. In 1983 a Polish electrician and union leader won the Nobel Peace Prize. Who was he?
   a. Lech Walesa
   b. Wojciech Jaruzelski
   c. Henryk Jankowski
   d. Roman Polanski

3. What fundamental American document was two hundred years old in 1987?
   a. the Declaration of Independence
   b. the treaty ending the Revolution
   c. the Constitution
   d. the Bill of Rights

4. On June 6, 1984, leaders of eight Western nations gathered in Normandy, France, to observe the anniversary of
   a. D-Day
   b. the end of World War II
   c. the storming of the Bastille
   d. President Mitterand's birthday

5. Fifteen years after his death, black leader Martin Luther King, Jr., was honored by a U.S. federal holiday. On what day does it fall?
   a. January 15
   b. the third Monday in January
   c. the second Friday in February
   d. the third Monday in February

**6.** In 1986 a famous American university celebrated its 350th birthday. What university was it?

   **a.** Harvard

   **b.** Stanford

   **c.** Princeton

   **d.** Columbia

**7.** Sisquoc and Tecuya, two California condors, are the first

   **a.** to be born in captivity

   **b.** to produce more than one offspring in a year

   **c.** to produce offspring in captivity

   **d.** captive-born condors to be reintroduced to the wild

**8.** In 1980 the aircraft *Challenger* set a record. What was it?

   **a.** It was the first entirely solar-powered airplane without batteries.

   **b.** It was the first human-powered airplane.

   **c.** It was the first glider to cross the English Channel.

   **d.** It was the first successful robot-piloted small plane.

**9.** Why did 4150 followers of the Reverend Sun Myung Moon gather in Madison Square Garden in July 1982?

   **a.** to get married

   **b.** to attend Unification Church services

   **c.** to induct new members into the Unification Church

   **d.** to be baptized into the Unification Church

**10.** What was the name of the airplane that circled the globe without refueling in 1986, setting a record for the longest flight made without a stop?

   **a.** *Challenger*

   **b.** *Atlantis*

   **c.** *Explorer*

   **d.** *Voyager*

**11.** What birthday did the first baby boomers celebrate in 1986?

   **a.** fortieth

   **b.** thirty-fifth

   **c.** forty-fifth

   **d.** fiftieth

**12.** Which Canadian city hosted Expo 86, the 1986 World's Fair?

   **a.** Vancouver

   **b.** Toronto

   **c.** Ottawa

   **d.** Montreal

**13.** What happy family event did the Kennedys celebrate in 1986?

   **a.** Teddy Kennedy's twentieth year in Congress

   **b.** the wedding of Caroline Kennedy

   **c.** the hundredth birthday of Rose Kennedy

   **d.** the wedding of John Kennedy, Jr.

**14.** What token borrowed from a country-western song became a symbol of hope for the return of the fifty-two hostages held in Iran in 1980 and 1981?

   **a.** the American flag

   **b.** a yellow ribbon

   **c.** a yellow rose

   **d.** a candle in the window

**15.** Which two Western countries in the 1980s enacted laws to ensure equal rights for women?

   **a.** the United States and Great Britain

   **b.** West Germany and Sweden

   **c.** Switzerland and Australia

   **d.** France and Belgium

**16.** In 1988 one group in a certain country celebrated its two-hundredth anniversary, and another group observed a Year of Mourning. What was the country?

a. Australia

b. France

c. the United States

d. Canada

**17.** What world-famous black leader won the 1984 Nobel Peace Prize?

a. Nelson Mandela

b. Martin Luther King, Jr.

c. Desmond Tutu

d. Jesse Jackson

**18.** In 1989, France celebrated the bicentennial of what event in its history?

a. the Fronde

b. the French Revolution

c. the French and Indian War

d. the crowning of Napoleon as emperor

**19.** In 1986 more than 5 million Americans joined in a celebration called "Hands Across America." What was the reason for this event?

a. to call attention to poverty and homelessness

b. to celebrate the unity of ethnic groups in the nation

c. to call a halt to environmental pollution

d. to spotlight the problem of illiteracy

**20.** What Middle Eastern country celebrated its fortieth birthday in 1988?

a. Israel

b. Kuwait

c. Iran

d. Syria

**21.** What famous American bridge turned one hundred in 1983?

   **a.** the Brooklyn Bridge

   **b.** the Verrazano-Narrows Bridge

   **c.** the George Washington Bridge

   **d.** the Whitestone Bridge

**22.** In 1986 five thousand new U.S. citizens were sworn in by Chief Justice Warren Burger on the one-hundredth anniversary of what American symbol?

   **a.** the Liberty Bell

   **b.** Ellis Island

   **c.** the Statue of Liberty

   **d.** the Washington Monument

**23.** What comic book hero celebrated his fiftieth birthday in 1989?

   **a.** Batman

   **b.** Superman

   **c.** the Incredible Hulk

   **d.** Spiderman

**24.** In 1989 the United Nations celebrated its

   **a.** fortieth birthday

   **b.** two-hundredth member

   **c.** tenth year of peacekeeping

   **d.** centennial

**25.** In 1988 students at Gallaudet University, the only liberal arts college in the United States for the hearing-impaired, won the right to

   **a.** a deaf president

   **b.** conduct all school business in sign language

   **c.** a deaf majority on the Board of Trustees

   **d.** all of the above

**26.** What group had something to celebrate in 1985 when the Rabbinical Assembly, the organization of Conservative rabbis, agreed to extend membership to them?

   **a.** women

   **b.** married men

   **c.** converts

   **d.** Israeli immigrants

**27.** In 1981, Britain's Prince Charles married Lady Diana Spencer. How did Britons celebrate?

   **a.** with a chain of bonfires

   **b.** with a $16,000 firework display

   **c.** by wrapping themselves in British flags

   **d.** with all of the above

**28.** The thirty-fifth anniversary of the People's Republic of China was marked by

   **a.** a student uprising

   **b.** a display of military might

   **c.** a series of anti-Communist demonstrations

   **d.** all of the above

**29.** The year 1989 marked the fiftieth anniversary of television. How was television first introduced in the United States in 1939?

   **a.** by RCA at the New York World's Fair

   **b.** by the Smithsonian Institution

   **c.** in theaters on Movietone News

   **d.** In the window of Gimbel's department store in New York

**30.** John Steinbeck's novel *The Grapes of Wrath* was fifty years old in 1989. What group of Americans does this book describe?

   **a.** Depression-era migrant workers (Okies)

   **b.** East-coast aristocrats

   **c.** plantation owners of the Old South

   **d.** mountain men of the Old West

**31.** What cake treat celebrated its seventieth birthday in May 1989? Hint: It has a seven-loop squiggle design on top.

    a. Twinkies

    b. HoHo's

    c. Ding Dongs

    d. Hostess cupcakes

**32.** What art form was 150 years old in 1989?

    a. neon signs

    b. watercolor

    c. photography

    d. papier-mâché

**33.** In 1986 an expedition of American scientists explored for the first time the sunken wreckage of what famous ship?

    a. *Andrea Doria*

    b. *Lusitania*

    c. *Titanic*

    d. *USS Arizona*

**34.** Why did Sandra Day O'Connor, at age fifty-one, make headlines in 1981?

    a. She was the only woman in Reagan's cabinet.

    b. She was the first woman appointed to the Supreme Court.

    c. She was the president of the National Organization for Women (NOW).

    d. She headed the first national task force on AIDS.

**35.** Democrat Geraldine Ferraro was the first woman to be

    a. appointed U.S. ambassador

    b. nominated as the vice presidential candidate of a major party

    c. elected governor of a state

    d. appointed to the president's cabinet

**36.** In the 1980s the British celebrated the births of two little princes, the sons of Prince Charles and Princess Diana. What are their names?

   **a.** Harry and William

   **b.** Charles and William

   **c.** James and Harry

   **d.** George and William

**37.** Once the tallest building in New York City, this skyscraper celebrated its fiftieth anniversary in 1980.

   **a.** the Empire State Building

   **b.** the Chrysler Building

   **c.** the Woolworth Building

   **d.** Rockefeller Center

**38.** What animated cartoon character celebrated his or her sixtieth birthday in 1988?

   **a.** Donald Duck

   **b.** Minnie Mouse

   **c.** Mickey Mouse

   **d.** Pluto

**39.** What famous French landmark celebrated its one-hundredth anniversary in 1989?

   **a.** Nôtre Dame

   **b.** the Eiffel Tower

   **c.** Chartres Cathedral

   **d.** the Moulin Rouge

**40.** The fiftieth anniversary of the first transatlantic flight by a woman was marked in 1982. Who was the woman?

   **a.** Beryl Markham

   **b.** Florence Barnes

   **c.** Marjorie Stinson

   **d.** Amelia Earhart

# TEST 11: Explanatory Answers

1. **(d)** First in line is his brother, Prince Charles. Second and third in line are the two sons of Charles and his wife, Diana. Andrew married red-haired Sarah Ferguson, a graphic designer, before 1800 invited guests at Westminster Abbey. The wedding ring was of Welsh gold. Before the wedding, Queen Elizabeth II conferred the title of duke of York on Prince Andrew, making his wife the duchess of York. The last duke and duchess of York were Andrew's maternal grandparents.

2. **(a)** Lech Walesa, leader of the first independent trade union movement in the Soviet bloc, won the Nobel Prize in recognition of his struggle for workers' rights to establish their own organizations. The Polish regime, which had crushed Walesa's union (Solidarity), called the choice "politically motivated." Walesa worked as an electrician at the Lenin Shipyards in Gdansk when he first gained international attention in 1980. He was on his way to a day of fishing and gathering mushrooms when he learned he had won the Peace Prize.

3. **(c)** A controversial document, the U.S. Constitution was called "our ark of the Covenant" by nineteenth-century congressman Caleb Cushing but "the handiwork of Satan" by abolitionists, who deplored the fact that it recognized slavery. (In Article 1, Section 3, it stipulated that representatives would be apportioned for the House by a formula that added "three fifths of all other persons" [slaves] to the "whole number of free persons.") Drafted by fifty-five men and completed on September 17, 1787, the Constitution took effect after it was ratified by nine states. The Bill of Rights was appended in 1791. Since then sixteen more amendments have been added, bringing the total number to twenty-six. Though an incredibly flexible and time-tested document, it has had its flaws. For example, it did not grant the vote to everyone. Women were disenfranchised until the Nineteenth Amendment was passed in 1920.

4. **(a)** On June 6, 1944, five thousand ships ferried Allied troops to the beaches of Normandy to begin an invasion of Nazi-occupied France that is considered to be the turning point in the Allied victory in World War II. Fifty years later, at Utah Beach, U.S. president Ronald Reagan and French president François Mitterrand met for a commemorative ceremony with

an audience that included Queen Elizabeth II of Great Britain, Prime Minister Pierre Trudeau of Canada, King Olav V of Norway, Queen Beatrix of the Netherlands, King Baudouin I of Belgium, and Grand Duke Jean of Luxembourg. The celebration, attended by ten thousand spectators, was marked by marching bands and eight warships out in the English Channel symbolizing the five thousand ships there at D-Day. The West Germans were not there, and the Soviets called it an "American show" that slighted the significance of the Eastern front in World War II.

5. **(b)** In 1983 the U.S. Congress voted to establish a national holiday, beginning in 1986, that would commemorate the birthday (actually January 15) of civil rights leader Rev. Martin Luther King, Jr. Both houses of Congress passed the bill with large majorities: 78 to 22 in the Senate and 338 to 90 in the House. Yet nearly a dozen states still refuse to recognize the only federal holiday that honors a black.

6. **(a)** In 1986, the 350th anniversary of its founding, the oldest university in the United States recalled its prestigious graduates. John Hancock was one of eight Harvard men who signed the Declaration of Independence. Among other graduates are former secretary of state Henry Kissinger, Pakistani prime minister Benazir Bhutto, composer Leonard Bernstein, six U.S. presidents, more than twenty Nobel Prize winners, and many creative artists and scholars. Harvard celebrated its anniversary by stretching a plastic rainbow over the Charles River and spelling out John Hancock's name in fireworks. A marionette of the university's benefactor, John Harvard, danced to the music of an all-female samba group, the Batucada Belles.

7. **(a)** Condors, really black buzzards, are America's largest land birds. The result of a controversial program to breed endangered species in captivity, Sisquoc and Tecuya were born at the San Diego Zoo in 1983. At the time of their birth only nineteen of the birds still survived, partly because they are not prolific, producing only a single offspring every two years, and take as long as seven years to mature. After the 7-ounce chicks hatched, they were placed in isolation and fed chopped-up mice with the help of a puppet glove that looks like a condor head—so they would know they are condors.

8. **(a)** Designed by Paul MacCready of Pasadena, California, the *Challenger* was the first aircraft powered by electricity drawn

*directly* from the 16,128 solar cells spread over the top of its 47-foot-long wings and 13-foot horizontal stabilizer. (Other planes had flown on solar energy, but they used batteries to store it.) The plane was aloft for 5 hours and 23 minutes during its flight from Corneilles-en-Vexin, France, to Manston Royal Air Force Base on the southeastern coast of England, but the actual Channel crossing took only 85 minutes. The total cost of the flight was $725,000. MacCready also designed the *Gossamer Condor*, the first craft to fly a 1.15-mile course with human muscle power alone. It accomplished this feat in 1976. His *Gossamer Albatross*, also human-powered, crossed the English Channel in 1978, the first plane of its type to do so.

9. **(a)** The Reverend Sun Myung Moon performed 2075 marriages in the Madison Square Garden mass wedding. He personally matched up the couples, many of whom had met for the first time only days before. The devoted followers of the South Korean evangelist and founder of the Unification Church, the "Moonies," regarded him as a manifestation of God and zealously collected funds by selling flowers on the street. He later was convicted of tax evasion in the state of New York and of not reporting interest on a $1.6 million bank account.

10. **(d)** Made primarily of cloth, paper, and glue, the experimental aircraft *Voyager* made the first flight around the world without stopping or refueling. Piloted by Dick Rutan and Jeanna Yeager, the plane weighed only 9750 pounds, fuel included, and carried seventeen fuel tanks loaded with 1200 gallons of 100-octane gasoline. It had no toilet. The 25,012-mile flight, which began December 14, 1986, took 9 days, 3 minutes, 44 seconds. The average speed was 115.8 miles per hour. On December 23 the plane touched down at Edwards Air Force Base in California with 8 gallons of usable fuel left, having nearly doubled the previous distance record of 12,532 miles set in 1962. The plane was designed by Burt Rutan, brother of the pilot.

11. **(a)** Because of the large number of children born during the postwar years, the period between 1946 and 1964 is known as the baby boom. Approximately 76 million Americans were born in those years. In 1986 the first of the baby boomers reached forty, including actor Sylvester Stallone, comedian

Gilda Radner, and financier Donald Trump. In 2030, when the baby boomers will reach old age, 21.2 percent of the population will be over sixty-five, compared with 12 percent today.

12. **(a)** During the opening ceremony of the fair a flotilla of more than one hundred boats—big and small, warships to sailboats—filled Vancouver Harbor. The fair was officially opened by Prince Charles and Princess Diana of Great Britain. More than fifty nations and forty corporations were represented at Expo 86.

13. **(b)** Caroline, age twenty-eight, daughter of Jacqueline Kennedy Onassis and the late President John F. Kennedy, tied the knot on July 19, 1986. Her husband, Edwin A. Schlossberg, president of a design company specializing in museums, was forty-two on the day of the wedding, which was held in Centerville, Massachusetts. Caroline's uncle, Senator Edward M. Kennedy, gave her away; and her brother, John F. Kennedy, Jr., was the best man. The reception was held at the Kennedy compound, the house of Rose Kennedy, Caroline's ninety-five-year-old grandmother.

14. **(b)** "Tie a Yellow Ribbon Round the Ol' Oak Tree," composed by Irwin Levine and L. Russell Brown in 1973, sold over 100 million copies. However, the yellow ribbon as a symbol of a lost one's return existed long before that. Penelope Laingen, wife of hostage L. Bruce Laingen, chargé d'affaires in Iran when the hostages were seized, tied a yellow ribbon to an oak tree in their yard shortly after the seizure of the American embassy in Teheran. The symbol became popular with the rest of the country and adorned everything from hairdos to buildings after the release of the hostages. When Bruce Laingen came home, he tore the faded ribbon off the tree in front of a crowd of about two hundred neighbors.

15. **(c)** On March 7, 1984, the Australian parliament passed, 86 to 26, a sweeping bill to eliminate discrimination on the basis of sex, marital status, or pregnancy. The bill outlawed discrimination in the areas of employment; education; the provision of goods, facilities, and services; accommodation; the disposal of land; the activities of clubs; and the administration of Commonwealth laws and programs. On June 14, 1981, an equal rights provision was added to the Swiss constitution.

The new amendment specifies that the phrase "all Swiss" means both men and women and states further that the two sexes enjoy equal rights, which apply particularly to family, education, and work. The vote was 797,679 to 525,950. Swiss women had won the right to vote in 1971.

**16. (a)** On January 26, 1988, the two-hundredth anniversary of the landing of British ships carrying the first white convict-settlers to Australia, 2.5 million people watched eleven ships reenact the prisoners' arrival in Sydney Harbor. Events included cockroach races and a melon seed-spitting contest. Aboriginal leaders, who saw the landing of the British as launching an era of oppression, declared 1988 a Year of Mourning.

**17. (c)** South African Anglican bishop Desmond Tutu, fifty-three, was awarded the Nobel Peace Prize for his attempts to eliminate apartheid. He was the first black to hold the position of secretary general of the Anglican South African Council of Churches. A believer in nonviolence, Tutu supported the African National Congress, South Africa's outlawed black underground organization. Tutu was the second South African to win the Peace Prize. Albert John Luthuli, former head of the African National Congress, won the award in 1960.

**18. (b)** According to popular belief, the French Revolution of 1789 ended the old regime of absolute monarchy and inaugurated a hopeful new era of participatory democracy. Bicentennial ceremonies began in Paris's Tuileries Gardens in January 1989 with the ascension of a blue-and-gold hot air balloon representing a "salute to liberty" and a reading by an actor of the 1789 Declaration of the Rights of Man and the Citizen. It was only the beginning. The French celebrated the controversial event all year, remembering and arguing about the success of what has been touted as a victory for *Liberté, Egalité,* and *Fraternité* but that also ushered in the bloody Terror and the repressive reign of Napoleon. François Furet, a French historian, says that the revolution "was a magnificent event that turned out badly."

**19. (a)** At 3 P.M. EST on May 25, 1986, Americans joined hands for fifteen minutes to help raise money and consciousness for the homeless. The human chain reached across 4150 miles through 16 states and 550 cities from Battery Park in New

York City to the wharf of the Queen Mary in Long Beach, California. There were some gaps, especially in the California desert, but the scale and excitement of the event won out. Each participant contributed $10 to $30 to the cause. President Ronald Reagan, his wife, Nancy, and daughter Maureen took part, as did Raquel Welch, Liza Minnelli, Sean Lennon, Cicely Tyson, Dudley Moore, Ben Vereen, and Kenny Rogers.

**20.** **(a)** Israel was declared an independent state on May 14, 1948. For many of the world's Jews, it fulfilled the two-thousand-year-old dream of the "promised land" for which they had been praying since the original diaspora—"Next year in Jerusalem . . ." Britain's Balfour Declaration in 1917, announcing British approval of a "national home in Palestine for the Jewish people," set a precedent, and Palestine became a haven for Jews fleeing the Holocaust during and after World War II—687,000 of them. The state was established on land the Arabs also claim as Palestine; fighting accompanied the birth of the new nation and continues today. Nonetheless, Jews from over one hundred countries have emigrated to Israel.

**21.** **(a)** The Brooklyn Bridge, which connects Manhattan and Brooklyn, was the technological marvel of its day. It took fourteen years to build, and twenty workmen died building it. A mile long, the bridge was designed and engineered by John Roebling. At the time of the construction the two 267-foot-high stone towers were the tallest buildings in the nation. To celebrate the birthday eighteen thousand people and one elephant marched across the bridge, led by a barefoot woman in white and a man carrying a small American flag in his teeth. The city also put on a $200,000 fireworks display that included ten thousand rockets and roman candles.

**22.** **(c)** Given to the United States by the people of France, the statue *Liberty Enlightening the World*, designed by Frederic Auguste Bartholdi, has stood in New York Harbor since 1886. The four-day celebration of its anniversary (July 3–6) included tall ships, fireworks, and the swearing-in of five thousand new citizens on Liberty Island. Twenty thousand more were simultaneously sworn in by satellite telecast. Still more ceremonies were held on October 28, 1986, the actual birthday of the statue.

**23.** **(b)** During the fifty years since he made his debut as a superhero in April 1939 on the cover of the first issue of *Action*

*Comics*, Superman has fought for "truth, justice, and the American way" and against evil-doers like his archenemy, the mad scientist Lex Luthor. Superman is aided by his super-powers, including x-ray vision and the ability to leap tall buildings in a single bound! Created by Jerry Siegel (the writer) and Joe Schuster (the artist) in 1934, Superman was born on the doomed planet Krypton, then escaped to Earth, where he lived both as mild-mannered Clark Kent, bespectacled reporter, and the blue-caped Man of Steel. Perenially in love with reporter Lois Lane, especially in his persona of Clark Kent, he has also had flings with more exotic women, such as Lori the mermaid and Wonder Woman.

**24. (a)** The United Nations celebrated its fortieth anniversary on October 24, 1985. Beginning with 50 member nations, the UN today has 159 members. During the week of its birthday, eighty heads of state and government—including U.S. president Ronald Reagan and British prime minister Margaret Thatcher—met at UN headquarters. Of these, twenty-five ate a power lunch at a round table. Ambassador Herbert Okun, a U.S. delegate to the UN, said that the birthday was "not a celebration. The United Nations is in a mid-life crisis." Former Israeli foreign minister Abba Eban said of the organization, "The U.N. is an umbrella which folds up every time it rains." However, since its founding in the last days of World War II, the United Nations, although it has not fulfilled one of its original goals—to keep the peace—has alleviated a great deal of human suffering. Its agencies have placed refugees and prevented disease.

**25. (a)** On October 21, 1988, the Washington, D.C., university installed its first deaf president, I. King Jordan. He was chosen to fill the post after student and faculty protests against the previous choice of Elisabeth Ann Zinser, who is not deaf. The protests also resulted in the replacement of Jane Bassett Spilman, head of the board of trustees, with Phillip W. Braven, who is deaf.

**26. (a)** The Reform branch of Judaism has ordained women since 1972, but Conservative Jews had not allowed women to act as rabbis until the Rabbinical Assembly, the organization of Conservative rabbis in the United States and Canada, agreed to admit anyone trained by the Jewish Theological Seminary.

The seminary began to train and ordain women in 1983, and the first female seminarian graduated in 1985. Orthodox Jews still do not allow women to be rabbis because it is against traditional religious law to do so.

**27.** **(d)** The royal wedding on July 29, 1981, seemed to unite the people of Britain, who, except for a few leftists, celebrated enthusiastically, punks and skinheads included. The day was declared a national holiday. The night before the wedding, $16,000 worth of fireworks lit up Hyde Park. A chain of bonfires blazed all over the kingdom in celebration. The wedding was held in St. Paul's Cathedral from 11 A.M. to noon. The twenty-year-old Lady Diana wore a dress of silk taffeta made from silk produced at Britain's only silk farm; it had a 25-foot train. Some three quarters of a billion people watched on television. About a million lined the route from Buckingham Palace to the cathedral, among them flag-wrapped spectators and young people who had painted their faces with the Union Jack. The 2700 invited guests included royalty and heads of state from around the world. The thirty-two-year-old prince's brothers, Andrew and Edward (the latter was best man), attached a lipsticked "Just Married" sign to the horse-drawn carriage that took the couple to Waterloo Station, from which they left for a country home in the Broadlands. Cost: at least $1 million to put on the show. London police officials assessed: "We hoped for a happy day to mark an historic occasion. Our wildest hopes have been exceeded."

**28.** **(b)** On the thirty-fifth anniversary of the People's Republic of China in October 1984, Deng Xiaoping, at eighty the senior member of China's politburo, presented the first public review of the country's military in thirty-five years. The parade lasted two hours: six thousand soldiers, together with tanks, artillery, and missiles that were all made in China, including submarine-launched CSS-NX-4 rockets with a range like that of early U.S. Polaris missiles (1200–1500 miles).

**29.** **(a)** When television was introduced at the 1939 World's Fair, screens were tiny and there were only a handful of TV stations in the entire country. Regularly scheduled broadcasting began after World War II. To commemorate the anniversary, the Smithsonian Institution put on an exhibit titled "American Television: From the Fair to the Family, 1939–89." Its angle:

that television was an important influence on the postwar consumer age. Early advertising for television promoted it as an agent of family togetherness. Some items at the exhibit were a Captain Video board game, a Lone Ranger deputy badge, Fonzie's jacket, and J. R. Ewing's hat.

**30.** **(a)** The novel was awarded the Pulitzer Prize in 1940 and is termed by many critics the greatest example of worker fiction of the 1930s and of the victory of the human spirit. It is the odyssey of the Joads, forced to leave their Dust Bowl farm in Oklahoma for California, where they look for work picking fruit. In the end, even after many tragedies, the family remains strong. Steinbeck's wife, Carol, who typed and edited the manuscript of the novel, chose the title, a phrase from the "Battle Hymn of the Republic."

**31.** **(d)** D. R. (Doc) Rice of the Continental Baking Company saved the cupcake from a downhill slide of bad sales after World War II and sugar and chocolate rationing. To perk up the cupcake he tried a straight line of icing, then changed it to squiggles, thinking them more upscale. Rice also played a part in developing the other Continental Baking Company cakes: Twinkies, HoHo's, Snoballs, and Ding Dongs. In 1988, Americans ate about 4 billion Hostess cupcakes.

**32.** **(c)** Two inventors—Louis Jacques Mandé Daguerre (French) and William Henry Fox Talbot (English)—laid claim to the creation of photography in 1839. Talbot called it the "pencil of nature." Cameras were used mostly by the wealthy until 1888, when George Eastman introduced the Kodak, which many people could afford. It brought the age of amateur photography. Museums all over the world commemorated the anniversary with retrospectives.

**33.** **(c)** The "unsinkable" *Titanic* went down in 1912 off the Newfoundland coast after hitting an iceberg. The Woods Hole Oceanographic Institution's team investigated the ship's remains and concluded that the hull's steel plates had separated, flooding the ship. One year later a French expedition caused a furor by recovering salvaged objects from the wreckage, which had been declared an undersea memorial by the U.S. Congress.

**34.** **(b)** President Reagan's first Supreme Court nominee, Sandra Day O'Connor, was easily approved by the eighteen male members of the Senate Judiciary Committee. She is the first woman to be nominated to or to serve on the court. A conservative with keen intelligence, O'Connor had served for only eighteen months on a court of appeals and one term on a county superior court in her home state, Arizona. She had, however, been majority whip during two terms in the Arizona state senate and had built a private law practice in Phoenix from 1957 to 1969. Newspaper accounts at the time of her appointment did not fail to mention that she had been married for twenty-nine years, that she had taken five years out early in her career to have three sons, and that she was an excellent cook.

**35.** **(b)** Geraldine Ferraro was nominated for vice president on the 1984 Democratic ticket with Fritz Mondale as the presidential candidate. Born in 1935, Ferraro put herself through Fordham Law School at night by working as a schoolteacher during the day. She passed the bar in 1960 and pursued a career in law. In 1978 she became the first female representative from the 9th Congressional District in New York and was reelected in 1980 and 1982. A liberal Democrat, she was an advocate of the Equal Rights Amendment and was pro-choice on the abortion issue. Scandal marred the campaign: she was forced to defend several shady financial transactions involving her husband, John Zaccaro, a real estate executive. Although charges against the couple, including tax evasion, were eventually cleared, Ferraro's political career suffered.

**36.** **(a)** The sons of the Prince and Princess of Wales are named William and Harry, born in 1982 and 1984, respectively.

**37.** **(a)** Built during the skyscraper war of the 1930s, the Empire State Building was specifically planned to top New York's then tallest structure, the Chrysler Building. At 1250 feet and 102 floors, the Empire State Building remained the world's tallest building until the World Trade Center in New York and the Sears Tower in Chicago surpassed it decades later.

**38.** **(c)** For the sixtieth anniversary of the creation of Mickey Mouse, Disney pulled out all the stops. Year-long festivities included a traveling twelve-story hot air balloon of Mickey, new lines of merchandise and video cassettes, a TV gala, and at Disney theme parks special parades and offerings such as the new Mickey's Birthdayland at the Magic Kingdom in

Florida. Mickey, who has grown younger with the years, even appeared "reanimated" at the 1988 Academy Awards presentation, and Disney took out a thirty-page ad supplement in *People* magazine to publish tributes from Mickey Mouse fans.

**39.** **(b)** Standing 985 feet tall, the Eiffel Tower, built by engineer Gustave Eiffel, is one of the world's most recognizable structures. To celebrate its hundredth anniversary in May 1989 a group of French backers wanted to send a chain of Mylar balloons into space, but for environmental reasons the idea was rejected. The French spent the better part of the year celebrating the event. Over and over again the historical facts were repeated: the tower stands on a brick foundation that is 50 feet deep; it was constructed from twelve thousand girders; 2.5 million bolts hold the tower together.

**40.** **(d)** In 1932, five years to the day after Charles Lindbergh flew from the United States to Paris, Amelia Earhart became the first woman to fly solo across the Atlantic. She scored many more distance and altitude records before her mysterious disappearance in the Pacific in 1937 while she was attempting to fly around the world.

AP/Wide World Photos

# *TEST 12*

# *Endings*

*Life is a great surprise. I do not see why death should not be an even greater one.*

—*VLADIMIR NABOKOV*

1.  What major Hollywood director (1906–87) directed the Academy Award–winning performances of both his father and his daughter?

    a.  Alfred Hitchcock

    b.  John Huston

    c.  John Cassavetes

    d.  Billy Wilder

2.  After John Lennon was assassinated outside his New York City apartment building on December 9, 1980, how did friends, colleagues, and associates honor him?

    a.  The remaining Beatles recorded a song.

    b.  Yoko Ono released an album.

    c.  New York City dedicated a monument.

    d.  all of the above

3.  The founder of the Youth International Party (Yippies), Abbie Hoffman committed suicide in April 1989. Which of the following statements about him is true?

    a.  He was a defendant in the Chicago Seven trial in 1969.

    b.  He lived underground for six years in the 1970s.

    c.  He led an environmentalist movement in the 1980s.

    d.  all of the above

4.  When did it become public that Rock Hudson was a victim of AIDS?

    a.  three months before his death, when he sought treatment in Paris

    b.  upon his death in October 1985

    c.  when his companion Marc Christian filed a lawsuit

    d.  at a press conference in 1984

5.  George Meany (1894–1980) held a nationally visible position through six presidential administrations. What was his job?

    a.  secretary of labor

    b.  ambassador to the United Nations

   **c.** president of the AFL-CIO

   **d.** commissioner of the National Football League

**6.** Who was the Arab leader assassinated in 1981 as he watched a military parade?

   **a.** Sadegh Ghotzbadeh

   **b.** Bashir Gemayel

   **c.** Anwar el-Sadat

   **d.** King Khalid

**7.** The author of *Tropic of Cancer* and other books that were banned in the United States died in 1980. What was his name?

   **a.** D. H. Lawrence

   **b.** Jack Kerouac

   **c.** Henry Miller

   **d.** William Burroughs

**8.** What former film star was fatally injured in a 1982 car accident in France?

   **a.** Simone Signoret

   **b.** Jean Seberg

   **c.** Grace Kelly

   **d.** Edie Sedgwick

**9.** Mohammed Reza Pahlevi died in Cairo, Egypt, in July 1980, eighteen months after he was exiled from his home country of

   **a.** Iraq

   **b.** Iran

   **c.** Lebanon

   **d.** Saudi Arabia

**10.** What happened to the Onassis fortune when Christina Onassis died of a heart attack in 1988?

   **a.** It reverted to the treasury of the Greek government.

   **b.** Thierry Roussel, Christina's fourth husband, inherited it.

    c. Christina's three-year-old daughter inherited it.

    d. It was divided among Roussel, Christina's daughter, and several charities.

**11.** The founder and artistic director of one of America's leading ballet companies died in March 1988. Named Abdullah Jaffa Bey Khan at birth, he was known to the American public as

    a. Sir Frederick Ashton

    b. Robert Joffrey

    c. Patrick Bissell

    d. Mikhail Baryshnikov

**12.** What is the name of the existentialist writer who died in 1980, sixteen years after refusing to accept a Nobel Prize in literature?

    a. Albert Camus

    b. Jean-Paul Sartre

    c. Simone de Beauvoir

    d. Jean Genet

**13.** The star of the 1930 film *Public Enemy* came out of retirement in 1981 for a leading role in the movie *Ragtime*. Who was this actor, who died in 1986?

    a. Ralph Bellamy

    b. James Cagney

    c. Henry Fonda

    d. Jimmy Stewart

**14.** Which of the following movies did *not* star John Belushi, the actor/comedian who died of a drug overdose in 1982?

    a. *National Lampoon's Animal House*

    b. *Continental Divide*

    c. *The Blues Brothers*

    d. *Trading Places*

**15.** When Jesse Owens died in 1980, what was his most lasting achievement?

   **a.** He was world heavyweight champion.

   **b.** He won four gold medals at the 1936 Olympics.

   **c.** He set world records in auto racing.

   **d.** He was a winning pitcher in four World Series.

**16.** Statesman Averell Harriman died in 1986 at the age of ninety-four. What position had he held?

   **a.** ambassador to Moscow

   **b.** European administrator of the Marshall Plan

   **c.** emissary to the 1967 Paris peace talks on Vietnam

   **d.** all of the above

**17.** The naturalist who spent nearly eighteen years studying the Rwanda mountain gorilla was murdered on December 27, 1985. What was her name?

   **a.** Dian Fossey

   **b.** Jane Goodall

   **c.** Mary Leakey

   **d.** Joy Adamson

**18.** What was author Jim Fixx doing when he suffered a heart attack and died on July 20, 1984?

   **a.** lecturing

   **b.** running

   **c.** swimming

   **d.** sleeping

**19.** The only prisoner of Spandau Allied War Crimes Prison died on August 18, 1987. What was his name?

   **a.** Rudolf Hess

   **b.** Joseph Mengele

   **c.** Heinrich Himmler

   **d.** Hermann Göring

**20.** Lucille Ball (1911–89) starred in how many television series?

   **a.** one

   **b.** two

   **c.** three

   **d.** four

**21.** Malcolm Baldridge died in 1987 from injuries sustained while trying to rope a steer. Who was he?

   **a.** ambassador to Brazil

   **b.** U.S. secretary of commerce

   **c.** an international banker

   **d.** a noted Hollywood stuntman

**22.** What is the name of the hero of the Serbs and Croats who died in 1980?

   **a.** Aleksei Kosygin

   **b.** Willy Brandt

   **c.** Josip Broz (Tito)

   **d.** Bashir Gemayel

**23.** In the 1933 movie that established him as a leading man, Mae West asked him, "Why don't you come up sometime and see me?". Who was this debonair actor who died in December 1987?

   **a.** Gary Cooper

   **b.** Cary Grant

   **c.** Bing Crosby

   **d.** Clark Gable

**24.** Who was the famous photographer of Yosemite and other national parks who died in 1984?

   **a.** Edward Weston

   **b.** Imogen Cunningham

   **c.** Jacques-Henri Lartigue

   **d.** Ansel Adams

**25.** Why did William J. Casey (1913–87), director of the U.S. Central Intelligence Agency, resign his post during the heat of the Iran-*contra* affair?

  **a.** Congress forced his resignation.

  **b.** He took another position in the Reagan cabinet.

  **c.** He took a job in the private sector.

  **d.** none of the above

**26.** During the 1980s two of America's great lyricists died. One of them wrote lyrics for *Camelot* and *My Fair Lady*; the other wrote *Funny Face* and co-authored the libretto for *Porgy and Bess*. What were their names?

  **a.** Allen Jay Lerner and Ira Gershwin

  **b.** Frederick Loewe and George Gershwin

  **c.** Ira Gershwin and Kurt Weill

  **d.** Allen Jay Lerner and Jerome Kern

**27.** When Joy Adamson, author of *Born Free*, was murdered in Kenya, the first accounts of her death reported that she had been killed by a(n)

  **a.** gorilla

  **b.** rhinoceros

  **c.** lion

  **d.** elephant

**28.** Two years before his death in 1987 a prominent entertainer revealed that he owned seventy-five "lost" episodes of his highly successful 1950s television program. Who was he?

  **a.** Jack Benny

  **b.** Ozzie Nelson

  **c.** Desi Arnaz

  **d.** Jackie Gleason

**29.** At the time of his death in 1983, R. Buckminster Fuller held two thousand patents. What was his best known invention?

    **a.** the aerosol can

    **b.** the geodesic dome

    **c.** airbags for automobiles

    **d.** the trash compactor

**30.** Marlon Brando, Laurette Taylor, Burl Ives, and Jessica Tandy all appeared in plays written by which playwright, who died in February 1983?

    **a.** Thornton Wilder

    **b.** George S. Kaufman

    **c.** Tennessee Williams

    **d.** Eugene O'Neill

**31.** Which of the following famous Moores is best known for sculpting reclining figures and died in September 1986?

    **a.** Melba Moore

    **b.** Henry Moore

    **c.** Marianne Moore

    **d.** none of the above

**32.** When she died in June 1986, all-American singer Kate Smith left behind a huge legacy of music, but she is best known for her rendition of

    **a.** "The Star-Spangled Banner"

    **b.** "God Bless America"

    **c.** "Stars and Stripes Forever"

    **d.** "Battle Hymn of the Republic"

**33.** In December 1936 King Edward VIII abdicated his throne in order to marry the socialite divorcee Wallis Warfield Simpson (1937–86). Before marrying Edward, Simpson had been divorced

    **a.** once

    **b.** twice

    c. three times

    d. four times

**34.** Dubbed one of the most important film directors of the twentieth century, François Truffaut (1932–84) was also

    a. an actor who appeared in *The Green Room*

    b. an actor who appeared in *Close Encounters of the Third Kind*

    c. a film critic

    d. all of the above

**35.** Son of a Welsh coal miner and an actor in more than fifty movies and Broadway plays, Richard Burton (1926–84) was also

    a. married five times to four different women

    b. knighted by Queen Elizabeth

    c. an Academy Award winner for his performance in *Who's Afraid of Virginia Woolf?*

    d. all of the above

**36.** Lillian Hellman, noted playwright and author who died in July 1984, is often quoted as saying "I cannot and will not cut my conscience to fit this year's fashions" in response to questions regarding why she

    a. never married fellow playwright Dashiell Hammett during their thirty-one-year relationship

    b. never wore haute couture fashions to the openings of her plays

    c. would not answer certain questions before the House Committee on Un-American Activities

    d. never denounced the excesses of Stalinism as had many of her contemporaries

**37.** When he died in 1984, Ray Kroc was best known as the

    a. owner of the Los Angeles Dodgers baseball team

    b. inventor of the milkshake machine

    c. founder of the McDonald's franchise business

    d. co-owner of Burger King

**38.** Legendary boxer Sugar Ray Robinson (1921–89) had a career that spanned

    a. ten years

    b. fifteen years

    c. twenty years

    d. twenty-five years

**39.** Spanish painter Salvador Dali (1904–89) was associated with what school of art?

    a. surrealism

    b. impressionism

    c. cubism

    d. expressionism

**40.** The "King of Swing" died in June 1986. He was

    a. Benny Goodman

    b. Glenn Miller

    c. Duke Ellington

    d. Guy Lombardo

# TEST 12: Explanatory Answers

1. **(b)** John Huston, who directed forty-one films over forty-six years, cast his father, Walter, in *Treasure of Sierra Madre* and his daughter Anjelica in the 1985 movie *Prizzi's Honor*. Each won an Academy Award for the role. Huston said his filmmaking was eclectic because he tried not to duplicate himself. His legendary work includes *The Maltese Falcon, The Asphalt Jungle, The African Queen, Moby Dick,* and *The Man Who Would Be King.* He died at the age of eighty-one after a long battle with emphysema.

2. **(d)** Paul McCartney and Ringo Starr played on George Harrison's single "All Those Years Ago." McCartney also released his own musical tribute to Lennon, "Here Today," on his 1982 *Tug of War* album. Lennon's widow, Yoko Ono, first released *Season of Glass* in 1981 and subsequently helped to create several other Lennon albums of live recordings as well as the 1988 film *Imagine.* New York City dedicated a portion of Central Park to Lennon and renamed it Strawberry Fields.

3. **(d)** Activist Abbie Hoffman was charged and acquitted with six others, including Tom Hayden and Jerry Rubin, for conspiracy to incite a riot at the 1968 Democratic Convention in Chicago. His radical pranks and antics in the 1960s included organizing fifty-thousand anti-Vietnam demonstrators in an attempt to levitate the Pentagon and throwing dollar bills onto the floor of the New York Stock Exchange. In 1974, charged with selling cocaine to undercover police, Hoffman went underground. He settled in Fineview, New York, under the name Barry Freed and led a successful movement to stop a dredging project on the St. Lawrence River. In 1980 he surrendered to authorities and served eleven months in jail. Hoffman's death in 1989 was attributed to an overdose of phenobarbital pills.

4. **(a)** The public learned of Rock Hudson's fatal illness when he flew to Paris in July 1985, hoping to be treated with an experimental drug. When no alternative treatments were offered by the French doctors, Hudson returned to his Los Angeles home on a stretcher in a chartered Boeing 747. Upon learning of his condition, the Hollywood community rallied its forces in support of Hudson. His colleagues held an AIDS benefit in September that raised $1 million and focused the

world's attention on the disease and its mostly homosexual victims. Hudson was too ill to attend the benefit and died less than a month later.

5. **(c)** George Meany became the first president of the AFL-CIO when the two labor unions merged in 1955, and he retired in 1979, only a few months before his death. An outspoken former plumber from the Bronx, Meany took his labor demands directly to whichever president was in office, overstepping the respective secretary of labor. Meany said, "When you have a problem with the landlord, you don't discuss it with the janitor."

6. **(c)** Anwar el-Sadat, president of Egypt, was shot by men in military uniforms as he watched a parade in Cairo commemorating the 1973 war against Israel. His assassins were never captured, but it is suspected that they were Muslim fundamentalists or Coptic Christians, two of the dissident groups that Sadat had tried to suppress. Sadat's popularity had waned in Egypt in the last year of his rule, but his international reputation as a peacemaker remains. His historic visit to Israel in 1977 set the stage for the Camp David peace accord, which he signed with Menachem Begin and Jimmy Carter in 1979. The treaty called for Israel to return, in phases, the entire Sinai Peninsula to Egypt. The agreement did not, however, provide a timetable for full self-determination for the West Bank Palestinians. For that omission, Sadat earned the enmity of other Arab leaders. Upon Sadat's death Hosni Mubarak became president and assured the world that Egypt would honor its treaties.

7. **(c)** Brooklyn-born author Henry Miller wrote *Tropic of Cancer,* his most famous book, in Paris, where he lived a bohemian life throughout the 1930s. The autobiographical novel was banned in the United States for its sex scenes until 1964, when the U.S. Supreme Court ruled that the book could no longer be suppressed. Miller's other works include *Tropic of Capricorn*; a collection of letters to author Anaïs Nin; and *Sexus, Nexus,* and *Plexus*, the trilogy he wrote in Big Sur, California. Miller spent the last years of his life with his fifth wife in Pacific Palisades, California, pursuing a career as a painter.

**8. (c)** Grace Kelly, the American actress who gave up her movie career to marry Monaco's Prince Rainier, died from injuries sustained in an automobile accident after she suffered a stroke while at the wheel of her 1972 Rover. Accompanied by her seventeen-year-old daughter Stephanie, the princess was driving through the steep French mountains above the principality of Monaco when she lost control of the car. Initial speculation that the underage and unlicensed Stephanie had been driving was based on the fact that Stephanie was pulled from the wreckage on the driver's side of the car; she survived with broken vertebrae. Kelly's most notable films were *To Catch a Thief, High Noon, Rear Window,* and *High Society.*

**9. (b)** Mohammed Reza Pahlevi, the shah of Iran, died in Egypt eighteen months after he was deposed by traditionalist Muslims who rallied behind Ayatollah Ruhollah Khomeini. The shah, who succeeded his father at age twenty-one, had previously been forced into exile in 1951 but regained the throne two years later with the help of the CIA. During his rule the shah directed the rapid modernization of Iran with the help of billions in oil revenues, a strong military, and the SAVAK secret police. The shah died of lymphatic cancer at the age of sixty.

**10. (c)** When Christina Onassis died near Buenos Aires on November 19, 1988, her three-year-old daughter Athina Onassis became the sole inheritor of the $1 billion legacy. Christina's fourth and last husband and father of the child, French businessman Thierry Roussel, took custody of Athina, but an Onassis trust manages the estate.

**11. (b)** Robert Joffrey, born in Seattle to an Afghan restaurant owner and his Italian wife, formed the Robert Joffrey Ballet in 1956 with only six dancers. The Joffrey Ballet has become known for its wide-ranging artistic expression, its grooming of young dancers, and its support of innovative, contemporary choreographers such as Twyla Tharp and Laura Dean.

**12. (b)** Jean-Paul Sartre refused to accept the Nobel Prize in literature in 1964 because he did not wish to be "transformed into an institution." The action was characteristic of the French writer, political activist, and existential philosopher who believed that each individual creates his or her own "situation" and alone must bear the responsibility for that situation. Sartre had a lifelong relationship with fellow writer and thinker Simone de Beauvoir, who died in 1986. Sartre's works include the philosophical tract *Being and Nothingness*, the play *No Exit*, and the autobiographical novel *Nausea*. He became well known for his resistance work in France during World War II and throughout his life lectured on and demonstrated for leftist causes. Sartre died at the age of seventy-four in Paris.

**13.** **(b)** Director Milos Forman persuaded James Cagney to return to Hollywood after a twenty-year retirement to play the police commissioner in *Ragtime*. Cagney was one of the country's highest-paid actors during the 1930s in a series of successful tough guy roles. His early training in vaudeville paid off in several musicals, including *Yankee Doodle Dandy*. His other memorable movies included *White Heat, Man of a Thousand Faces*, and *Mister Roberts*. Cagney died in 1986 at the age of eighty-six at his farm in upstate New York.

**14.** **(d)** *Trading Places* starred Dan Ackroyd and Eddie Murphy, two comedians who, like John Belushi, achieved fame on "Saturday Night Live." As one of the "Not Ready for Prime Time Players" on "Saturday Night Live" from 1975 to 1979, Belushi impersonated a killer bee, a samurai warrior, and many other popular characters. Among his movie roles he is best remembered as the toga-wearing, food-throwing college boy in *Animal House* and as a white soul singer with partner Dan Ackroyd in *The Blues Brothers*. Belushi died in 1982 after a five-day drug binge. Cathy Evelyn Smith, who is believed to be the last person to see him alive, was sentenced in 1986 to three years in prison for involuntary manslaughter. She had pleaded no contest to supplying drugs to the actor and injecting him with a series of "speedballs," a mixture of cocaine and heroin.

**15.** **(b)** At the 1936 Olympics in Berlin, Jesse Owens won four gold medals. His gold-medal events were the 100-meter run, the 200-meter run, the running broad jump, and the 400-meter relay. Adolf Hitler, who hosted the Olympic games to showcase the feats of his Aryan "supermen," left the stadium rather than congratulate a black athlete. Official U.S. recognition of his feats did not come until forty years later, when Owens was invited to the White House to receive the Presidential Medal of Freedom. In his later years Owens ran a marketing and public relations firm, first in Chicago and then in Phoenix, where he died at the age of sixty-seven.

16. **(d)** Averell Harriman, born in 1891, took to heart the advice of his railroad magnate father that "great wealth is an obligation." Harriman, a Democrat, served as ambassador and emissary for five U.S. presidents. As ambassador to Moscow during World War II he helped Franklin D. Roosevelt sustain the alliance between Stalin and Churchill and spent more time with Stalin than any other American statesman. In Harry Truman's administration he shepherded the Marshall Plan for Europe. Under John F. Kennedy he negotiated the Limited Test Ban Treaty in 1963. For Lyndon Johnson he was the emissary to the Paris peace talks, and at the age of eighty-four he went to Moscow for Jimmy Carter to talk to Leonid Brezhnev about arms control. In addition, he served one term (1955–58) as governor of New York, his home state.

17. **(a)** Dian Fossey, author of the 1983 book *Gorillas in the Mist* and subject of the 1988 movie of the same name, was found murdered in her remote jungle cabin on December 27, 1985. Fossey had made it her life work to study the rare mountain gorillas in their natural habitat in Rwanda in central Africa. She befriended them as well and defended them against poachers. Although her colleagues suspected she was murdered by a poacher, the government of Rwanda issued an arrest warrant nine months after her death for Wayne McGuire, an Oklahoma PhD student who was working with Fossey. When McGuire learned about the warrant, he fled to the United States. Nonetheless, Rwandan officials tried him in absentia and pronounced him guilty. McGuire continues to proclaim his innocence from afar; the United States does not have an extradition treaty with Rwanda.

18. **(b)** Jim Fixx died of a heart attack during his daily 10-mile run. The author of the 1977 best-seller *The Complete Book of Running*, Fixx was the guru of the long-distance running craze in the United States. He took up the sport at the age of thirty-five in order to lose 61 pounds and rejuvenate himself after quitting a two-pack-a-day cigarette habit. Although he died at the young age of fifty-two, some experts said that his seventeen years of running may have prolonged his life by a

decade; his father died of a heart attack at the age of forty-three. Fixx's autopsy revealed that his main coronary arteries were 70 to 99 percent blocked.

**19.** **(a)** Rudolf Hess, the only prisoner at West Berlin's Spandau Prison for twenty years, was the last survivor of the nineteen German officials convicted at the Nuremberg Trials in 1946. Hess was one of the first members of the Nazi party and was named top deputy after Hitler became chancellor of Germany in 1933. When World War II began, Hess was eclipsed by his assistant, Martin Bormann. In 1941 Hess pulled a stunt that continues to baffle historians. He flew a fighter plane to Scotland, parachuted down near Glasgow, and demanded to speak to Churchill to offer peace terms on behalf of Germany. Although Hess claimed he was on a "mission of humanity," the British believed he was acting alone and interned him in the Tower of London. Hitler disavowed Hess. He remained an enigma until his death at the age of ninety-three.

**20.** **(d)** Lucille Ball is best remembered for her role as Lucy Ricardo in "I Love Lucy," co-starring Desi Arnaz, her then real-life husband, and Vivian Vance and William Frawley as their neighbors, the Mertzes. The CBS show made its debut on October 15, 1951, and ran for 179 episodes. Lucille Ball had two more successful series—"The Lucy Show" and "Here's Lucy"—but her 1986 show on ABC, "Life with Lucy," did not last the season. When the unquestioned queen of television comedy died of a ruptured abdominal aorta on April 26, 1989, millions of people around the world felt a personal loss, for Lucy's face is one of the most recognized faces on earth. Reruns of "I Love Lucy" have been played and replayed in virtually every country in the world.

**21.** **(b)** Malcolm Baldridge was one of the three original members of Ronald Reagan's cabinet who served the president into his second term. As U.S. secretary of commerce, Baldridge made headlines before his death in 1987 for advocating high tariffs against Japanese electronic imports. Outside of politics, Baldridge was a successful businessman and a serious rodeo rider who was admitted to the Cowboy Hall of Fame in 1984. He died of internal bleeding after his horse reared and fell on him while he was trying to rope a steer.

**22.** **(c)** Tito, the Marxist hero who ruled Yugoslavia for more than thirty-five years, died on May 4, 1980. After severing ties with

Stalin after World War II, Tito developed his own brand of communism that allowed for some free-market practices. Tito is credited with forging a united nation after the war from Yugoslavia's diverse regions and ethnic populations. The country has some seventeen nationalities—including Croats, Serbs, and Slovenes—six languages, and three major religions. Tito is also remembered for establishing in the 1950s the "non-aligned" movement, to which most Third World nations now profess allegiance, and for his princely life-style that included châteaus, hunting preserves, a yacht, and a private zoo.

**23.** **(b)** Mae West, who died in 1980, said her famous and often-misquoted line to Cary Grant. The movie was *She Done Him Wrong*, in which Grant played a lawman disguised as a missionary; it was his first leading role. During his career, Grant made seventy-two films, including four suspense movies with Alfred Hitchcock and several comedies co-starring Katherine Hepburn (*Bringing Up Baby*, *The Philadelphia Story*, *His Girl Friday*). Born Archibald Leach to a working class family in an industrial English town, Grant was devastatingly handsome and was considered the epitome of elegance and charm. Although he was nominated twice for an Academy Award, it was not until 1970, after his retirement from Hollywood, that Grant won a special Oscar for his lifetime achievements in the movie industry.

**24.** **(d)** Ansel Adams, born in San Francisco in 1902, was one of America's most famous photographers. Although he took his first pictures of Yosemite Valley in 1916 (with a Brownie box camera), he did not become a professional photographer until 1930. Along with Edward Weston and Imogen Cunningham, Adams was responsible for establishing photography as a legitimate and distinct art form. He was an ardent conservationist and served as director of the Sierra Club from 1936 to 1973. His stunning black-and-white photographs capture the majesty of the natural American landscape in the High Sierra, Yosemite, and other national parks.

**25.** **(d)** William Casey resigned as director of the CIA after he underwent surgery for a malignant brain tumor in December 1986. He was hospitalized just one day before he was scheduled to testify before a Senate panel about the CIA's role in the Iran-*contra* scandal. Casey became director of the Central

Intelligence Agency in 1981 after managing Reagan's 1980 presidential campaign. A multimillionaire, Casey held a number of high government posts, including chairman of the Securities and Exchange Commission from 1971 to 1973. Casey died on May 6, 1987, at the age of seventy-four, without giving any public testimony about his role in the Iran-*contra* affair.

**26.** **(a)** Allen Jay Lerner, wordsmith to composer Frederick Loewe, died in 1986. Ira Gershwin, brother and lyricist to composer George Gershwin, died in 1983. Lerner wrote rich, romantic musicals—*Camelot, My Fair Lady, Paint Your Wagon*—that became Hollywood movies, usually with a screenplay written by Lerner. Ira Gershwin, with his brother George (who died in 1937), shaped popular music in the 1930s, most notably with songs from *Porgy and Bess*, "I Got Rhythm," "The Man I Love," and many musical hits from a succession of Fred Astaire movies. Ira Gershwin won the first Pulitzer Prize for a lyricist in 1931.

**27.** **(c)** The first accounts of Joy Adamson's death reported that she was mauled by a lion near her camp 230 miles north of Nairobi. Later it was determined that she had died of wounds from a sharp instrument. A disgruntled employee from her camp was later tried and convicted of her murder. The Austrian-born author wrote *Born Free* in 1960; it is the story of a lion cub that she and her husband raised and then released into the wild. The book became both a movie and an American television show. Adamson wrote two sequels to the book, donating the royalties from the books to conservation causes.

**28.** **(d)** In 1985, Jackie Gleason released seventy-five "lost" episodes of "The Honeymooners," which he had preserved in an air-conditioned vault. "The Honeymooners" originated on the hour-long "Jackie Gleason Show," where Gleason perfected the role of Ralph Kramden, the grumbling bus driver, in skits with Audrey Meadows, who played Ralph's wife. Although Gleason had a long career that included theater, movies (*The Hustler, Requiem for a Heavyweight, Smokey and the Bandit*), and thirty-five record albums, the rotund actor is best remembered for his pioneering work in television. He was seventy-one years old when he died of cancer at his home in Fort Lauderdale, Florida.

**29. (b)** Buckminster Fuller patented the geodesic dome in 1947. The structure, made of lightweight materials and built on a framework of triangles to reduce stress and weight, embodied Fuller's philosophy of balance and efficiency. Largely self-taught, the philosopher/engineer/architect believed that technology could "save the world from itself, provided it is properly used." Fuller's other inventions included a three-wheeled car that could reach a speed of 120 mph using a standard 90-hp engine, and a flat world map that showed the full surface of the earth without distortion. He also wrote some twenty-five books, including *Synergetics* and *Operating Manual for Spaceship Earth*. He died in Los Angeles, his hometown, at the age of ninety-eight.

**30. (c)** Tennessee Williams wrote *The Glass Menagerie*, starring Laurette Taylor; *A Streetcar Named Desire*, starring Marlon Brando and Jessica Tandy; and *Cat on a Hot Tin Roof*, starring Burl Ives. Born Thomas Lanier Williams on March 26, 1911, Williams changed his name to Tennessee when he was twenty-eight. He wrote more than twenty-four full-length plays. His poetic dramas are laced with dramatic tension and brilliant dialogue. In addition, he was a master of stage effects and scene construction.

**31. (b)** Born in the coal-mining town of Castleford, England, on July 30, 1898, Henry Spencer Moore became one of the most celebrated sculptors of the century. His works in wood, stone, cement, marble, and bronze are characterized by smooth organic shapes that include empty hollows. Moore's most favorite subjects were mother with child and the reclining figure. According to Moore, "The sensitive observer of sculpture must . . . feel shape simply as shape, not as description or reminiscence." He received more public commissions than even Auguste Rodin, and his major commissions include huge reclining figures for the UNESCO building in Paris and for Lincoln Center in New York City.

**32. (b)** Written by Irving Berlin and made famous by Kate Smith, "God Bless America" became the unofficial national anthem of the United States. Smith was singing at church socials at the age of five, and by age eight she was performing for the troops at army camps in Washington, D.C., during World War I. She made her radio debut at age twenty-two and first sang "God Bless America" when she was twenty-nine. Her singing career spanned forty-five years, during which she recorded almost three thousand songs. Berlin and Smith did not accept royalties from performances of "God Bless America" but instead turned over the proceeds to the Boy Scouts of America and the Girl Scouts of America.

**33. (b)** In 1916, at the age of twenty, Wallis Warfield married a twenty-seven-year-old aviator, Lieutenant Earl Winfield Spencer. The couple separated in 1921, and in 1927 Mrs. Spencer was granted a divorce on the grounds of desertion. Her second husband was Ernest Simpson, who headed a British shipping business. While living in London, the Simpsons became friends with Benjamin Thaw, first secretary of the American embassy, and his wife, Consuelo, who introduced Wallis to the Prince of Wales and future king of England. When his father, George V, died in 1936, Edward succeeded to the throne but was never crowned. That same year he abdicated the throne with a dramatic and unforgettable speech: "I have found it impossible to . . . discharge my duties as King . . . without the help and support of the woman I love." Wallis obtained a divorce from her second husband in April 1937, and she and Edward were married the following June. As the duke and duchess of Windsor, the couple lived in self-imposed exile in France.

**34. (d)** François Truffaut began his movie career as a film critic and went on to become the director of such award-winning films as *Day for Night*, for which he earned an Academy Award for best foreign film in 1973. Truffaut made many other noteworthy movies; among them, *Shoot the Piano Player* (1960) and *Jules and Jim* (1961). *The 400 Blows* (1959) won him a Cannes Film Festival prize as well as entrée into the group of French moviemakers known as the New Wave. Among Truffaut's acting credits are appearances as a newspaperman in his own film *The Green Room* and as a French scientist in Steven Spielberg's *Close Encounters of the Third Kind*.

**35. (a)** Although he was critically acclaimed as a film and stage actor, Burton was never knighted by Queen Elizabeth, nor did he win an Academy Award for his performance in *Who's Afraid of Virginia Woolf?* (co-star and future wife Elizabeth Taylor did win an Oscar for her performance in that movie). However, Burton did marry four different women a total of five times.

He was first married to Sybil Williams in 1949. He was catapulted into international fame with his second and third marriages to Liz Taylor in 1964 and 1975. Burton's fourth and fifth marriages were to Suzy Hunt in 1976 and Sally Hay in 1983.

**36.** **(c)** Hellman, one of the most important playwrights of the American theater, wrote *The Children's Hour*, *The Little Foxes*, *Watch on the Rhine*, and *Toys in the Attic*. Critical as well as popular successes, the plays were controversial, as was her three-volume set of memoirs. A political activist, Hellman was affiliated with many left-wing causes and was always outspoken about her beliefs. In 1952 she was called before the House Committee on Un-American Activities, which was investigating links between American leftists and the Communist party in the United States and abroad. It was in a written reply to the committee that Hellman wrote, "I cannot and will not cut my conscience to fit this year's fashions." She did appear before the committee but refused to give information about other people. As a result of her convictions, Hellman was blacklisted by the film industry.

**37.** **(c)** Although at one time Kroc sold milkshake machines for a living, he did not invent them. However, selling milkshake machines paid off because two of his clients were Richard and Maurice McDonald, owners of a hamburger stand in San Bernardino, California. Kroc and the brothers worked out a deal whereby Kroc started a hamburger franchise business patterned on the McDonald operation in return for paying the brothers a small percentage of the gross profits. The first McDonald's franchise opened in Chicago in 1955, and by the time he died, Kroc had built his hamburger empire into a chain of more than 2500 outlets in nine countries with sales of over $1 billion. Kroc was also the owner of a baseball team, the San Diego Padres, which he bought in 1974 for $10 million.

**38.** **(d)** His manager called him "sweet as sugar," but Sugar Ray Robinson was anything but sweet when he entered the ring. A welterweight and middleweight champion, Robinson won 175 fights in his twenty-five-year career, and 110 of the victories were knockouts; he lost only 19 bouts. Known for his crippling punches and fancy footwork, he retired in 1965. Boxing historians call Robinson "pound for pound, the world's greatest fighter."

**39. (a)** Dali, whose trademark was his waxed mustache, worked in the surrealist style. For example, he expressed *The Persistence of Memory* as a group of melting watches in a bleak landscape, a visual image of the permeability of time. In his later years Dali moved into commercial arenas, selling signature dishware and deodorant.

**40. (a)** A clarinettist and jazz musician, Benny Goodman was a musical pioneer of the big band swing era. He introduced concert jazz to Carnegie Hall in 1938 and was the first major bandleader to break the color barrier by integrating his bands. As he put it, "If a guy's got it, let him give it. I'm selling music, not prejudice." Two of Goodman's biggest hits were "Sweet Georgia Brown" and "Stompin' at the Savoy."